O9-AHS-605

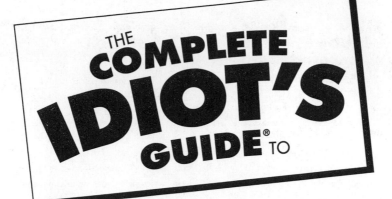

THE
COMPLETE
IDIOT'S
GUIDE® TO

Girlfriend Getaways

by Lisa Kasanicky

ALPHA

A member of Penguin Group (USA) Inc.

For my mom, grandma Roselia, grandma Rose, grandma Stauffer, aunt Dolly, and all the amazing women who I have been blessed to have in my life.

ALPHA BOOKS

Published by the Penguin Group

Penguin Group (USA) Inc., 375 Hudson Street, New York, New York 10014, USA

Penguin Group (Canada), 90 Eglinton Avenue East, Suite 700, Toronto, Ontario M4P 2Y3, Canada (a division of Pearson Penguin Canada Inc.)

Penguin Books Ltd., 80 Strand, London WC2R 0RL, England

Penguin Ireland, 25 St. Stephen's Green, Dublin 2, Ireland (a division of Penguin Books Ltd.)

Penguin Group (Australia), 250 Camberwell Road, Camberwell, Victoria 3124, Australia (a division of Pearson Australia Group Pty. Ltd.)

Penguin Books India Pvt. Ltd., 11 Community Centre, Panchsheel Park, New Delhi—110 017, India

Penguin Group (NZ), 67 Apollo Drive, Rosedale, North Shore, Auckland 1311, New Zealand (a division of Pearson New Zealand Ltd.)

Penguin Books (South Africa) (Pty.) Ltd., 24 Sturdee Avenue, Rosebank, Johannesburg 2196, South Africa

Penguin Books Ltd., Registered Offices: 80 Strand, London WC2R 0RL, England

International Standard Book Number: 978-1-59257-821-4
Library of Congress Catalog Card Number: 2008931266

12   11   10   09   8   7   6   5   4   3   2   1

Interpretation of the printing code: The rightmost number of the first series of numbers is the year of the book's printing; the rightmost number of the second series of numbers is the number of the book's printing. For example, a printing code of 09-1 shows that the first printing occurred in 2009.

Printed in the United States of America

Note: This publication contains the opinions and ideas of its author. It is intended to provide helpful and informative material on the subject matter covered. It is sold with the understanding that the author and publisher are not engaged in rendering professional services in the book. If the reader requires personal assistance or advice, a competent professional should be consulted.

The author and publisher specifically disclaim any responsibility for any liability, loss, or risk, personal or otherwise, which is incurred as a consequence, directly or indirectly, of the use and application of any of the contents of this book.

Most Alpha books are available at special quantity discounts for bulk purchases for sales promotions, premiums, fund-raising, or educational use. Special books, or book excerpts, can also be created to fit specific needs.

For details, write: Special Markets, Alpha Books, 375 Hudson Street, New York, NY 10014.

Publisher: *Marie Butler-Knight*
Editorial Director: *Mike Sanders*
Senior Managing Editor: *Billy Fields*
Executive Editor: *Randy Ladenheim-Gil*
Development Editor: *Lynn Northrup*
Senior Production Editor: *Janette Lynn*

Copy Editor: *Lisanne V. Jensen*
Cover Designer: *Rebecca Harmon*
Book Designer: *Trina Wurst*
Layout: *Ayanna Lacey*
Proofreader: *Laura Caddell*

Contents at a Glance

Contents

Appendix

Introduction

In the words of pop/rock artist Lenny Kravitz, "I want to get away. I want to fly away." Yeah, yeah, yeah, I'm with you, Lenny. But can I bring my girlfriends along? This book is meant to inspire you to fly away on an adventure laced with girl talk, giggling, gawking, and good fun with the women who bring out your best: your girlfriends.

So, wherever shall you go? The possibilities are truly endless. But in the pages that follow, we'll explore destinations that lead down the path to fun, freedom from the constraints of everyday life, and tightening the bonds of friendship. With some 75 destinations across North America (plus more than 50 other ideas for places to explore), you'll have no excuses for not getting away with the girls.

How This Book Is Organized

This book is broken down into six parts. In the first part, we focus on the business of planning and preparing for your getaway. In the next five parts, we dive right into the juicy details of where to go. Each of the destination sections focuses on a theme and within each chapter, you'll get ideas on where to stop along the way and where to plop at the end of the day.

Part 1, "Plan, Prep, and Primp," lays the groundwork for turning talk of a getaway into reality with advice on planning, organizing, prepping, and packing for your trip. We'll look at tools for collaborating on the travel planning process, the pluses and minuses of different modes of getting to your destination, and tips for not stressing over the details.

Part 2, "Shop 'Til You Plop: Adventures in Retail Therapy," explores destinations where the first order of business is finding that fabulous pair of shoes, killer deals, or trophy pieces for your home. We'll bust out our walking shoes for big-city shopping trips, stroll along sidewalks of smaller cities where boutique shops radiate with local charm, and hunt down beautiful home décor items that will long remind you of your shared shopping adventure.

Part 3, "Head Trips: Mind and Body Retreats," takes you to blissful destinations that do a mind, body, and spirit loads of good. We'll dip our tired toes into spas where blissful relaxation tops the to-do list and hit resorts that merge a luxury experience with healthy eating and fitness. Finally, we'll take a walk down sandy beaches that will clear your head and hearten your spirit.

Part 4, "Culture Club: Excursions that Feed Your Mind and Appetite," fuels your inquisitive side with destinations where learning comes with a picturesque backdrop. We'll look at places where you can sharpen your cooking skills, learn to paint, or deepen your appreciation of photography. We'll refine your palate with wine and food excursions and brush up on history with trips to cities that have rich pasts.

Part 5, "Friends Who Play Together Stay Together: Adventure Trips," leads you on a quest for the thrills and spills of adventure vacations. Test your physical and mental endurance by riding the rapids, climbing giant rock formations, or pedaling along hidden paths. Slow down your pace with a hike through the wilderness or a horse trot down a country road.

Part 6, "The Road Less Traveled: Quirky, Wacky, and Wild Excursions," takes you on off-the-beaten-path journeys—from purposeful volunteer getaways and trips with a spooky side to festivals and fantasies. We'll wrap up our walk on the wild side with a place where "over the top" is an everyday occurrence: Las Vegas.

A Little Help on the Side

Throughout each chapter, you'll find tips and tidbits for making the most of your getaway.

Powder Room

Why do women go to the ladies' room in groups? Because that's where we spill our best secrets and advice. Duh! These tips are meant to offer insight or further information about destinations that will enhance your trip.

STOP *Bad Trip*
Remember that vacation where you scratched yourself silly thanks to a poison ivy outbreak? These are little (or big) annoyances to watch out for that could spoil an otherwise memorable getaway.

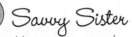 *Chick Wit*
What do I know? That it's best to go to my girlfriends for their own words of wisdom on traveling with gal pals. These are quotes from the mouths of babes who know a thing or two about girlfriend getaways.

Savvy Sister
How many uses does a bandanna have during a hike through the wilderness? You'll find out with these tidbits that are meant to shine a brighter light onto the subject at hand. Plus, they're good conversation starters.

You'll also find that phone numbers and names of important destinations throughout the book are placed in **bold.** Look for bold when you want to locate information about the fabulous girlfriend getaways at a glance.

A Word About Rates

While accurate at the time of publication, current rates and offers may fluctuate. Unless otherwise noted, rates quoted herein are based on double occupancy, per person, per night. Be sure to confirm prices and details directly with the businesses in question when making your travel arrangements.

Acknowledgments

Author of *The Complete Idiot's Guide to Reading with Your Child*, Helen Coronato, gave me a nugget of wisdom that stuck with me throughout the process of writing my first book. "It's a lot of work," she said. "But you'll have the most fun writing the acknowledgments and thanking everybody who helped you do it." She was right.

A huge thank you first to literary agent Jacky Sach for thinking of me for this amazing opportunity. Thanks also to executive editor Randy Ladenheim-Gil and the entire team at Alpha Books for their dedication to this project, and especially to development editor Lynn Northrup for her patient guidance and enthusiasm for the subject matter.

My deepest appreciation goes to all the public relations and visitor bureau professionals who provided a wealth of information for this book. Big props to my friend and Portland connection Angela Fenske and to my new buddy Bill DeSousa-Mauk of Michael Patrick Communications who led me on a virtual tour of the entire Northeast. Also to my super-fab aunt, Cyndy Murrieta, and her crew of insightful friends and colleagues for their witty travel advice.

Big hugs all around to my girlfriends, especially Anita Malik, Kari Stolley, Carrie Severson, Morgan Long, and Carolyn Anger for keeping me sane during this process. Also to BFFs Laura Hebbard, Karen Ankner, and Marci Russell. Drinks are on me at the next get-together.

Also, I am extremely grateful to my network of fellow writers, editors, and media colleagues in the Phoenix area for their encouragement and support. An extra-long belly rub goes to Sophie the spa dog for keeping me company during the late-night writing marathons. Finally, my deepest love and appreciation to my dad, Bob Florer, and his wife, Val, my entire extended family, my ever-patient husband and best friend Chaz Kasanicky, and my mom who was with me in spirit throughout the process to remind me to stop biting my fingernails and to not sit so close to the computer screen.

Finally, for SPANX, Frownies, zit concealer, my hairdresser, and my aesthetician—the second-best friends a girl could have.

Trademarks

All terms mentioned in this book that are known to be or are suspected of being trademarks or service marks have been appropriately capitalized. Alpha Books and Penguin Group (USA) Inc. cannot attest to the accuracy of this information. Use of a term in this book should not be regarded as affecting the validity of any trademark or service mark.

Part

1

Plan, Prep, and Primp

The term "girlfriend getaway" has become a buzzword in the travel biz for trips and tours designed for women. But heck, isn't *any* vacation with a friend, mom, daughter, sister, aunt, and so on a girlfriend getaway? In my book, it is. In fact, that's what makes the decisions of "When?", "Where?", "Why?", and "How soon can we go?" seem nearly insurmountable. The first hurdle is giving yourself permission to go (just do it, and let's move on!). The second obstacle is planning, organizing, and prepping for your trip. In the chapters that follow, we look at ways to help you decide which direction to head, travel options, collaboration tools, and home matters.

Desert vistas, camaraderie, and prickly pear cactus margaritas mark the highlights of the Giddy-Up Gals Getaway in Wickenburg, Arizona.

Destination Unknown

In This Chapter

* Why we need girlfriend getaways

* About the getaways in this book

* Choosing a getaway that matches budgets and expectations

* Getting there: planes, trains, and road trips

When I first set sail on the journey of writing this book, a friend congratulated me on having landed the project—but then innocently added, "Why you? You're practically a shut-in."

"I travel!" I remember shooting back defensively.

And then I lit into all the exciting travel adventures that I'd experienced in my 39 and a half years: whitewater rafting in

West Virginia, scaling mountains in North Carolina, cycling through Napa Valley wine country, and plunging down a snowy Colorado mountainside with skis strapped to my feet.

My friend responded, "Yeah, but wasn't that like 10 or 15 years ago?"

Why a Girlfriend Getaway?

Okay—truth be told, I'm your typical "everywoman" trying to juggle a full-time job with a part-time career, subsisting on "health" bars and vitamin water, down-dogging my way to some semblance of sanity, and convincing myself that getting my roots dyed is "me time." I know women who actually do all this *and* raise kids. How is that even possible? How do any of us do what we do? And how are we supposed to tuck a vacation into our whirlwind schedules? You'd think it was the 1980s all over again, when we wore Wonder Woman bras under our shoulder-padded power suits. But it's not. It's life.

We need a vacation—a vacation far away from the kids, the husband, the laundry, the demands of being everything to everybody. We need a vacation that plucks us up out of our normal lives and whisks us away to a tropical paradise, a peaceful retreat, or a life-changing adventure—a vacation that reminds us who the heck we are sans the to-do lists, the e-mails and text messages, and the nagging voice in the back of our heads that reminds us that the toilets need to be cleaned.

Hope for the Weary

You've heard the speech: you have to take time for yourself before you can fully reach your potential as a loving friend, mom, daughter, wife, or partner. But honestly, who has time for that?

When crafting this book, I made it my mission to keep that very point in mind. My hope is to alleviate the research and planning on your part so you can get to the business of actually booking a trip and going. I focused on mining out places that not only cater to women traveling in groups but that also offer options for varying budgets.

A Personal Perspective

Before we plunge ahead, allow me to recount a recent getaway experience that taught me the rewards of trading the daily grind for a few days of connecting with like-minded women. As a journalist, I was invited to experience a "Giddy-Up Gals Getaway" cowgirl adventure at a working ranch in Wickenburg, Arizona (read more about the ranch in Chapter 16). This Old West town is just an hour drive from my home in Scottsdale. As I kissed the hubby and dog goodbye and hopped in my Beetle for the trip, I was overwhelmed by all the things I should be doing rather than jumping ship for three days of freedom.

The women who were to be my accomplices for the long weekend came from California, Georgia, and Arizona. Besides me, the cast consisted of three early 30-something moms who had known each other since high school, two bubbly women in their 50s, and four friends on the cusp of 60 who had been close chums for decades. One trail ride, many drinks, and one three-course dinner later, our lives began to overlap.

By the end of the second day, which included a team cattle penning competition and a desert cookout, we had bonded like old friends. We had nicknames for each other, knew who did what, who was married, who was single (and looking or not looking), and who had kids, dogs, and how many of each. My new posse nicknamed me "Pen" because they knew that I was frantically journaling every detail of the trip. By the sounds of the laughter that fluttered nightly from the rooms of the women who originally arrived together, their bonds were clearly renewed and strengthened. But women have a way of reaching out beyond party lines to create new connections. Trite as it might sound, women have an innate need for connection. We connect on an emotional level. So it sticks—and that's exactly what happened.

The entire ride home, I was practically giddy. The relationships that I forged with my new "girls," the incredible female wranglers who led the trail rides—one a Grammy-winning opera singer and another a decorated rider and graduate student—and even my horse for the weekend, Santana, had fed my spirit a burst of energy and gratitude. The picture-perfect weather, the healthful food, and the spa massage only heightened the experience.

Just as I turned into my neighborhood, my cell phone jostled me out of my happy place. "Honey," said the sleepy voice of my husband. "Are you almost home? I'm hungry and I haven't eaten since you left."

Good golly, I thought. A woman's work truly is never done. Hear me roar. Grrr.

So the fact is, you really don't need a reason to get on the horn now with the girls and start pulling together a getaway plan of action. If you really need an excuse, we can find one—a when-did-40-happen birthday celebration, post-holiday meltdowns, knocked up, tied the knot, finally divorced that jerk, found God—the list goes on. But the best reason is that for most of us, it has been 5, 10, maybe 15 years since you've shrugged off all your responsibilities for a good belly laugh or two with the girls.

> ### Chick Wit
>
> Make a great music mix and give everyone a copy. There's nothing better than hitting the open road with a self-made soundtrack for your trip. Best of all, when the experience is over, the music will remind everyone of the fabulous time shared.
>
> —Helen, author, mother, and road-tripper

How Do We Decide?

Choosing which direction to point your compass can be daunting. Trust me, I know. I changed my mind exactly 564 times as I chiseled down the final destinations featured in this book. What you really need to consider is timing, budget, and the common interests of each of the girls.

The good news is that most of the women who I've grilled about their favorite girlfriend getaways say it was the simple things that made it fun: hunkering down in a cabin in the woods for a weekend of Mahjong and martinis or perhaps plopping down on a beach somewhere and catching up between chick-flick movie marathons.

On the flip side, the most common complaints I've heard centered on the group being mismatched financially or that they were socially out of sync with what they wanted to do. One girl invariably just wanted to sit by the hotel pool and bury her nose in a book while another wanted to hit the town. This doesn't mean you have to share the same income levels to share a vacation. It means you need to seek out a destination with economical accommodations that offers plenty of activities at every end of the spectrum.

The same is true if the likes and dislikes of the girls are out of sync. One might love theater, one might love shopping, and one might hate both. It happens. But can you say, "New York City"? Hit a place that offers a little bit of everything. Send the one who hates both (what's up with her, anyway?) to a museum and come up with a few activities that include everyone.

Timing is also critical. If summer is the best time for everyone to get the necessary time off for good behavior, don't head to the desert Southwest. It's hot. *Really* hot. Instead, seek out an outdoor adventure or a lazy beach destination that takes advantage of the weather but isn't overrun by tourists and families. If a post-holiday meltdown is what the girls want, consider a winter wonderland ski trip or a fitness-focused trip that starts off the new year on a good foot.

The first step toward figuring out where to go and setting yourselves up for a good time is making sure everyone's needs are met.

How Do We Get There?

Ah, the ol' planes, trains, and automobiles question. The answer depends on budget and how much time you have.

Planes ...

Making a case for jetting to your destination is easy, especially if you're meeting up with friends spread across the country. But these days, the downsides of air travel are piling up. Besides strategic packing (more on that in Chapter 3), most airports request a two-hour lead time for security processing, and delayed flights are the norm—and most recently, you'll be met with a barrage of nickel-and-dime fees.

In May 2008, U.S. Airways and United began charging $25 for check-in of a second bag. A third bag can run you between $25 and $100 on most airlines (if the carrier allows it at all). And you may want to invest in that huge handbag you've been eying—some airlines are limiting you to one carry-on that includes your purse (gasp!). If hunger strikes at 30,000 feet, you can drop up to $10 on snacks and meals. An in-flight movie can be another $5. And be prepared with cash and plastic, because several airlines such as Frontier and JetBlue accept credit and debit cards only for incidentals while Continental and Southwest accept only cash.

And then there's the issue of booking your flight. One-stop booking sites such as Travelocity, Expedia, and Orbitz make the process of booking flights, hotels, and rental cars easy as a few mouse clicks and usually provide competitive fare rates. But beware of booking fees. Airfare comparison site, **Airfarewatchdog** (www.airfarewatchdog. com) recently found a travel site that charged a processing fee of $35 per ticket booked. Most add between $5 and $10 but may also charge a change, refund, or cancellation fee upward of $75. With the mass proliferation of travel websites, a trend is growing toward minimal or no booking fees (currently being offered by Priceline)—and with hope, we'll see other sites follow suit.

What's the best course of action? Browse the "Terms & Conditions" or "FAQ" pages on these sites for fee disclosures. Also, formidable travel expert Peter Greenberg suggests on his website, www.petergreenberg. com, using a combination of online booking and calling a reservation agent to see which shakes out the best rate. To save time, he recommends a site called **Get Human** (www.gethuman.com), which lists direct phone numbers and tips that allow you to bypass the automated customer support service and speak with a live agent more quickly.

The bottom line? Although flying is becoming more challenging, until warp-speed teleportation becomes a reality, planes are still your fastest option.

Savvy Sister

Some popular all-in-one booking sites include **Travelocity** (www. travelocity.com), **Expedia** (www.expedia.com), **Orbitz** (www.orbitz. com), and **Hotwire** (www.hotwire.com). Travel search engine sites include **Kayak** (www.kayak.com), **SideStep** (www.sidestep.com), **Mobissimo** (www.mobissimo.com), **Priceline** (www.priceline.com), **Cheapflights** (www.cheapflights.com), and **TripAdvisor** (www. tripadvisor.com).

Trains ...

When my husband and I were preparing to relocate from Florida to Arizona in 1999, I drove one of our cars out on a house-finding mission. To return home to Florida, I had the option of a ridiculously priced one-way plane trip or hopping on board Amtrak for a leisurely three-day trip from Tucson to Orlando. I opted for the latter and had one of the best solo traveling experiences of my life. I passed the days with my nose plunged deep into a book only looking up occasionally to take in expansive views of the countryside, joined a lively crowd of seniors for wine and cheese happy hours (which started around 3 o'clock), and enjoyed three perfectly acceptable well-rounded meals, including vegetarian selections, that came with my fare.

That's not to say there weren't challenges. I had a bumpy shower experience, and nights in my private "roomette" in the sleeping car were long as I adjusted to the jostling train vibrations. But there's something romantic about traveling by train, and I can only imagine how much more fun it would have been sharing the experience with girlfriends. I will say that train travel is not for everybody, but it is extremely affordable. **Amtrak** continually offers weekly specials, tour packages, and discounted weekend getaway fares. For example, at the time of this writing, a weekend jaunt from Philadelphia to Penn Station in New York City was $45 (round trip). The cheapest airline ticket for the same trip was $320 into John F. Kennedy International Airport. What's more, the train travel time was only about 30 minutes longer than the non-stop flight.

Yes, just like in the airline industry, railroad travel delays do happen. But here's a little factoid to chew on if you're concerned about getting stuck on a delayed train: Amtrak allows you to bring aboard two carry-ons, each up to 50 pounds *plus* personal items such as laptops and purses. You'll be able to fire up your laptop or move about the cabins while you wait. It's just not the same as being strapped into a plane seat waiting for take-off clearance.

For more information, call Amtrak at **1-800-872-7245** or visit www.amtrak.com.

Powder Room

In June 2008, Amtrak unveiled a new look for the Coast Starlight, which operates daily along the scenic route between Los Angeles and Seattle. Enhanced amenities and services include a specialty coffee bar, newly redesigned theater with 50-inch plasma HD monitors, refurbished Parlour Cars, daily tastings of regional wines, and new dining items such as Pacific Bay scallops. The **Coast Starlight** is among several long-distance trains to be upgraded in the past few years (others include the **Empire Builder** and **City of New Orleans**).

... and Road Trips

Road tripping can be a blast as long as there are no more than four girls (unless you've rented a very large bus) and the trip is less than six hours. Through a completely unscientific survey of my girlfriends, any longer than six hours and you cross over into dangerous territory.

I just recently hit the road with three friends on a four-hour trek from Phoenix to San Diego (see, I travel!), and here are a few sound bites from the audio portion of the trip:

"Isn't this fun?"

A flurry of excited conversation followed by deep silence.

"Have you seen Cindy's* face? Can lip injections actually stretch out your bottom lip so much that you can never close your mouth again? She looks so weird." (*Name changed to protect the innocent's overzealous cosmetic surgeon.)

Long stretch of silence.

"Oh my gosh, that trucker guy is so checking you out. Wave!"

Chuckles followed by a short silence.

"Oh geez, that truck is totally following us. Why did you wave at him?"

One girl talks with her dad on a cell phone with bad reception while the driver softly sings, "Papa, Can You Hear Me?" from the 1983 movie *Yentl*.

An open-mouth belly laugh from the back seat (the girl on the phone is too young to remember *Yentl*).

"God, I need to get out of this car."

Silence interrupted by occasional snores.

"Wasn't that fun?"

That's what you've got to love about road trips. You and your girls are rolling along toward your destination in a private cabin on wheels with Red Bull and giant donuts within arms' reach. You can say anything, make impromptu fast food stops, play games, and belt out show tunes or priceless movie theme songs—all things you really can't do on an airplane.

Powder Room

Portable car navigation systems are not only handy for road trips but also if you plan to drive in an unfamiliar city once you reach your destination. You'll find basic vehicle GPS units at most electronics stores for $180 and up.

Where Do We Go?

In the pages that follow, you'll find detailed shopping excursions, adventure trips, spa getaways, and much more. My goal was to mine out getaways so juicy and rewarding that they must be shared. And while some are based on my own experiences, most explore destinations recommended to me by others in the know or by those on my own must-do list.

So, stay with me through the next few chapters as we fly through ways to plan your trip, and you'll be off on a fabulous getaway in no time!

Crash Course in Travel Planning

In This Chapter

* ⚹ Tips on breezing through the planning phase of your getaway

* ⚹ Tools for creating and sharing your trip itinerary

* ⚹ How to prepare your family to get along without you (it can be done!)

* ⚹ The four girlfriend getaway agreements

Still with me? Congratulations—you have graduated to Round 2 of basic getaway training! Survive this section, and you're almost there. In this chapter, we'll look at how to make the tricky job of planning your trip as easy as possible as well as paving the way for a smooth departure. We round out the chapter with a few ideas on how to deal with those little annoyances that can otherwise ruin the perfect getaway.

Communicating with the Girls

You'd think that in this day and age of the Blackberry, iPhones, Bluetooth, and whatever new-fangled gadgets are invented between now and when this book hits the shelves, planning would be a breeze. But if you ask me, all the electronic doohickeys in the world can't streamline the planning phase of your trip if everyone doesn't have clear tasks and goals. In fact, I think the menagerie of communication tools can complicate the matter. How many times lately have you searched in vain for an important e-mail or accidentally erased a voicemail? Someone has to take charge, muddle through all the ideas, streamline the process, and make a clear plan of action.

My suggestion is to empower each girl in your group with a major task. Make it fun, and enjoy the journey of planning your getaway!

Here are some possible roles that your cast and crew can play in the planning process:

* **Transportation Babe (TB).** This person will take on the job of researching the best way to get to your destination. If you decide on a road trip, the TB will be armed with maps, driving directions, and a checklist for your road trip stash. If you decide to fly, the TB will research the best carriers and flights and disseminate the information necessary for each girl to book her own seat. She will also be the person with gum.

Powder Room

For planning road trips, check out the Rand McNally TripMaker Planning Tool. It's free, but for the low-low price of $19.95 for a Premier Membership, you can print a nifty trip guide with detailed maps, estimated driving times and distance between stops, and explicit driving directions. The girls will be impressed, trust me. For more information, visit www.randmcnally.com.

* **Motor Maiden (MM).** The right-hand woman to the Transportation Babe, the MM will make car rental and airport shuttle arrangements as necessary. She will also be the designated backseat driver on road trips.

* **Home Girl (HG).** The holder of this position will comb through accommodation options to find the most perfect home away from home as possible. Her duties will include scouring the Internet for killer deals, making sure everybody has a comfortable place to sleep at night, and booking the rooms. The HG will bring the ear plugs.

* **Entertainment Diva (ED).** Also referred to as the cruise director, the ED will be given the almighty job of keeping the troops entertained. She will compile a list of must-hit restaurants, recreational options, shopping excursions, and other diversions. She will be armed with tissues and hand sanitizer at all times.

* **Cyber Sister (CS).** The smarty pants of the group, the CS will compile and manage trip details via an online travel tool described in the following section. She will work closely with the TB, HG, and ED to draft flexible daily itineraries that all members of the group check and approve. Optional duties during the trip will include programming the GPS navigator and waving cell phones wildly in the air to establish reception.

* **The Secretary of Expense (SE).** This position is dedicated to the all-important task of tracking shared expenses such as lodging, cab fare, shuttle fees, activities, and tips. If you decide that expenses will be split among the group equally after the trip is over, the SE will be the keeper of all shared receipts and will disseminate financial damages after the trip. During the trip, she should be armed with cash for tips and will also be the keeper of all coupons.

* **The Kids.** These are the gals in the group with no particular skills. We love them, and we need them for their wit and good humor—but because their hidden talents have yet to surface, they just have to show up. However, the Kids will have last dibs on showers and will be relegated to sleeper sofas and rollaways when necessary (sorry—someone has to sleep on them).

Powder Room

Start your lodging search on **Hotels.com**. Not only do they offer comprehensive listings, special deals, and value packages, but they also have a price-match guarantee. If you find a lower hotel rate through another means, the site will either refund the difference or cancel your reservations without penalty. For more information, visit www.hotels.com.

Creating Your Itinerary

The key to creating an itinerary that the group will embrace is balancing flexibility with planned activities. And a central storage point for organizing all this information is key. Consider starting an online trip blog (free at sites such as www.blogger.com and wordpress.com) or using an online planning tool such as www.ImIn.com. One caveat: remember to set up your blog or online tool in a private, invite-only, or password-protected mode so the world doesn't know your travel plans.

The advantage of planning your trip online is that you and your travel companions can share thoughts, questions, and suggestions all in one place throughout the planning process. You'll also be able to print itineraries or access them online from your laptop or portable devices.

Here are a few cool tools to check out:

* **Trip Planner at Yahoo! Travel.** Yahoo!'s Trip Planner allows you to create a trip, share it with friends, add activities, and post photos. The best feature of this handy site is the blog-style listing of group questions, thoughts, and suggestions rather than streams of e-mails and phone calls. For more information, visit www.travel. yahoo.com/trip.

* **TripWiser.** Akin to a social networking website for travelers, TripWiser offers a clean, fresh space for planning your getaway. Create your trip, invite your pals, and plan your itinerary for each day of the trip. Add destinations, activities, and restaurants. Facebook users can add TripWiser's Going Places application to their profile. For more information, visit www.tripwiser.com.

* **AAA TripTik.** This nifty tool was just recently made free to non-AAA members and takes the cake for online mapping. You can automatically format a trip plan with detailed maps, hotels, restaurants, and activities. The plan can be printed and taken along with you or e-mailed to all the members of your travel group. For more information, visit www.aaa.com.

Prepping Your Family

In my experience, even with just my tight little nebula of one dog and one husband, preparations must be made.

Here are some simple steps toward preparing your family for your departure:

* **Embrace frozen foods.** I guarantee your family won't starve while you're gone—especially if you stock the freezer with frozen pizzas, meat patties or veggie burgers, fries, macaroni and cheese, bags of mixed vegetables, and frozen sweet treats. They might gain a few pounds, but they won't go hungry. If you're the type who feeds your family organic, meticulously balanced homemade meals on a daily basis, then you need this getaway more than any of us. Precook the meals, and freeze those suckers in microwave-safe containers. Stock the pantry with buns, bread, peanut butter, pasta, sauce, and healthy snacks. If you're truly worried that scurvy might ravish your family while you're gone, then you worry too much (and should stock the fridge with orange juice).

Chick Wit

The first time I left my baby in someone else's care, I practically needed a U-Haul to carry everything that I packed for her. And I was only going away *one* night. My best advice to new moms is don't overpack. Make sure you have food, clothes, and diapers, and everything else can be improvised.

—Tiffany, computer programmer and new mom

* **Plan a home tour.** It totally amazes me that after nearly ten years of living in the same house, my husband doesn't know where anything is. Call the family together and lead them through the house, pointing out the locations of the Band-Aids, first-aid kit, fire extinguisher, list of emergency phone numbers, vacuum, spare keys, kitty litter box, doggy pooper scooper, mailbox, and main trash bins. If you have kids, make it a scavenger hunt (whatever it takes to familiarize the fam with all things not related to the TV).

* **Write up your pet projects.** Here's your chance to inform the spouse, the kids, and so on about how to actually care for all the pets they've adopted. Write step-by-step care instructions including feeding times and amounts, potty times, medications, treat allocations, and the phone numbers and locations of the veterinarian's office and the closest pet emergency clinic. Point out where pet supplies like carriers, brushes, and treats are kept.

* **Designate a spy.** If you are truly paranoid about leaving home for whatever reason, ask a trusted neighbor or friend who lives close by to keep an eye on your homies.

I'm telling you these things not because I think your family members are total idiots—but instead, because I want you to relax. Women worry. We know that. The point is to alleviate anxiety so you can enjoy a fun, guilt-free getaway. When you return, both the kitty litter box and the mailbox will likely be overflowing—but after a rewarding vacation, it just won't matter. Right?

Powder Room

Single ladies, here's your chance to save a few bucks while racking up good Earth karma points. Unplugging your appliances when you leave for a vacation adds up to a smaller carbon footprint, according to authors of *The Green Book: The Everyday Guide to Saving the Planet One Simple Step at a Time* (Three Rivers Press, 2007). Close shades and curtains and set your thermostat to 50°F (10°C) during winter and 85°F (29°C) in summer months (unless you have animals staying at home under the care of a pet sitter). Depending on how long you're gone, you could save up to $100 a year.

Setting the Ground Rules

You're almost there. Now comes the delicate task of setting the groundwork for healthy group dynamics. Rather than tiptoeing around issues such as who has to share a bed, who gets to sleep alone, who snores, who pinches pennies, who overspends, and so on, tackle these matters beforehand. What seems like small things can become major annoyances that can spoil a trip (and sometimes friendships).

Here are the four girlfriend getaway agreements.

Be Present

Put a limit on how many times each gal is allowed to pine for the kids, the dog, the boyfriend, the new job, and so on. If someone seems clearly obsessed with something outside the task at hand (having a good time), then initiate a Whine Jar. Each time someone goes over her limit, she has to plunk five bucks in the jar. The money, of course, goes toward a bottle of wine on the final evening. Obsessive calling and texting counts, too. The point is that time with your girlfriends is a rare treat that should be savored.

Be Practical

Agree up front on how expenses will be shared. Nothing spoils a trip more than constant worry over money. I personally think all shared expenses (shuttles, cabs, rooms, and so on) should be tracked and split equally after the trip. However, exceptions do arise. Inevitably, someone drinks like a fish while someone else doesn't touch alcohol. And that can add up. In those cases, consider separating drink costs from shared meal bills.

I'll be the first to admit that I will down a margarita (or three) on vacation, and my math skills are easily impaired by tequila. If you agree to separate drinks as an individual expense, make it easier by counting the number of drinks rather than trying to keep track of actual cost. Make brews and house wines equal to $5 and cocktails $10. Adjust accordingly, but if you do that throughout the trip, it will average out and be easier to track. Perhaps someone in your group is barely scraping by financially and will sleep on the floor just for a few days away from reality. In those cases, work out something so that she doesn't feel like a burden but still contributes what she can to the bottom line.

Be Fair

Who gets the lumpy sleeper sofa, and who gets the cushy king-size bed? Maybe it's the gal who made the least effort in the planning process—but then again, maybe she just came through a major life change and didn't have time to participate but needs this getaway more than anyone. Consider pulling a number out of a hat, applying different price points to different bedrooms or agreeing to switch halfway through the vacation.

> **STOP** *Bad Trip*
> Whatever you do, don't go with the first-come, first-served rule. You're setting yourselves up for resentments to creep in. Deal with it in a way that satisfies everyone, and you'll sleep tight at night.

Be Tolerant

Speaking of sleeping arrangements, you really get to know someone when you sleep with them—in the close quarters of a shared hotel room, that is. All of us have idiosyncrasies when it comes to our nocturnal habits. Some of us need a light on and *Conan O'Brien* softly crooning on the TV. Others read or prefer total darkness, and the mere sound of someone else breathing can drive them to the point of madness. If you're the latter, you don't want to hold the entire breathing thing against your best friend. Bring ear plugs and sleep masks.

Ear plugs in a shared bunking situation are a girl's best friend. Bring enough to share. Any quality foam plugs will do, but the Sleep Pretty in Pink Women's Ear Plugs are shaped for a woman's ear and run about $3.99 in most drugstores for a pack of seven. For more information, visit www.sleepinpink.com.

Primping, Packing, and Final Deck Check

In This Chapter

* Tips for scheduling your pre-travel grooming needs

* Strategic packing tips: what to carry on and what to check in

* A beauty addict's top picks for travel-friendly beauty

I once ran into an old boyfriend at an airport en route to Puerto Vallarta, Mexico, where I was meeting up with a college roommate for a week of lounging on the beach. My freshly highlighted hair was crammed carelessly into a scrunchie, and my fabulous new faux-tanned skin was hidden under a gigantic sweatshirt (which I always travel in because of its dual role as a pillow). I was horrified because finally, here was my opportunity to make him regret all his past mistakes and to marvel in my confidence and hotness. But I missed the chance because I was a mess from having been up all night frantically washing laundry, portioning my beauty potions between tiny travel bottles and zip-top baggies, and packing—all while trying not to smudge my freshly painted nails.

I'm not saying you have to get all gussied up just to sit pretty in a tin can while you jet off to your destination. Heaven knows you'll probably end up sitting next to creepy Carl who keeps "accidentally" brushing your knee or desperately trying to engage you in something that resembles a conversation. But it does help to be prepared. Remember that we're enjoying the journey even before we get there. So, give yourself plenty of time to plan your pre-travel beauty regimen, vacation wardrobe, and packing schedule so that you can smoothly transition into vacation mode.

Before-You-Go Beauty

Low-maintenance gals have my permission to skip this section. But first, here's a little advice from my beauty philosophy book (excuse me while I climb onto my soapbox). True beauty comes from confidence and an inner core draped in peace and health. The path to beauty radiates with reverence, kindness, and knowing not to take yourself too seriously. (We know that, right?) Now, all that aside, there's a lot to be said for well-groomed brows, manicured nails, and a drop-dead awesome haircut—especially when you need that kick of confidence to set off on a new adventure.

Here's a checklist for your path toward external, pre-travel beauty:

* **Face.** If you're like me, just below the surface of your skin lies a pimple the size of Texas waiting to erupt. According to my face-saving aesthetician, pimples are formed weeks before they decide to make their grand entrance. All it takes is a stress-induced spike in hormones and voilà—pimple vacation interruptus. What's worse, if you plan to hit the spa on your getaway, a pimple can rear its ugly head after a facial treatment. If you can, a month before your trip schedule a deep-cleansing facial with a local skin-care guru who can coax those suckers to the surface and initiate the healing process. If you can't, stash a pimple concealer product in your cosmetic bag. My favorite beauty weapon against the

bump is the Judith August EraseZit Antiseptic Concealer (www.
judithaugustcosmetics.com).

* **Nails.** Schedule a manicure and pedicure a few days before the
trip. The general rule of thumb is to keep your fingernails neutral
and go bold with your toenail polish color. Pack bottles of your
polishes if you're worried about chips.

* **Hair.** There's nothing like a fresh cut and color or even just a
home hot-oil conditioning treatment to get you revved up for a
vacation. Schedule your hair appointment a week before your trip
or on the same day as your nail appointments, and make it a day
of beauty.

* **Brows.** Two or three days before your trip, tame those little suckers into submission with a professional brow waxing, threading, or
tweezing service. Well-shaped brows open your eye area and trim
years off your perceived age. But don't schedule a brow wax the
day before your trip because of possible redness.

* **Bikini.** Even if you're not going to a beach destination, you might
have a dip in the hot tub or pool on your agenda. Don't be caught
unprepared. Schedule a bikini wax or try a home depilatory kit.
Just like a brow wax, give it a day or so before your trip for any
redness to subside.

Savvy Sister

The first question on any virgin bikini waxer's mind is, "Does
it hurt?" Heck yeah, it hurts. Your hair is being yanked out by its
tiny little follicles. Keep the ouch to a minimum by getting a skilled
waxer's name from a trusted friend, and never get a bikini wax right
before your menstrual cycle. The best time for a wax job is the week
after your period when your pain threshold is at its highest. Trust me,
the two to three weeks of hair-free freedom are worth the couple
seconds of oh-good-golly-that-smarts pain.

* **Body scrub.** It doesn't matter what part of the country you live
in. Dull, drab skin happens. For vacation-ready skin, use a home
body scrub product a few days before your trip. Freshly buffed
skin better absorbs moisturizer and treatments such as cellulite
creams and self-tanners.

The beauty aisles are flooded with exfoliating body products. Save a few bucks with this home concoction: mix about $1/3$ cup fine sea salt with a little less than $1/3$ cup safflower oil. Grate the peel from one fresh orange into the mixture for an extra kick. Gently massage the scrub all over, avoiding your face. Focus on your knees, feet, and elbows. Go easy on areas such as your chest and décolletage.

* **Faux glow.** For my fair-skinned sisters headed to warm climates, a touch of bronzer gives the illusion of healthier skin. I personally think a tan makes me look thinner and taller, but that's just my twisted thinking. Smooth on your self-bronzer at least a day or two in advance of your trip—or schedule a bronzing treatment at a local day spa, where you can get an all-over self-tanner applied in hard-to-reach spots such as your back and the backs of your legs. In a crunch, grab a box of self-tanning towelettes at the drugstore and stash them in your overnight bag (try L'Oreal Sublime Bronze Self-Tanning Towelettes, available at most mass retailers).

Packing for Your Adventure

Proper packing technique, like yoga, is a skill that I practice but will never truly master. Back in the good old days of unlimited baggage, I would empty my closet *and* the kitchen sink into my luggage and hope for the best. Nowadays, airline restriction weight and bag limits make strategic packing a must (even more so with road trips, when you're sharing the trunk with your gal pals).

Chick Wit

Get organized during the packing process with my best friend, Ziploc baggies. Fill each bag with panties, bras, or swim wear; remove the extra air, and seal. It saves on luggage space and is a lifesaver if your hotel room is short on drawer space.

—Chrissy, food broker

Ask yourself some honest questions when you set about packing. Do you really need all that makeup for a vacation with your girlfriends? Are laundry facilities available where you're staying? Are six pairs of shoes really practical for a three-day weekend? You get the picture. Start with the basics, and add only what you think you'll need. If the worst happens and you run short on clothes, plan an impromptu shopping excursion.

Beauty and Grooming Essentials

When you travel by plane, aim to take the least amount of items as possible in your carry-on bag. By the same token, keep in mind flight delays, cancellations, lost luggage, and other unforeseen circumstances that might separate you from prescription medications and other necessities.

Here's a beauty checklist broken down by items you may want to place in your checked bags and those you may prefer to pack in your carry-on bag.

Check it:

❏ Makeup

❏ Shampoo, conditioner, and hair styling products

❏ Band-Aids

❏ Makeup remover

❏ Facial cleanser and moisturizer

❏ Sunblock for face and suntan oil/lotion for body

❏ Body wash and pouf, loofah, or whatever else you soap up with and that you can't live without

❏ Body lotion

❏ Hair brush and other hair accessories

❏ Razor and shaving cream

❏ Cotton swabs

❏ Eye mask

❏ Nail polish and nail polish remover

❏ Travel candle

Powder Room

The Transportation Security Administration (TSA) has come up with a nifty 3-1-1 rule to help us remember airline carry-on restrictions: 3-oz. bottles, packed in 1 zip-top bag, and 1 bag per passenger. Here's a translation: all liquids, gels, and aerosols must be in 3-oz. or smaller containers, which should be crammed in 1 quart-size, zip-top, clear plastic bag. Stick to the 3-1-1 rule and security check-in will go faster. For more information about airline restrictions, go to www.tsa.gov.

Carry on:

❏ Lip balm

❏ Toothbrush, toothpaste, and dental floss

❏ Hand lotion and hand sanitizer

❏ Nail file

❏ Baby powder

❏ Mini hairbrush or comb

❏ Contact lenses, case, and contact lens solution

❏ Eye drops

❏ Eyeglasses and sunglasses

❏ Deodorant

❏ Feminine products

❏ Pain reliever and prescription medications

❏ Ear plugs

Avoid spillage and the "mystery goo" phenomenon with travel-ready grooming products. Look for TSA-friendly sample sizes, single-use treatment packets, and mini sizes that you can tuck into your makeup bag. The beauty store Sephora offers an Airplane-Approved Beauty list on www.sephora.com, listing a full selection of travel kits and mini-size beauty finds.

Another trick in avoiding leaks is to fill containers only three-quarters full so contents have room to spread out, especially at high altitudes. But just to be safe, still pack checked-in liquids in zip-top or washable, reusable cosmetic bags.

As a self-proclaimed beauty addict, I've looked high and low for effective products that travel well. Here are some items from my own overnight beauty bag:

* LUSH Solid Shampoo Bars and Travel Tins: www.lush.com

* Ojon Rub-Out Dry Cleanser To Go (for giving hair a pick-me-up while diminishing oils and smells): www.sephora.com

* Almay Hypo-Allergenic Eye Makeup Remover Pads: available at most drugstores

* Olay Daily Facials Express Wet Cleansing Cloths (for cleansing on the run): available at most drugstores

* Facial blotting tissues from The Body Shop (to absorb excess oil): www.thebodyshop.com

* Lippmann Collection The Stripper To Go (one-use nail polish remover finger mitts): www.lippmanncollection.com

* Philosophy Booster Caps (one-use ampules with a nightly hit of anti-aging retinol): www.philosophy.com

* Bodhi Balm by Buddha Nose (a mini tin of aromatherapy to calm nerves and cover icky smells—think about getting sandwiched between creepy Carl and sweaty Sam on the plane): www.buddhanose.com

* C. O. Bigelow Chemists Mentha Lip Balm Stick (with SPF 15 and a hint of mint for fresh breath): www.bigelowchemists.com

* SweetSpot Labs on-the-go mini wipettes (for "on the spot" freshness in basil grapefruit or geranium lavender scents): www.sweetspotlabs.com

* Emergen-C Vitamin C fizzy packs (single-use energy boosters that mix with water): available at most health food stores

Powder Room

I once had the chance to interview a past Miss Arizona, and she let me in on her beauty secret for keeping her tresses fabulous during a long day of running from event to event: baby powder. Midway through a long day, rub a small amount in your hands and then massage into your scalp to freshen up the scent and keep oils at bay.

Wardrobe

Besides undergarments and comfy PJs, your wardrobe should be based on the daily itineraries you and the girls have drafted during the planning stage. The goal is to travel light, and if you're heading to a shopping destination, keep the door open to add a few new items to your wardrobe during your trip.

Through a series of unfortunate events, I recently found myself watching *The Bachelor* reality TV show. One of the bachelorette contestants brought an entire suitcase full of shoes. Granted, she was trying to snag the man of her dreams—but please girlfriend, *twenty* pairs of shoes?

Shoot for three pairs max for your getaway. Pick one pair based on the central theme of your trip: flip-flops for beach getaways, athletic shoes for adventure trips, cowgirl boots for ranch vacations, and so on. Your second pair should be for dressing up and dinners out. The third pair is on your feet during travel.

Finally, your itineraries are planned, your bags are packed, and you're one step closer to a getaway to remember.

Here's the last-minute checklist:

❏ Wallet

❏ Driver's license or photo ID

❏ Passport (if necessary)

❏ Credit cards, cash, traveler's cheques

❏ Address book or PDA

❏ Small notebook and pen

❏ Pillowcase or travel pillow

❏ Magazines or books

❏ Snacks

❏ Sunglasses

❏ Camera, camera accessories, and extra batteries (if necessary)

❏ Plane tickets or boarding passes

❏ Confirmation numbers for rental car, shuttle, and hotels

❏ Travel agent contact information (if necessary)

❏ Directions and maps

Powder Room

If you're a list maker, check out the handy "Make a List" tool at www.girlawhirl.com. Create a "What's a Girl to Pack? List" and then print it, e-mail it to yourself, and send it to your travel pals. There are no excuses for someone forgetting their swimsuit!

Fasten Your Seatbelts, and Off You Go!

Posy, an advertising agency executive and a friend of a friend, recently relayed a story to me of how she and her 40-and-fabulous girlfriends set out on a getaway to Aspen, Colorado—only to be delayed by a 10-hour layover in Salt Lake City, Utah. Catching wind of a "free" shuttle bound for bargains and margaritas, they hopped on board a bus to kill some time.

"One of us really should have noticed the bus driver's name tag and more importantly, his title: Bill, Missionary," she says. As they whizzed past the Macy's and Crate & Barrel and pulled into the parking lot of The Church of Jesus Christ of Latter-Day Saints headquarters, it dawned on them that Coach bags and afternoon cocktails were out of the question. Through a series of hilarious misadventures from feigning a diabetic coma to hobbling down unknown streets in stiletto boots, they finally made their way back to the airport by hitching a ride in the bed of a truck—full-length fur coats and all. "Our adventure was officially underway," she says.

As Posy's story demonstrates, you never know where a girlfriend getaway might take you (and you should also be wary of "free" shuttles). Your getaway may not go off without a hitch, but you'll be creating precious memories that'll last a lifetime. Go with the flow, and be in the moment.

Part 2

Shop 'Til You Plop: Adventures in Retail Therapy

Besides the obvious, what's the major difference between men and women? Most men equate shopping with the throbbing pain of slamming a finger in a door. But most women view shopping as therapy. In this section, we lace up our walking shoes and head to the big cities and mega malls for shopping excursions. We also stroll through boutiques in cities with small-town character and pound the aisles of outlets in search of killer bargains. Finally, we dig up treasures for our homes and head to places where quality handcrafted items rule.

(Photo courtesy of Hollywood & Highland Center.)

Tinseltown glam meets shop-until-you-drop therapy at the Hollywood & Highland Center in Los Angeles.

Big-City Power Shopping

In This Chapter

* ✳ The importance of sensible shoes

* ✳ Bargain buys and shopping highs in New York City

* ✳ Finding fame and fashion in Los Angeles

* ✳ Miracle miles meet designer duds on the streets of Chicago

* ✳ One-stop shopping in Minnesota's mother of all malls

* ✳ More shopping destinations in major cities

For some of us, shopping is a sport. Throngs of hungry shoppers, the din of cash registers, and miles of shiny racks only make you stronger. If this describes you and your girlfriends, you've landed in the right chapter. While the focus of this chapter is big-city shopping excursions, I've also dug up accommodations at various price ranges, hot spots for refueling, and a few diversions along the way. So, lace up your walking shoes and get set for a serious slice of retail therapy.

Sole Mate

Speaking of shoes, nothing spoils a power shopping trip like sore soles. So, make room in your suitcase for a pair of sensible shoes. And no—they don't have to be frumpy. Supportive, low-heeled Mary Janes, skimmers, or hip sneakers look cute with just about any getup. My personal favs are Børn, Privo, and Merrell because they blend comfort with some attempt at fashion. Heck, even Keds are cute these days—and the sport versions offer heel cups and arch support.

> ## Powder Room
> For a solid selection of sensible shoes as well as road-tested clothes and accessories, check out **TravelSmith** at www.TravelSmith.com or call **1-800-950-1600** to order a catalog.

Fashion Central: Manhattan

What better way to kick off a chapter dedicated to shopping meccas than to charge right into the heart of Manhattan? But with the endless options, planning a big-city shopping excursion is no easy task.

In fact, the hair on the back of my neck stands up just thinking about my first **New York City** shopping trip. It was my sixteenth birthday, and I was a typical wide-eyed Catholic school girl who had rarely ventured from my home state of Florida. Bright and early on our first day in the city, my mom and I popped on our '80s power pumps and made a beeline to Barney's. No one told us the store was 10 sprawling floors. The day was a blur of crowded escalators, miles of clothing racks, near starvation ("We're not eating until we buy something!" was my mother's determined mantra), and throbbing feet. Overwhelmed, we left hours later—beaten, battered, and without a single shopping bag. To make matters worse, we spent the next day at a swanky salon, where my signature side ponytail was transformed into a giant mound of teased blond locks worthy of a Country Western singer circa 1972. Don't let this happen to you. Bad hair happens (and looking back, I don't know which was worse—a lopsided ponytail or the mile-high 'do). But armed with a solid game plan, bad shopping trips can be avoided.

Depending on who you talk to, the **Manhattan** shopping scene encompasses more than a dozen hot blocks and districts. You've got your biggies: **Bloomingdale's, Bergdorf Goodman, Barney's, Henri Bendel, Saks Fifth Avenue,** and **Takashimaya.** And you've got your trendy and trying-not-to-be-trendy neighborhoods where flagship stores and boutiques abound: **SoHo, NoLita, Greenwich Village, East Village,** and the **Meat-Packing District** to name a few. We're talking urban retail la-la land of mega proportions.

The best way to navigate the landscape while keeping track of your shopping mates is to book yourselves a shopping tour. The tours are cheap by New York standards and are led by savvy insiders. And here's the best part: not only will you be privy to special discounts, but you'll also get access to the wholesale showrooms of the city's famed **Garment District** (normally open only to the general public during sample sales).

Garment District Tour

New York designers are the world's preeminent fashion innovators, and there's only one way to travel deep into the international heart of the world's emerging fashion scene: through the one-square-mile jungle of the Garment District. But you can't get into the halls of the wholesale showrooms on good karma alone. You need an "in," and Pamela Parisi of **The Elegant Tightwad** is the one to call when you and the gals have your minds set on mining out designer duds at wholesale prices and below.

A former showroom model and retail manufacturing insider, Parisi and her personal shoppers lead walking tours of groups up to 12 on shopping excursions. Their mission is simple: save dough while hunting down gorgeous pieces to add to your wardrobe. Her most popular tours, **Garment District Diva** (four hours, $90) and **Accessory Addict** (two hours, $45) hit the wholesale showrooms—but she also offers consignment, vintage, and custom excursions if you and the gals prefer a private tour. Another advantage of booking your shopping stint through

Elegant Tightwad is that once you schedule the tour, the company will follow up with a questionnaire regarding sizes and special needs and provide an informational sheet on what to expect and what to wear. *1-800-808-4614.* *www.theeleganttightwad.com.*

Other Shopping Tours

Professional fashion stylist and owner of **Style Guide** shopping tours, Carrie Gjermundsen can guide you through the more eclectic neighborhoods such as NoLita and the Meat-Packing District. Plus, she has collaborated with many of the boutiques on her tour for exclusive discounts. Tours are approximately four hours and range from $100 each for groups, $150 for two people, and $225 for a private tour. Custom tours are available for shorter or longer durations. *718-935-9883.* *www.styleguidenyctours.com.*

Shop Gotham is practically a city institution and offers daily group walking tours as well as private excursions. The two-hour SoHo excursion combines upscale boutique shopping with bargain hunting through NoLita and SoHo for $36 per person. The three-hour Garment Center tour winds through sample sales, wholesale showrooms, and retail stores for $63. *917-599-6650.* *www.shopgotham.com.*

> 👄 *Chick Wit*
>
> My favorite girlfriend trips happen in big cities—like New York City—because big cities always seem to bring on a right-of-passage for me and my life. I walk away realizing something bigger and better about myself and I love experiencing that with a bunch of really important women in my life.
> —Carrie, publicist

Discount Detours

What gal doesn't like a good deal? The underbelly of the city's shopping scene beats with amazing deals if you have the patience to dig them out. **Filene's Basement** and **Loehmann's** are solid choices for rock-bottom pricing on designer threads, bags, shoes, and home accessories. **Century 21 Department Store** used to be the city's best-kept secret until Zagat outed it as "the No. 1 discount store in New York" (and for good reason: prices are slashed up to 70 percent).

> **Filene's Basement.** Broadway: **212-873-8000.** Avenue of the Americas: **212-620-3100.** Union Square: **212-358-0169.** www.filenesbasement.com.

> **Loehmann's.** Upper West Side: **212-882-9990.** Chelsea: **212-352-0856.** www.loehmanns.com.

> **Century 21 Department Store.** Manhattan: **212-227-9092.** www.c21stores.com.

Weekends were made for trolling the streets of the **Hell's Kitchen Flea Market,** an open-air fair free to the public with an eclectic mix of antiques, art, vintage clothing, jewelry, and collector's items. *Located between 9th and 10th Avenue on 39th Street. Open Saturdays–Sundays 10 A.M.–6 P.M.* ***212-243-5343.*** *www.hellskitchenfleamarket.com.*

For a departure outside the city, head an hour north to **Woodbury Common Premium Outlets**—home to some 220 stores ranging from designer duds to specialty gifts (Barney's, Burberry, Diane Von Furstenberg, Jimmy Choo, Kate Spade, and Salvatore Ferragamo, to name a few). ***845-928-4000.*** *www.premiumoutlets.com.*

Diva Diversions

No doubt you've heard that the city offers a dizzying array of activities—but no girlfriend getaway would be complete without walking in the footsteps of the four very fashionable, very fictional icons of *Sex and the City.* Even after hitting the rerun syndicate, *Sex and the City* tours are still as hot as Samantha's nooner with the Worldwide Express guy in Episode 70.

Created by **On Location Tours,** the *Sex and the City* HotSpot Tour is a three-and-a-half-hour bus jaunt hosted by professional actresses or stand-up comedians versed in show trivia. You'll make stops at hangouts such as the **Magnolia Bakery,** where Miranda and Carrie stopped for cupcakes in Episode 35, and the sex shop where Charlotte meets "The Rabbit" in Episode 9. Because the tours sell out, you'll need to grab them at least two weeks in advance. Bachelorette packages, complete with a Pleasure Chest gift kit (I'll leave the contents to your imagination), and custom tour packages are available. Even if you're not a fan of the show, the interactive tour is an engaging way to see the city. *Tickets: $40 per person.* **212-683-2027.** *www.screentours.com.*

When you're ready to trade those sensible shoes for a night out in your new Jimmy Choos, make reservations at **Buddakan,** a hip spot where eclectic Asian cuisine meets downtown chic. **212-989-6699.** *www. buddakannyc.com.*

For casual drinks, dinner, or just gawking at the pretty heads that pass by, head to **Hotel Gansevoort.** The roof-top lounge, **Plunge,** mixes stunning city views with trendy cocktails, while **Ono Restaurant** is celebrated for its neo-Japanese dishes. **212-206-6700.** *www. hotelgansevoort.com.*

You can also raise your glasses to girl-time at **Flute** in midtown Manhattan. Located in a space that was once a speakeasy, this gathering place is home to a menu of savory small plates, champagne by the flute, and creative cocktails. Call ahead to reserve a table. **212-265-5169.** *www.flutebar.com.*

Where to Stay

For the budget conscious, **Apple Core Hotels** offers five centrally located, midtown Manhattan hotels with rates starting at $109. The five hotels offer a typical hotel chain décor, but what they lack in personality they make up for in features such as free wi-fi access and complimentary breakfast and fitness centers. Choose from the La Quinta Inn Manhattan (17 West 32nd St.), Red Roof Inn Manhattan (6 West 32nd St.), the smoke-free Comfort Inn Midtown (129 West 46th St.), Super 8 Hotel Times Square (59 West 46th St.), and the Ramada Inn East Side (161 Lexington Ave.). **1-800-567-7720.** *www.applecorehotels.com.*

For a boutique experience, **The Shoreham** and **The Mansfield** hotels in midtown Manhattan both offer luxurious touches such as pillow-top mattresses with plush linens and seasonal packages ideal for power shoppers. You'll also find seasonal packages at both that cater to women. Standard rooms at The Shoreham start at $299. **1-800-553-3347** *or* **212-247-6700.** *www.shorehamhotel.com.* Standard rooms at

The Mansfield start at $499. *1-800-255-5167 or 212-277-8700. www.mansfieldhotel.com.*

The **W New York** is another option. Home to **Bliss Spa,** the W stocks its ultra-contemporary rooms with Bliss products. Rates fluctuate, and a stay at the W can range from $300 to $700 per night. *212-755-1200. www. starwoodhotels.com.*

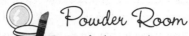

Powder Room

For further reading, pick up *The Complete Idiot's Guide to New York City* (Alpha Books, 2008) by Anita Gates. The book chronicles the ins and outs of navigating the city, from nightlife and theater to dining and accommodations with insider tips along the way.

Walk of Fame: Los Angeles

Why do we love Los Angeles? Parking is a hassle, air pollution is off the charts, and the freeways are consistently ranked as the worst in the country for sun-up to-sun-down traffic jams. But despite all that, you've got to love it—the culture, the cuisine, the glamour, and the colorful vibe that radiates from the tips of the city's ruby slippers to the top of its bottle-blonde locks. The City of Angels is fun, especially for a bunch of gals on the fashion prowl.

And it's all here: Rodeo Drive, Melrose Avenue, Montana Avenue, Sunset Plaza, Westwood Village, and so on. **Los Angeles** might just have as many shopping beats as New York City. But navigating them is another story. My advice is to map out days for window shopping and days for serious down-and-dirty, hit-the-pavement shopping. For the power shopping days, consider a guided romp through the Los Angeles **Fashion District.**

Fashion District Tour

Home of the apparel industry's West Coast hub, the Los Angeles Fashion District spans some 90 blocks of downtown Los Angeles and is flanked by a bustling mix of retailers, wholesalers, and unique vendors. The area is also home to a textiles market, the largest flower market in the United States, and a **Jewelry District** that is second in size only to

New York City's. You can tackle the retail areas yourselves, but the Los Angeles wholesale marts are not generally open to the public except during sample sales and are a jungle to navigate. Los Angeles Fashion District sample sales are generally held the last Friday of every month. For more on the Los Angeles Fashion District, including shopping tips and terms, visit www.fashiondistrict.org.

Enter Christine Silvestri of **Urban Shopping Adventures.** Backed by a retail marketing background and more than twenty years as a Los Angeles resident, Silvestri offers three-hour strategic walking tours that take you inside the four massive clothing marts of the Los Angeles Fashion District. She is also generous with advice on navigating other Los Angeles shopping neighborhoods, dining, and sightseeing. Choose from the Luxury Coach Adventure for $54, the Walking Adventure for $36 (her most popular), or the Mini-Shuttle Adventure for $50. All packages include optional lunch and custom services. Tours of Melrose Heights, Pasadena, and Rodeo Drive are also available. *213-683-9715. www.urbanshoppingadventures.com.*

Shopping in Hollywood

To immerse yourself in all that is Tinseltown, head to **Hollywood & Highland Center**—a mall and entertainment complex that's central to the action on Hollywood Boulevard. Heck, 15 million people can't be wrong (which is about how many visitors flock to the center each year). Connected to the historic Grauman's Chinese Theatre (also known as Mann's Chinese Theatre), Hollywood & Highland features more than 60 retailers, nine restaurants, two nightclubs, the Mann Chinese 6 Theaters mega movieplex (**323-461-3331,** www.manntheatres.com*)*, and the high-tech Lucky Strike Lanes bowling alley and bar. Hollywood & Highland Center also houses the Kodak Theatre, where the Academy Awards ceremonies have been held since 2002. *323-467-6412. www. hollywoodandhighland.com.*

As for stores, all the usual suspects are here—**Gap, Victoria's Secret, Sephora**—plus specialty stores such as the **Virgin Megastore**'s West Coast flagship with cool tees, electronics, books, and a full selection of music and DVDs (yes, you can still buy music in a store). Other retailers include the duty-free **DFS Galleria, XXI Forever, Vino100, GUESS, ISSI, Giordano, H&M,** and a newly expanded **Louis Vuitton.**

Between hitting the stores, you can meet up for a tour of **Grauman's Chinese Theater** (run by Mann Theatres). Learn the rich history of the Chinese Theatre, dating back to 1927, along with fascinating facts about the legendary forecourt where you can walk in the footprints of stars such as Frank Sinatra and Marilyn Monroe. *Open seven days a week. Admission $5.*

Guided thirty-minute walking tours of the **Kodak Theatre** are also available. You'll catch a glimpse of an authentic Oscar statuette, see where celebrities sat during recent ceremonies, and visit a VIP backstage room. *Open seven days a week. Admission $15. Kodak Theatre,* **323-308-6300.** *www.kodaktheatre.com.*

Powder Room

Before you go, sign up for a free VIP Elephant Card at www. hollywoodandhighland.com and get discounts at participating stores and restaurants. Also get 10 percent off at the Renaissance Hotel and buy one, get one free tickets for the Kodak Theatre guided tour.

Diva Diversions

Once your shopping appetite has been quenched, try your hand at the small screen or plan some star gazing with a movie set tour. And don't forget to eat!

Be part of a studio audience. Everybody loves Ellen! You can request tickets online to *The Ellen DeGeneres Show* at www.ellen.warnerbros. com/tickets. The show fills up months ahead of time, but a limited number of standby tickets are made available during the day of taping. To snag day-of tickets, call **818-260-5585** before noon (Pacific Standard Time) on the day you want tickets, and follow the voicemail instructions. For other shows, there's **Audiences Unlimited** (sitcoms, pilots, and specials) at www.tvtickets.com and **On Camera Audiences** (*Chelsea Lately, American Idol*) at www.ocatv.com.

Tour a movie set. Board an electric car and explore backlot streets, sound stages, sets, and craft shops of **Warner Brothers Studios.** Offered Monday through Friday and select weekends, the VIP Tour is $45 and just over two hours. The Deluxe Tour is five hours and includes lunch at the Commissary Fine Dining Room (where you might spot a celebrity or two wolfing down lunch) for $150 per person. *818-846-1403. www2.warnerbros.com/vipstudiotour.*

You can also check out the **Sony Pictures** Studios Tour (**310-244-8687,** www.sonypicturesstudios.com). Or, tour **Paramount Pictures**. (**323-956-1777,** www.paramount.com).

If celeb-spotting is on your agenda, reserve a table at the **Ivy** (**310-274-8303**)or **Dolce Enoteca e Ristorante** (**323-852-7174,** www.dolcegroup.com.). The trademark white picket fence of the Ivy marks the spot for classic comfort foods and the Hollywood experience. Co-owned by a dozen celebrity investors including Ashton Kutcher, Dolce is a trendy Italian joint with a cozy, dark vibe and a menu laden with tempting seafood and pasta entrées. For breakfast or brunch, make your way to **Tart** at the **Farmer's Daughter** hotel (**323-937-3930,** www.tartrestaurant.com), which is a cute place to stay if you like barnyard chic. Offering farm-fresh, creative cuisine such as chocolate strawberry flapjacks, Tart is a short walk from the Farmers Market (www.farmersmarketla.com), an excellent spot to walk off a filling breakfast. Finally, for a taste of Old Hollywood, head to **Musso and Frank Grill** (**323-467-5123** or **323-467-7788**). Practically unchanged since it opened in 1919, this is the place for sipping a classic martini on hallowed Hollywood ground.

Powder Room

Who says nobody walks in Los Angeles? *Walking L.A.: 36 Walking Tours Exploring Stairways, Streets, and Buildings You Never Knew Existed* (Wilderness Press, 2005) by Erin Mahoney details walking routes that explore the city from a pedestrian's perspective, including maps, detailed directions, and points of interest along the way. Love it. Get it.

Where to Stay

On the downtown front, the Moroccan-themed **Figueroa** (also known as the "Fig") is a stone's throw from the **Staples Center** and **Nokia Theatre** and offers amenities such as a restaurant, bar, and an otherworldly pool and Jacuzzi area. The brightly appointed rooms start at $104, with suites at $205. *1-800-421-9092 or 213-627-8971. www.figueroahotel.com.*

The hip digs of both the downtown and Hollywood locations of **The Standard Hotel** offer a colorful, mod appeal along with 24/7 restaurants, free wi-fi, and platform beds with oversized down duvets and pillows. Rates at the downtown location start at $245, where you and the gals can kick back at the chic rooftop bar and pool with vibrating waterbed pods. The Hollywood location offers similar amenities with "budget" rooms that start at $160. *213-892-8080. www.standardhotels.com.*

If the Hollywood & Highland Center is on your agenda, the center's **Renaissance Hollywood** is a hop and a skip from the action. Modern luxury meets classic Hollywood charm at this upscale hotel padded with amenities such as a full-service spa, restaurant, fitness center, and an outdoor pool with a great view of the Hollywood sign. Rooms are $259 and up. *323-856-1200. www.renaissancehollywood.com.*

Designers in Motion: Chicago

In 2006, Mayor Richard M. Daley launched the Mayor's Fashion Council Chicago to support and promote the city's fashion community. Before then, aspiring local designers hightailed to New York City or Los Angeles. But with Mayor Daley's fashion initiative, the wind-blown city has experienced a surge in its shopping appeal and has blossomed into a fashion hotbed for local designers and unique retailers.

To you, that means tons of great shopping districts peppered with the Midwest charm and personality that permeates the streets of **Chicago.**

Magnificent Mile and Oak Street

Chicago's **Magnificent Mile** (www.themagnificentmile.com) spans more than 3 million square feet of retail space, 460 stores, 275 restaurants, museums, and attractions galore. Parkway gardens, flower-filled medians, towering trees, and awe-inspiring architecture are among the picturesque visions that shape the Magnificent Mile district. Power shopping stops abound: **Bloomingdale's, Neiman Marcus, Saks Fifth Avenue, Lord & Taylor, Marshall Fields,** and **Nordstrom** along with high-end boutiques such as **Cartier, Hermès, Giorgio Armani, Salvatore Ferragamo, Anne Fontaine, La Perla, Ermenegildo Zegna,** and **Tiffany & Co.**

Bordering the northern tip of the Magnificent Mile is the one-block stretch of upscale shopping on **Oak Street** (www.oakstreetchicago. com), between Michigan Avenue and State Street. Making their marks on this stretch of converted townhouses are **Tod's, Donald J. Pliner, Kate Spade, Hermès of Paris,** and **Prada** (among others). If nothing else, the street is an excellent window-shopping detour, but do make time to pop by **Bravco** for a mega dose of beauty. The two-story beauty mecca offers an endless variety of head-to-toe beauty brands, from drugstore regulars to hot new must-haves.

Lincoln Park

Tree-lined streets, Victorian row housing, and ornate architecture set the backdrop for Chicago's northside neighborhood of **Lincoln Park.** The heart of the shopping scene lines **Armitage Avenue, Halsted Street,** and **Webster Avenue**—easily accessed via the mass transit Brown Line.

The area offers a mix of local and national retailers. Must-see stores include **Aroma Workshop, B Boutique, Cynthia Rowley, She, Tabula Tua, Art Effect, Intermix, Barney's Co-op, Blues Jean Bar, Stinky Pants** (kids' clothing), and **LUSH.** Visit www. lincolnparkshopping.com for a full list of retailers.

Lincoln Park is also bustling with great bites. Grab a patio seat for tex mex and margaritas at the **Twisted Lizard (773-929-1414,** www. kincadesbar.com/twisted). **Tilli's Restaurant (773-325-0044,** www. tillischicago.com) is the happening place for fine wine and people watching. Treat yourselves to a sugar fix at **Sweet Mandy B's (773-244-1174)**, the home of good-time desserts such as snickerdoodles and whoopie pies.

Shopping Tour

By now, you've caught on to my enthusiasm for shopping tours. And to tap into the Chicago style vibe, book a date with Julie Cameron of **Urban Shop Guide.** Backed by more than fifteen years in the retail industry, Julie has a bubbling enthusiasm that spills out during her power shopping excursions. Her most popular tours are the two and a half hour Walk Out Tour, where you'll hit the shops of Lincoln Park or Bucktown on foot for $40 per person, and the **Neighborhood All-Stars,** a four-hour jaunt through boutique hotspots via luxury transportation starting at $125 per person. She also offers a four-hour Chicago Designers Tour (starting at $125), a two and a half hour Happy Hour Tour ($40) and private tours at various price points. *312-533-1256. www.urbanshopguide.com.*

Diva Diversions

Grab your hats and hit the water for a historical perspective on Chicago's rich architectural heritage. Architectural boat excursions are a great way to relax after a day of store hopping. For a ninety-minute river cruise, check out Chicago's **First Lady.** *Open seven days a week May–November. Admission Monday–Friday $28, weekends and holidays $30. 847-358-1330. www.cruisechicago.com.*

For a shorter cruise, check out the hour-long Chicago River Architecture Tour on **Wendella Boats.** *Open seven days a week April–November. Admission $22. 312-337-1446. www.wendellaboats.com.*

Where to Stay

Like any metropolitan area, you won't find a shortage of hotels—but for an affordable yet sophisticated option, check into the **Inn of Chicago.** Just a half block from the Magnificent Mile and Rush Street (bar and eatery central), the recently renovated hotel offers a modern vibe that streams through the lobby, bar, and contemporary rooms that start as low as $89. *1-800-557-2378. www.innofchicago.com.*

Located on the Magnificent Mile above The Shops at North Bridge on Michigan Avenue, **The Conrad Chicago** is a contemporary hotel with views of the Chicago skyline or Lake Michigan from nearly every room. Amenities include a restaurant, lounge, free

Powder Room —

From bars to galleries and bookstores to yoga studios, **Centerstage Chicago** offers comprehensive neighborhood guides plus a Virtual L Navigator feature that lists hot spots along the city's mass transit routes. For more information, visit www. centerstagechicago.com.

wi-fi, and a skywalk to Nordstrom. Rooms start at $195. *312-645-1500. www.conradhotels.com.*

For a holistic departure from the usual, the **Ruby Room** offers eight suites, a day spa, boutiques, yoga, and outrageously comfortable rooms (think sleeping in a yoga studio) sans TVs and phones. Suites are available from $155. *773-235-2323. www.rubyroom.com.*

Mother of All Malls: Minnesota's Mall of America

Imagine a mall encompassing more than 520 stores, 50 places to nosh, and square footage so expansive that you could park 32 Boeing 747s inside its walls. In 1985, after the Bloomington, Minnesota, Port Authority bought the site of the old Metropolitan Stadium, a group of investors began to imagine just that. And in 1992, the **Mall of America** opened its doors to reign as the nation's largest retail and entertainment complex.

The mall boasts the largest indoor amusement park in the nation with more than 30 rides, including a spiraling roller coaster. The **Underwater Adventures Aquarium** offers an aquatic interlude with a 1.2 million gallon walkthrough aquarium voted "World's Best Shark Encounter" by The Discovery Channel. A 14-screen movie theater, an 18-hole miniature golf course, and a calendar full of events such as celebrity book signings and healthy cooking demos round out the entertainment options. But it's the mega dose of shopping that makes this the mother of all mall destinations. *60 East Broadway, Bloomington, MN 55425. 952-883-8800. www.mallofamerica.com.*

The Shopping

You won't need a guided shopping tour for this shopping excursion— just a pair of those aforementioned comfortable shoes and a mall directory (available at one of the four Guest Services Desks on Level One). Anchored by **Nordstrom, Bloomingdale's, Macy's,** and **Sears,** the mall encompasses almost four and a half miles of retail and dining space. You'll find posh haunts such as **Burberry** and **Coach** tucked between stores such as **J. Crew, Ann Taylor, Sephora, Steve Madden,** and Minnesota-based **Aveda.** Exclusive boutiques are planted inside department stores. Nordstrom hides **Gucci, Yves Saint Laurent, Chloé,** and **Chanel** boutiques; Bloomie's has an exclusive boutique for **Tag Heuer** watches; and Macy's a **LUSH** beauty boutique.

When hunger strikes, head to **Twin City Grill** for comfort food classics such as beer-dredged walleye and toasted macaroni and cheese chased with jumbo martinis. You'll also find **California Café, Napa Valley Grille, Tiger Sushi,** and **Nordstrom Café.**

Where to Stay

With some 35 hotels within a 5-mile radius of the mall, you'll find accommodations to fit most budgets—most hovering around the $100 per night mark.

A contemporary hotel with a boutique feel, **Le Bourget Aero Suites** (pronounced *Le-bur-'zhay)* offers free wi-fi, complimentary transportation to and from the airport and mall, a bistro and espresso bar, L'Occitane bath amenities, a heated indoor pool, a fitness center, and comfy beds with pillow-top mattresses and down comforters. Rooms start at $109. *1-800-449-0409. www.lebourgethotel.com.*

The **Hyatt Place Minneapolis Airport** also offers a modern décor and amenities such as free wireless, a fitness center and pool, complimentary breakfast with Starbucks coffee, and the bonus of a separate sitting area with queen-size sofa-sleeper beds—all starting at $99. *952-854-0700. www.hyattplace.com.*

Finally, the **Crowne Plaza Hotel** boasts all the cushy comforts you would expect from the brand—plus a women's-only floor with secure access, upgraded Bath & Body Works amenities, robes and slippers in every room, and complimentary snacks and beverages in the fully stocked refrigerator. Rates start at $129. *952-831-8000. www.cpmsp.com.*

Powder Room _____

Save time by booking your trip via **Destination Bloomington**'s Girlfriends Getaway package, which includes discounted rates at select hotels, a Mall of America map, coupons, a tote bag, and the option of adding transportation and activities all with one click. Visit www.bloomingtonmn.org or call **1-866-888-8501** for details.

More Big-City Shopping Destinations

Atlanta. Imagine two mega malls directly across the street from each other with upscale anchors such as **Bloomie's, Saks, Neiman Marcus,** and **Nordstrom. Lenox Square** and **Phipps Plaza** in Atlanta's Buckhead area offer just that, with hundreds of stores between them. Take it in by booking the **Buckhead Legendary Shopping Package** through the **Atlanta Convention & Visitors Bureau,** and save on accommodations and get extras such as a complimentary breakfast for two, free hotel transportation, and a $25 mall gift card. *1-800-285-2682 or 1-800-ATLANTA. www.atlanta.net.*

Boston. From **Newbury Street** to **Faneuil Hall Marketplace** and **Harvard Square** to **Back Bay,** Boston bustles with shopping destinations laced with history, good eats, and camera-snapping opportunities galore. Check out *The Boston Globe's* visitor's guide for travel tools and destinations. *www.boston.com.*

Miami. Metro Miami is dotted with sprawling malls such as **Aventura Mall** (www.aventuramall.com*)*, with storefronts from **Juicy Couture** to **Michael Kors;** the **Village of Merrick Park** (www.villageofmerrickpark.com) in Coral Gables with specialty stores such as **Diane Von Furstenberg** and **Donald J. Pliner;** and the **Bal Harbour Shops** (www.balharbourshops.com) with high-end haunts such as **Tory Burch, Versace, Prada, Chloé,** and **Lulu Couture.** For a vibrant mix of South Beach culture and retail delights, head to **Miami Beach.** *www.shoponmiamibeach.com.*

San Francisco. From eclectic **Haight Street** to **Chinatown** to the upscale digs of **Union Square,** the Bay Area is teaming with more than a dozen shopping districts. Pinpoint your destination by visiting the San Francisco Convention & Visitors Bureau website, where you can explore current package offers or order a free Visitor's Kit. *415-974-6900. www.onlyinsanfrancisco.com.*

Boutique Bound

In This Chapter

* Surf, sand, and laid-back store hopping in Santa Barbara

* Economical (no taxes!) and eco-friendly Portland, Oregon

* Cactus-free boutiques of sunny Scottsdale

* Retail trolling Texas-style in Austin

* Three more boutique-bound city destinations

If the fervid pace of big city stores and sprawling malls isn't your style, consider a getaway where retail therapy slows to a more thoughtful gait. In this chapter, we'll explore the shopping experience on a boutique level, where hidden storefronts and quaint plazas tell the story of the local language, flavor, and landscape.

Good Vibrations: Santa Barbara, California

Just 90 miles north of Los Angeles, **Santa Barbara** puts a screeching halt to fast-paced city life. This seaside town is a breezy mix of white-washed buildings with red tiled roofs, swaying palms, cascading bougainvillea, and a friendly vibe that reverberates in the cobbled streets and the people who call it home. Pedestrian-friendly retail districts and plazas are easy to navigate, and the eclectic shops and gourmet eateries make it a top destination for sun, surf, and boutique shopping.

Where to Shop

Dotted with plazas, enclaves, and open-air malls, State Street is Santa Barbara's main drag for strolling, shopping, and noshing.

Start your spree by making your way up State from Gutierrez Street. From there, pop into designer clothing store **beca:christian (805-884-4700,** www.becachristian.com) located on State Street and **A Tropical Affair (805-730-1625,** www.atropicalaffair.com) for hot lingerie and swimwear (just a block off State on Cota Street). Then, wind your way through charming **El Paseo** (www.santabarbara.com/community/shopping/el_paseo/), California's first shopping center. Built in the 1920s, this mixed-use plaza is home to unique gift shops and restaurants nestled within romantic gardens and Spanish courtyards.

Just across the street is shopping central at **Paseo Nuevo** (www.sbmall.com), a Mediterranean-style, open-air mall with courtyards alive with colorful tiles, fountains, sitting areas, and lush landscaping. Anchored by **Nordstrom** and **Macy's,** the center was originally the site of a thriving pueblo and now houses some 50 boutiques, jewelry, and clothing stores. Be sure to pop into **Wendy Foster** boutique **(805-966-2276,** www.wendyfoster.com), adored by locals for her carefully procured designer apparel and jewelry, just outside of the mall area.

From there, hit other local favs **K. Frank (805-560-7424,** www.kfrankstyle.com) and the **Blue Bee (1-866-258-3233,** www.bluebee.com) boutiques. Blue Bee is a string of five stores, each with an individual flair and focus—from designer collections to jeans, menswear,

and shoes. Stroll through nearby **La Arcada Court** (www.santabarbara.
com/community/shopping/la_arcada), a T-shaped Spanish paseo and
courtyard that spotlights a range of specialty stores and art galleries.
Victoria Court is another quaint village of shops located near the
landmark **Granada Theater** (**805-899-3000,** www.granadasb.org/
index.html). Its more than 30 stores, restaurants, and vendors are connected by winding paths and courtyards.

Wind up your trip at the **DIANI** trio of boutiques (**1-877-342-6474,**
www.dianiboutique.com), each dedicated to fashion in the form
of shoes, clothes, and wardrobe essentials. Located in **Arlington
Plaza,** DIANI is just steps from the historic **Arlington Theater**
(thearlingtontheatre.com). Wrap up with a stop at **Treat** (**805-966-
2336,** www.treatthyself.com) for luxury hair, face, and body essentials.

And if that's not enough, thanks to its wealthy residents, Santa Barbara
is also a hotbed for high-end vintage and secondhand designer finds.
Unearth ever-so-slightly used treasures at **The Closet** (**805-963-8083**)
and **Renaissance Fine Consignments** (**805-963-7800**) on State Street
and **Vintage Heart** (**805-963-6812,** www.thevintageheartboutique.
com), a few blocks away on West Canon Perdido Street.

Powder Room

Up the street without a paddle? Catch a ride back to your
starting point on an electric shuttle for an easy 25-cent fare. The
Downtown-Waterfront Shuttle along State Street and the Waterfront
area runs until 6 P.M. year round and until 10 P.M. on Fridays and
Saturdays from May through September.

Where to Stop

With all the good eats in Santa Barbara, belly grumblings are easily satiated. For Southern-style food with a California twist, pop into
Tupelo Junction Café (**805-899-3100,** www.tupelojunction.com)
for breakfast or brunch. **Quantum Kitchen & Cocktails** (**805-962-
5999,** www.quantumrestaurant.com) mixes up gourmet burgers, spin-
offs of the great comfort-food classics, and spiked milkshakes. **Opal
Restaurant & Bar** (**805-966-9676,** www.opalrestaurantandbar.com) is
another local hub with a great menu, moderate prices, and a bustling

atmosphere. Breezy beach evenings were made for the **Hungry Cat** (**805-884-4701,** www.thehungrycat.com), a dinner-only bistro featuring a raw seafood bar and freshly made cocktails. Or head to **Bouchon** (**805-730-1160,** www.bouchonsantabarbara.com), where the chef mixes up creative, seasonal, regional cuisine.

Between shopping and noshing, take a day off to catch a relaxing ride through the **Santa Ynez Valley** on a wine country tour. **Stagecoach Co. Wine Tours (805-344-4010,** www.winetourssantaynez.com) and **Wine Edventures (805-965-9463,** www.welovewines.com) both offer tours that start at $105 and include transportation to and from your hotel, tasting fees at four top wineries, a souvenir glass, and lunch. The tours are four and a half to five hours, and each can customize your excursion if a particular winery is on your hit list.

Where to Stay

Keep in mind that summer is the high season for Santa Barbara, and rates will generally increase while availability becomes scarce. As with any seasonal destination, book early and watch hotel websites for promotions and specials.

Central to the heart of downtown, the **Hotel Santa Barbara** offers an affordable option with the Shoppers Spree Package. The package includes a one-night stay in a double room, breakfast, a bottle of wine or sparkling cider, chocolates, two trolley passes, and retail discount vouchers—starting at $209 for two. The double queen rooms can sleep up to four. Rates start at $172. *805-957-9300. www.hotelsantabarbara.com.*

Stylish yet relaxed, the **Canary Hotel** is also convenient to the State Street scene. The **Shop Chill Nest package** includes two nights in a Junior Suite (a king bed with fold-out sofa), a $100 Saks or Nordstrom gift card, a personal shopper, and two 60-minute in-room spa treatments for $975 double occupancy. Amenities include a restaurant and pool. Standard room rates start at $229. *1-877-468-3515 or 805-884-0300. www.canarysantabarbara.com.*

On the pricy side but well worth it, the **Simpson House Inn Bed & Breakfast** is an historical landmark that dates back to 1874. Rates for the 15 plush rooms start at $233 and include a gourmet vegetarian breakfast, evening hors d'oeuvres with local wines, bikes, beach equipment, a trolley pass, and gratuities. *1-800-676-1280.* *www. simpsonhouseinn.com.*

For more information and a list of seasonal discounts, call the **Santa Barbara Conference & Visitors Bureau and Film Commission** at **805-966-9222** or visit www.santabarbaraca.com. Order or download a map that traces the stops in the movie *Sideways*, a Visitors Magazine, or Culinary Guide.

The World Is Your Oyster: Portland, Oregon

Why Portland? Can you say tax-free shopping? Besides being one of the few states in the country with no sales tax, **Portland** is home to a growing roster of boutiques—many of which are stocked with locally made goods. Downtown is home to **Pioneer Place Mall,** which spans more than four city blocks; and **Columbia Sportswear,** the flagship location of Portland's own outdoor wear headquarters. But it's the trendy neighborhoods that hide the real goods.

Where to Shop

An industrial wasteland of abandoned warehouses in its previous life, the **Pearl District** has evolved over the last couple decades into a hip hub of retail, restaurants, and residences. The name itself was coined during its makeover phase in the '90s when, as legend has it, a local gallery owner referred to the buildings in the warehouse district as "crusty oysters" and the galleries and artists' lofts within as "pearls." The heart of the über urban district is bordered to the south by West Burnside Avenue and to the north

Savvy Sister

If only she offered a shopping tour, I would love this gal even more—but for now, her blog will have to do. Local fashion guru and editor-in-chief of *Ultra* (a webzine for Portland fashion insiders), Lisa Radon blogs about local sales, new stores, and events at www.discoverportlandshopping. com. Plus, she offers an excellent breakdown of Portland's shopping neighborhoods and districts.

by Northwest Lovejoy Street (streets run alphabetically south to north) and is peppered with pricy condos and lofts, trendy eateries and cafés, posh day spas, and of course a bevy of boutiques.

Start your shopping excursion on the southern tip of the Pearl at **Powell's City of Books** (1-800-291-9676, www.powells.com), the largest independent bookseller in the world. This two-story bookstore spans several city blocks and sells new and used books. If you can't find a book at Powell's, it likely doesn't exist. You can also grab a free walking map of the Pearl District at Powell's.

From here, the world is—as they say—your oyster. Pry it open with a stroll up Northwest Tenth Avenue for boutiques such as **Nolita** (503-274-7114, www.nolitaonline.com) or **The Bee and Thistle** (503-222-3397, www.thebeeandthistle.com) for designer duds and accessories, **Judith Arnell Jewelry** (503-227-3437, www.juditharnell. com), **Hanna Andersson** (503-321-5275, www.hannaandersson.com) for "mommy and me" clothes, and **Urbane Zen** (503-227-8852, www. urbanezen.com) for spa and bath necessities. The district invites meandering, so mark these other local favorites on your map: local designer **Michelle DeCourcy Flagship Boutique** (503-227-2971, www. michelledecourcy.com), **Cheeky B** gifts and accessories (**503-274-0229,** www.cheekyboutique.com), **Bella Moda Designs** shoes (**503-224-9994,** www.bellamodadesigns.com), **Olivia Belle** designer outlet (**503-473-8900,** www.oliviabelle.com), and **Le Train Bleu** (503-222-2598, www.letrainbleu.com) for a colorful mix of fashion and apothecary items.

Get a listing of Pearl District businesses and download a walking map at www.explorethepearl.com.

Another area to hit is the **Northwest** and **Nob Hill Districts,** where you'll find a battery of restaurants, bars, bakeries, and coffee houses. The key shopping beat is the Northwest Twenty-Third Avenue strip, home to a series of boutiques hawking housewares, furniture, clothing, and body products. Of note, check out **Seaplane** (503-234-2409, www.e-seaplane.com) for West Coast independent designer collections, **Blush Beauty Bar** (503-227-3390, www.theblushbeautybar.com) for—you guessed it—beauty finds galore, and **Stella's** (503-295-5930, www.stellason21st.com) on 21st for a fun and funky selection of gifts and home accents.

Powder Room

The **Portland Streetcar** offers a fare-free zone called the **Fareless Square,** a service that offers free transportation throughout the downtown area. The Fareless Square encompasses most of the Pearl where it shoots through on 10th and 11th Streets. For maps and fares outside the Fareless Square, visit www.trimet.org.

Where to Stop

You won't go hungry in either of the shopping 'hoods. In the Pearl, grab a to-go cup of locally roasted specialty coffee at **World Cup Coffee & Tea (503-228-4152,** www.worldcupcoffee.com). For quick bites, the **Daily Café (503-242-1916,** www.dailycafe.net) and **Hot Lips Pizza (503-595-2342,** www.hotlipspizza.com) are both local faves. **Bluehour (503-226-3394,** www.bluehouronline.com) is adored by gourmands for its sophisticated Mediterranean-inspired cuisine and decadent weekend brunches. Make a date with **Fratelli's (503-241-8800,** www.fratellicucina.com) for happy hour or an evening of indulgent, eclectic Italian cuisine.

In the Nob, **Moonstruck Chocolate Café (503-542-3400,** www. moonstruckchocolate.com) is a must for a midday pick-me-up. Lunch and dinners at **Wildwood (503-248-9663,** www.wildwoodrestaurant. com) are an explosion of farm fresh flavors and possibly the most decadent desserts on the planet. **Lucy's Table (503-226-6126,** www. lucystable.com) makes Portland proud for both its inventive cuisine and cozy vibe.

For a diversion besides shopping and nibbling, take in the meticulous cultivations at the **Japanese Garden (503-223-5055,** www. japanesegarden.com) or the **Portland Classical Chinese Garden (503-228-8131,** www.portlandchinesegarden.org). The $8 admission to the Japanese Garden includes a guided walking tour and access to seasonal exhibits. The $7 admission fee to the Chinese Garden also comes with a walking tour and access to the gardens, which hide the two-storied **Tower of Cosmic Reflections** teahouse where you can sip quality Chinese loose-leaf teas.

For hotel discounts and more information on Portland, visit **Travel Portland** at www.travelportland.com or call **1-800-962-3700** to request a free travel guide.

Where to Stay

Portland has no shortage of places to stay—but depending on your budget, several are just quirky enough to capture the Portland spirit.

Close to the Pearl, **Hotel deLuxe** offers contemporary digs and special online packages for extra savings. The Babes on Broadway Package includes overnight accommodations with valet parking, a martini of choice for each upon arrival, a sampler box of cupcakes from St. Cupcake, a $40 gift certificate for a rejuvenating foot treatment at the Footbar in the Pearl, and an extended late check-out and breakfast for two. Rates for the package vary, but standard rooms start at $159. *1-866-895-2094. www.hoteldeluxeportland.com.*

A classic Tudor-style home on the outside, the **Heron Haus Bed & Breakfast** offers a bright, cozy interior and easy access to the Nob Hill district. All rooms have fireplaces and private bathrooms with rates starting at $135. *503-274-1846. www.heronhaus.com.*

The **Inn at Northrup Station** wears its 1970s history loud and proud. The playful, retro landing spot in the Northwest district offers a landscaped rooftop garden for afternoon lingering and suites starting at just under $100. *1-800-224-1180 or 503-224-0543. www.northrupstation.com.*

Cactus and Cocktails: Scottsdale, Arizona

Once a sleepy paradise to golfers and outdoor enthusiasts, **Scottsdale** has blossomed into a destination city where chic hotels, spas galore, a handful of the nation's best restaurants, and a string of boutiques dot the prickly landscape. Perpetually sunny skies, lush desert vegetation, and (honestly) one too many nips and tucks make the shiny, happy residents and scenery seem almost surreal.

Where to Shop

For the last couple years, a controversy has been brewing among the fashion-charged of Scottsdale. Should the neighborhood once endearingly called Old Town now simply be referred to as downtown? It's a clash that apparently will live on undecided, because the charm of **Old Town Scottsdale** and the budding new shops and eateries of the downtown-minded merge into a district underlined by urban cowboy hospitality. Thanks to city visionaries and a flood of discerning visitors, an area once marked by art galleries, tourist shops (with no shortage of dream catchers, tiny cacti, and scorpion paper weights), eateries, and bars is now also blooming with boutiques and high-end restaurants. So for our purposes, we'll call it downtown—but don't be surprised if a local store owner raises an eyebrow in disagreement.

The hippest hop in downtown is the **SouthBridge area,** bordered on the northern tip by the sprawling indoor **Scottsdale Fashion Square Mall**—home to **Neiman Marcus** and **Nordstrom**—and the **Scottsdale Waterfront,** a string of casual eateries and shops such as **Urban Outfitters** and **Sur la Table.**

The main shopping area of SouthBridge is a unique boutique cooperative called **The Mix.** A trendy two-storied fusion of food and fashion, The Mix consists of three buildings each clustered according to the themes Live, Nest, and Play. The central Live structure showcases designer collections and accessories in a pleasantly seamless maze that invites meandering. Apparel shops to note are **Studio Joy Li,** home of exclusive designs by local resident and nationally recognized designer Joy Li; and **Cici & Belle,** a stunning collection of cocktail and evening dresses procured by Jennifer Croll, the fashion innovator behind The Mix concept. Others to check off your list are **Garage** (children's clothes and cute accessories) and **Moody Blues** (high-end blue jeans for men and women).

Next door in the Nest building, **Nestledown** offers a luscious collection of luxury linens while **The Porch** overflows with meticulously cultivated plant arrangements and garden furniture. The Mix shops spill across the street where local beauty haunt **Glam Lounge** hides hard-to-find beauty apothecary items and cult-status cosmetics.

For more information and a complete list of shops, visit www. themixshops.com.

Outside downtown Scottsdale, boutiques are tucked into a string of shopping hubs that stretch up to the north tip of the city, which trails off into lush Sonoran desert. Most are off the city's main drag of Scottsdale Road, and you can hit them all in a day or two. Here are some worth the stop: **Estilo Boutique (480-664-0365**, www.estiloboutique.com) at the Scottsdale Waterfront, **Bijou** at **The Borgata (602-953-6311**, www.borgata.com), **Fleur't** at the **Shops at Gainey Village (480-609-6909**, www.theshopsgaineyvillage.com), **Jennifer Croll** at **Kierland Commons (480-348-1577**, www.kierlandcommons.com), and **Heidi Boutique (480-663-7777**, www.heidiboutique.com) in north Scottsdale.

Powder Room

Not one to go hightailing around unknown boutique territory? Enlist the help of a local shopping expert, Nancy Shina—owner of **Spree! The Art of Shopping**. A stretch limo will pick you and the girls up for a four-hour shop-hopping odyssey with Nancy as your guide while you sip champagne between stops. Hotel packages and custom tours are available. _480-661-1080. www. azshoppingspree.com._

Where to Stop

Scottsdale's culinary secret weapon and Arizona-native Sam Fox has created a string of trendy, casual eateries worth the stop. At the Scottsdale Waterfront, **Olive & Ivy Restaurant & Marketplace** is a bustling indoor-outdoor eatery with an East Coast vibe. At Kierland Commons, **Chloe's Corner** serves grown-up soda shop selections in a boutique setting while **North** is known for fresh-to-the-minute Italian dishes and **The Greene House** that pays homage to Craftsman architect Henry Greene. **Bloom** at Gainey Village makes its name in eclectic American cuisine. Information on all of these wonder eateries can be found at www.foxrestaurantconcepts.com.

The Mix's claim to fame is **Canal (480-949-9000**, www.canalaz. com), where you can catch a fashion show while noshing on their famed "30-Dollar Sandwich" (more affordable options are also available). In north Scottsdale, **Sassi** (**480-502-9095,** www.sassi. biz) serves up decadent southern Italian dishes with scenic city and mountain views as a backdrop. For an authentic Arizona experience, **Greasewood Flat** (**480-585-9430,** www.greasewoodflat.net) is a local hangout for the affluent biker crowd, where hearty burgers and beer are served from a historic bunkhouse.

For a diversion besides retail trolling and eating, Scottsdale may just have more spas per capita than any other city in the United States. Get your nails buffed or skin polished at the eclectic **Dolce Salon & Spa** at The Borgata, or take an entire day off to lounge at local favorite **The Spa** at the Marriott's Camelback Inn. For more information on the Scottsdale spa scene, visit www.arizonaspagirls.com.

Where to Stay

Get the lowest rates during the off-season from late May to early September. Rates are at their highest in the winter and spring months. If you travel to Scottsdale in high season, stay at a chain hotel but spa or dine at one of the many amazing resorts.

The closest spot to land near the downtown area is the **Hotel Valley Ho.** A landmark boutique hotel draped in 1950s Hollywood glam, "the Ho" offers a lively retro vibe punctuated by amenities such as a martini glass-shaped pool, boutique spa, fitness center, and updated rooms— some with soaking bathtubs in the middle of the room. Rooms start at $199. *1-866-882-4484 or 480-248-2000. www.hotelvalleyho.com.*

For luxury accommodations central to the city's action, the **Hyatt Regency Scottsdale Resort and Spa at Gainey Ranch** takes the cake. Two restaurants, 10 pools (including an adult-only pool and water play-ground), and a sprawling indoor-outdoor luxury spa with full amenities set the relaxing tone for your stay. Rooms start at $170. *480-444-1234. www.scottsdale.hyatt.com.*

The **Four Seasons Resort Scottsdale at Troon North** embraces the lush landscape that surrounds this luxury high-desert destination. Indulge in a cocktail at the resort lounge and gaze out over the Phoenix metro area and mountain vistas. The resort boasts casita-style suites, a restaurant, pool, spa, and fitness center with rooms starting at $165. *480-515-5700. www.fourseasons.com/scottsdale.*

Small City, Big Bite: Austin, Texas

Presidents and cyclists aside, **Austin** is home to an educated, artistic crowd of unhurried denizens who thrive off a laid-back culture laced with good music, spicy food, and an independent spirit. I don't know any better way to sum it up other than to say that Austin is just cool. And it's that laid-back coolness topped with a progressive attitude that has attracted a growing crop of lively shopping haunts.

Where to Shop

The **Domain** is Austin's slick new shopping mall. But if an immersion in the true Austin experience is your goal, head to the **South Congress District.** Dubbed "SoCo" by locals, the South Congress Shopping District is a primo shopping beat when you and the gals are ready for serious retail therapy.

This "hip zip" district encompasses most of the 78704 ZIP code and is bordered by Town Lake to the north and Oltorf Steet to the south. Start with a tour through **Parts & Labour (512-326-1648,** www. partsandlabour.com), a fun collection of silk-screened tees, intricate jewelry, reconstructed vintage clothes, handmade soaps, and children's wear—all crafted by local Texans. **Creatures Boutique (512-707-2500,** www.creaturesboutique.com) carries shoes and accessories with attitude, while **Blackmail (512-326-7670,** www.blackmailboutique.com) is a shop for lovers of all-black apparel. **Uncommon Objects (512-442-4000,** www.uncommonobjects.com/) is also a must—but do the rounds and don't be overwhelmed by the bulging collection of kitsch and oddities. Other stores to add to your shopping list are **By George (512-441-8600,** bygeorgeaustin.com), a posh designer mecca; **Love (512-442-5683,** www.loveaustintexas.com) for vintage-style threads with a rock 'n' roll twist; **Kick Pleat (512-445-4500,** www.kickpleat. com) for hot apparel and shoes; and **Maya Star (512-912-1475,** www. mayastar.com) for killer jewelry.

Powder Room _____

Plan your trip to coincide with the first Thursday of the month, when **First Thursdays** in SoCo light up the streets of South Congress. Live music wafts through the streets, stores keep their doors open late, and a varying schedule of special events keeps the crowd lively and entertained. For more information, visit www.firstthursday. info.

The **Second Street District** is also an emerging hot shopping beat. Winner of Best of Austin's "Best Street" Award, the Second Street neighborhood offers a high-end mix of shops such as **Eliza Page** jewelry and accessories (**512-474-6500**, www.elizapage.com), **Shiki** (**512-391-0123**, www.shikistyle.com), and **Girl Next Door** (**512-322-0501**, www.girlnd. com). Make a date at **Milk + Honey** day spa (**512-236-1115**, www. milkandhoneyspa.com) for an end-of-the-day Lux Pedi. For a complete list of Second Street shops, visit www.2ndstreetdistrict.com.

Where to Stop

Nothing pairs better with shopping than eating, and Austin serves up endless options in SoCo, Second Street, and the outskirts. The choices in SoCo are endless. Start by grabbing a cuppa joe or a light morning bite at **Jo's Hot Coffee and Good Food** (also on Second Street, **512-444-3800**, www.joscoffee.com). Famous for its New York-style "'za," share a pie at **Home Slice Pizza** (**512-444-PIES**, www.homeslicepizza. com). **Guero's Taco Bar** (**512-447-7688**, www.guerostacobar.com) is a must for inexpensive Tex Mex and is rumored to be a favorite of former U.S. President Bill Clinton (he orders the El Presidente combo, of course). Depending on your hunger meter, **Vespaio Ristorante** (**512-441-6100** or **512-441-7672**, www.austinvespaio.com) offers fresh pasta dishes and decadent desserts while the **Enteca Bistro** (**512-441-7672**) next door serves a lighter fare of pastries and a fantastic brunch menu. Curb your sweet cravings at the **Hey Cupcake** (**512-476-CAKE**, www.heycupcake.com) stand or **Amy's Soco** (one of 12 locations, **512-440-7488**, www.amysicecreams.com) for a hit of homemade spiked ice creams such as Bourbon Chocolate Walnut and Black Velvet.

Culinary haunts worth the jaunt outside SoCo include **Uchi** (512-916-4808, www.uchiaustin.com) for sushi with a Texan twist, **Jeffrey's** (512-477-5584, www.jeffreysofaustin.com) for creative seasonal dishes, and **Hudson's on the Bend** (512-266-1369, www.hudsonsonthebend.com) for an extensive wine list paired with a menu bursting with local flavors.

Shopping and eating might be tops, but nary a night goes by in Austin that you can't chill out to live tunes. Anointed as the "Live Music Capital of the World," you can find blues, country, rock, and everything in between. For current shows, pick up a copy of the *Austin Chronicle* or tune in to Austin's Music Entertainment Television on Channel 15. For more information, visit www.austinchronicle.com and www.metelevision.com.

Where to Stay

The city hosts plenty of chain hotels, but look for accommodations that offer a taste of authentic Austin.

Old becomes new at the family owned **Austin Motel** in the SoCo district. The "Cool Pool" built in the 1950s and gardens add a cheeky charm to this otherwise low-key lodge. The hip digs add a lively and fun touch to the refurbished rooms. Rooms start as low as $80. *512-441-1157. www.austinmotel.com.*

Just down the street, **Hotel San José** is another Austin staple with a trendy, retro vibe often frequented by visiting musicians. Rooms start at $95 and include access to the pool, bar, and breakfast room service. *1-800-574-8897. www.sanjosehotel.com.*

Redefining luxury Texas-style, **The Mansion at Judges' Hill** hotel and restaurant is architecturally breathtaking while relaxed and inviting. The Bed & Breakfast Package includes one-night's accommodations in a Queen Petite room and breakfast for two with complimentary Mansion mugs, starting at $209. On-site extras include a restaurant, bar, and limited room service. Rooms start at $139. *1-800-311-1619 or 512-495-1800. www.mansionatjudgeshill.com.*

Central to downtown, the **Driskill Hotel** is pricy but as authentically Austin as you can get. Opened in 1886, the historic landmark has undergone a recent facelift while retaining its grand-dame charm. The hotel houses two restaurants, a boutique spa, and fitness center. Rooms start at $320. *1-800-252-9367 or 512-474-5911. www.driskillhotel.com.*

Chick Wit

The key to successful girlfriend getaways for me is to leave it all behind. I find I have to stay away from my Blackberry: no checking on the husband, the dog, what's happening at home. Be present and let your family know you are taking some time for yourself. Emergency contacts only!

—Jacky, literary agent

Find out more about Austin attractions, events, tours, and special travel offers on www.austintexas.org, where you can also request a free Visitor's Guide.

More Boutique-Bound City Destinations

Framed by the Rockies and vibrant blue skies, **Boulder, Colorado,** is a laid-back urban community where a mix of professionals, nature lovers, sports enthusiasts, and college students set the pace for the diverse shopping scene. The awning-lined boutique beat of the **Pearl Street Mall** is the pedestrian-friendly home of mostly independently owned shops. The **Twenty-Ninth Street District** is the national retailers zone while **The Hill District** is an eclectic mix of shops in the heart of the college scene. Stay at the **St. Julien Hotel & Spa** for plush digs with an unpretentious attitude. Visit www.bouldercoloradousa.com to request a Visitor's Guide.

Fort Lauderdale, Florida, isn't just for bikini-clad college kids anymore. The sprawling seaside city is dotted with elegant malls and boutique shops. A stroll along tree-lined Los Olas Boulevard gives you a sense of "old" Florida while a trip to **Mizner Park** in nearby Boca Raton offers a more upscale appeal. Both offer great boutique shops and food finds. Splurge on the oceanfront **St. Regis Resort** and you'll be within less than a mile of **The Gallery at Beach Place** and **The Galleria Mall.** Pick up a free "e-guide" to greater Fort Lauderdale on www.sunny.org.

Nashville, Tennessee, is making a name for itself outside the twang of a country banjo. Crowned as one of the "best new shopping cities" by *Lucky Magazine*, Nashville blooms with boutiques and trendy eateries. Central to the growing retail community is the **Hill Center at Green Hills,** where swanky clothing stores such as **Posh, Jigsaw,** and **Hemline** are sandwiched between national retailers such as **Anthropologie** and **West Elm** home furnishings. Other shopping destinations include **The Mall at Green Hills** and the **Twelfth Avenue South Shopping District.** Download or request a Visitor's Guide at www.visitmusiccity.com.

Homebodies

In This Chapter

* Furniture trolling on the back roads of North Carolina

* Antique spotting in the Buckhead neighborhoods of Atlanta

* Chic and shabby finds along the famous streets of New Orleans

* Other destinations for home décor

If you've searched high and low for that one fabulous piece to bring your home interior to life and have still come up empty-handed, a getaway may just be what the decorator ordered. Delving into furniture and décor shops outside your own neighborhood can broaden your perspective on your home décor and inspire creativity. In this chapter, we'll explore excursions where the main goal is digging out that perfect accent chair for your living room or an antique lamp for your bedroom while the underlying mission is sharing some down time with the girls.

Furniture Heaven: High Point, North Carolina

Hailed as the home furnishings capital of the world, **High Point, North Carolina,** is crowded with furniture manufacturing operations, home showrooms, and even a Furniture Discovery Center and museum. About an hour and a half from Charlotte in the west and the same distance from Raleigh to the east, the city was named in the 1850s when it was the "highest point" on the North Carolina Railroad between Goldsboro and Charlotte (and therefore, the seat of commerce). Today, furniture industry professionals from all over the world flock to High Point's biannual **International Home Furnishings Market**—the largest event of its kind in the world.

Although the market is not open to the general public, High Point and its surrounding cities are home to hundreds of galleries, showrooms, and stores with everything from furniture and rugs to lighting and fabrics. From ultra contemporary and sleek Scandinavian to European imports and Colonial styles, you'll find elements that speak to every taste.

For more of furniture heaven, ensure you stop by the following destinations.

Powder Room

Craft hounds should plan a trip in November when the **Craftsmen's Christmas Classic Arts & Crafts Festival** comes to town at the **Greensboro Coliseum**—a holiday tradition in central North Carolina for more than 20 years. Find out more by calling **336-282-5550** or by visiting www.gilmoreshows.com.

Family owned and operated for two generations, the **Furnitureland South** complex (in Jamestown, 15 minutes from High Point) boasts more than one million square feet of retail and showroom space, including an expansive clearance center. A 400-foot glass-enclosed walkway connects the indoor showroom with the Hickory Furniture Mart, guarded by the world's largest highboy. *336-822-3000. www.furniturelandsouth.com.*

Boyles Furniture is a household name in North Carolina, with more than 10 stores scattered throughout the state. At the High Point store in Jamestown, you'll find upscale furniture collections (Baker, Bernhardt, Sherrill, Hancock & Moore, Henkel Harris, and Century Furniture, to name a few) at below-retail prices. *336-812-2200. www. boyles.com.*

Black's Furniture has been a player in the fine furniture market since 1964 and recently expanded into a new showroom and retail complex in Greensboro (about 20 minutes from High Point). Home to literally hundreds of brand names and styles—from casual contemporary to cottage and country—you can also shop green, sustainable furniture lines that do their part in preserving the environment. *336-886-5011. www. blacksfurniture.com.*

The hour-and-a-half drive to the **Hickory Furniture Mart** is worth the trek when you're ready to explore the largest home furnishings resource in the nation. The sprawling 20-acre complex offers a mix of more than 100 outlets, stores, and galleries with home furnishings, lighting, art, fine rugs, fabrics, and accessories. If you decide to crash in Hickory for the night, visit the furniture mart's website for special shop-and-stay packages. *1-800-462-MART. www.hickoryfurnituremart. com.*

Streamline your visit with a custom shopping tour. Shannon Neal of **Where You Need to Go** tours has been on the furniture beat for more than 20 years and will create a personal plan of attack for you and your crew based on your design preferences. The day-long tours are $250 per group and include door-to-door transportation in a luxury vehicle, access to private showrooms, and discounts of up to 50 percent at select stores along with a side of southern charm and insider tidbits. *336-317-2894. www. whereyouneedtogotours.com.*

STOP Bad Trip

Furniture stores in the High Point area are massive. The outdoor furnishings section alone at Furnitureland, for example, is as big as most free-standing furniture stores. Avoid getting overwhelmed by preplanning your needs and narrowing down furniture lines and styles before your trip. Order catalogs, if available, so you can show salespeople exactly what you want.

Where to Stop

Barbecue is such a major part of North Carolina culture that the state has its own official barbecue society. The **North Carolina Barbecue Society** exists to preserve the Tar Heel state's barbecue traditions and "to secure North Carolina's rightful place as the Barbecue Capital of the World" (more information is available at www.ncbbqsociety.com). So don't go skipping town without a taste.

Make a barbecue pit stop at **Kepley's Bar-B-Q (336-884-1021,** www.kepleysbarbecue.com), where traditional, slow-cooked pork "NC-BBQ" is served up with all the fixings. Family owned and operated since 1948, this beloved barbecue joint serves hand-chopped barbecue, homemade slaw, hush puppies, and chili. Grab a bottle of Kepley's mouth-watering Downhome BBQ Sauce to take home.

Other barbecue hot spots in town are **Carter Brothers BBQ & Ribs (336-841-2241)**, **Country BBQ (336-431-8978)**, and **Henry James (336-861-4846,** www.henryjamesbbq.com).

When you've had your fill of pork, head to **Bimini's Oyster Bar (336-886-3474,** biminisoysterbar.net) on Main Street. This casual, island-themed restaurant is a local favorite where you can order the fresh grilled catch of the day or a steam pot for two filled with seafood, corn, and fixings. There's also live music on weekends.

High Point offers a few unusual diversions—one of which is the **Doll and Miniature Museum (336-885-3655)** of High Point. A collection that was started by the late High Point resident Angela Peterson, the museum features more than 2,700 dolls including an extensive Shirley Temple doll collection, costumes, miniatures, and doll houses. It's open daily, and admission for adults is $5.

Another must-see (and hard-to-miss) wonder is the **World's Largest Chest of Drawers.** Built in the 1920s to mark High Point's place as the home furnishings capital of the world, two giant socks hang from the middle drawer of this eighteenth-century–style piece that stands almost 40 feet tall. For more information, call **1-800-720-5255.**

Where to Stay

Besides the furniture insiders who flood the town, **High Point University** also brings its fair share of visitors—so you'll find no shortage of affordable hotels in the area. One option is the **Biltmore Suites Hotel,** where rooms and suites come with conveniences such as complimentary breakfast, coffee makers, microwaves, and Jacuzzi tubs in some rooms. Rates start at $90 for rooms with two queen beds, or you can opt for an individual "cruise room," which sleeps one and resembles a cruise ship cabin ($69). Check the website for seasonal specials and deals. *1-888-412-8188 or 336-812-8188. www.biltmoresuiteshotel.com.*

For something with more local charm, the **J. H. Adams Inn** features 31 uniquely designed guest rooms and suites, each with robes, high-end linens, refrigerators with complimentary bottled water, large private baths, and king- or queen-size bedding. The on-site fine dining restaurant, **Hampton's,** offers French-New American cuisine and an extensive wine collection. Complimentary services include an extended continental breakfast, glass of wine, fitness studio access, a daily newspaper, and local discount coupons. Room rates start at $139. Ask about the Wine Tour package, which (for $345) includes a Champagne & Grapes welcome tasting, breakfast for two, two night's accommodation in a Gallery or Veranda room, an All-Day Wine Tour with lunch, and an evening wine reception. *1-888-256-1289 or 336-882-3267. www.jhadamsinn.com.*

For more information and a list of local events, call the **High Point Convention & Visitors Bureau** at **805-966-9222** or visit www.highpoint.org. Order a Passport to Savings discount book that includes a furniture shopping directory.

Antiques Central: Atlanta

The southeast's epicenter for shopping, **Atlanta** is home to some 20 indoor malls, five outlet centers in its outskirts, and pockets of neighborhood boutiques and specialty stores. But if antiques are your passion, lace up your walking shoes and hit the streets of **Buckhead.**

Just six miles north of downtown, the Buckhead community is considered a subcity of Atlanta and bustles with more than 1,400 retail stores, art galleries, and antique shops catering to all tastes and styles. The hot spots are the two major malls—**Phipps Plaza** and **Lenox Square**—but for art, antiques, and decorative accessories, the side streets and design districts are the places to head.

You should also visit the **Miami Circle Design District,** which is among Atlanta's most lively design and decorating destinations. Once designated as a warehouse district, the Miami Circle cul-de-sac is now home to more than 80 shops, galleries, and serious home décor stores. Shoppers can find museum-quality antiques; estate jewelry; rare book galleries; showrooms of unique lamps, lighting, and chandeliers; and other home wares for collectors and bargain hunters alike. If fabric is on your shopping list, head to **Curran Designer Fabrics & Furniture** (737 Miami Circle, **1-800-241-0178,** www.curran-aat.com), where you'll find thousands of fabric choices from discounted bolts to exclusive designer fabrics.

Just south of the Miami Circle off the 2,100 block of Peachtree Road, **Bennett Street** is home to an intriguing jumble of antique shops, galleries, studios, and restaurants. Bennett Street has lived many lives, from its beginnings as a quiet country road to a supply path that linked Atlanta to the surrounding countryside during the Civil War. Today, it's considered home base for some of the best antique and art shops in Atlanta. For Oriental rugs and an ever-changing selection of antiques, head to **John Overton** (25 Bennett St., **404-355-9535**).

The **Galleries of Peachtree Hills** (www.galleriesofpeachtreehills.com) boast a collection of more than 20 distinctive antique and art galleries. This luxury center is reminiscent of an antiques and art row, with the five-building complex designed in classical French style. The collectors, owners, and designers at The Galleries offer knowledgeable, experienced guidance and service.

Peachtree Hills is also home to the **Atlanta Decorative Arts Center** (**404-231-1720,** www.adacdesigncenter.com), a 550,000-square-foot design center with close to 80 showrooms and myriad furniture, fabric, kitchen, bath, fine art, antiques, lighting, accessories, mantels, home theater products, and floor and wall coverings stores. The center is only open to trade professionals, but the general public can enter with a designer or unaccompanied if your designer makes arrangements ahead of time with the center for your visit.

The heart of the original Buckhead community, the **West Village of Buckhead** offers an array of shops—from the quaint to the eclectic—along with a mix of galleries and restaurants. Located just west of Peachtree and Roswell Roads between West Paces Ferry Road, retail shops line the west side of Peachtree while the east side is the center of Buckhead nightlife. If you're into beadwork, stop by **Brina Beads** (3231 Cains Hill Place, **404-816-8230,** www.brinabeads.com) or call ahead to reserve space on "Bring Your Own Wine Thursdays," where for $5 per person you can learn basic stringing techniques while sipping vino.

Where to Stop

Cafés, casual eateries, and upscale dining choices abound in the Buckhead 'hoods. One stop to add to your itinerary is the **Atlanta Fish Market (404-262-3165,** www.buckheadrestaurants.com) on Pharr Road just off Peachtree. Marked by a three-story copper fish sculpture, the restaurant is a fun and funky joint where seafood lovers can chomp on batter-fried lobster tails, jumbo crab cakes, and daily grilled specials.

Another quintessential dining spot spiked with a nostalgic décor is the **Buckhead Diner (404-262-3336,** www.buckheaddiner.com) on Piedmont Road, where you'll find mouth-watering items such as homemade potato chips with warm Maytag blue cheese, sweet and sour calamari, artful salads, and the James Beard award-winning White Chocolate Banana Crème Pie. Sunday brunch is complete with Valencia-orange or ruby-red mimosas.

Spice up your getaway and learn to mix up your Latin dance moves at **The Sanctuary (404-262-1377,** www.sanctuarynightclub.com) on Paces Ferry Place, Atlanta's longest-running Latin nightclub. Every Friday night, the club holds beginner and intermediate salsa classes for the price of admission. Spend the rest of the evening practicing your salsa steps.

Where to Stay

Located in the bustling Buckhead financial district, the **Doubletree Hotel Atlanta Buckhead** is a short walk to the mass transit system (MARTA) and close to shopping and businesses. Guests are greeted with the hotel's signature chocolate-chip cookies. Rooms feature Sweet Dreams by Doubletree plush-top beds, jumbo hypoallergenic down pillows, Neutrogena bath amenities, Internet access, and coffee makers.

Savannah's Restaurant offers casual southern fare while **Beauregard's** is a cozy club for casual dining. Room service and complimentary use of a nearby fitness center is available. Room rates start at $109. *404-231-1234. www.doubletree.com.*

Powder Room

If the antique bug is still biting, head to the **Lakewood 400 Antiques Market (770-889-3400,** www.lakewoodantiques.com) in Cumming, Georgia, about 30 minutes from Buckhead. The market is housed in a 75,000-square-foot, climate-controlled building with more than 500 dealer spaces, abundant parking, and a full-service restaurant. It's open the third weekend of every month, Friday through Sunday, for $3 admission.

The **Laurel Hill Bed & Breakfast** is a quaint retreat six miles outside Buckhead where five elegantly decorated suites offer a cozy place to crash. The Dudley Suite might be your best option because it accommodates up to four in the separate Red and Green Rooms. You can also enjoy a full breakfast cooked to order. Rates start at $139. *404-377-3217. www.laurelhillbandb.com.*

The **Ritz-Carlton Buckhead** guest rooms and suites feature bay windows with views of the city skyline. Rooms have fully stocked mini bars, plush terrycloth bathrobes, feather-top beds, down and non-allergenic foam pillows, Bulgari bath products, complimentary newspapers, Internet access, and evening turndown service. Rates vary, but check the website for seasonal promotions and discounted packages. The Reconnect package includes deluxe accommodations for two, complimentary daily breakfasts for two, and complimentary valet parking daily, starting at $219. *404-237-2700. www.ritzcarlton.com.*

For more information on restaurants, hotels, shopping, or to order the Buckhead Guidebook ($3.50), call **1-800-935-2228** or visit www.buckhead.net.

Shabby Chic: New Orleans

Shabby chic is the epitome of a casual, unassuming style underlined with elegance and peppered with personal expression. The style is generally defined as an eclectic melding of soft colors, vintage-inspired fabrics, delicate glass chandeliers, cottage-style furniture, and a smattering of antiques. And there's no better place to point your compass than **New Orleans** when your chic home interior needs a punch of character.

And yes, New Orleans is a destination with much more of a draw than home décor. But if you're looking for that one special piece to spice up your home, the lively streets of New Orleans hold treasures unlike anywhere else in the country.

The city is the place to immerse yourself in a sea of French antiques, vintage furnishings, and unique home accessories. And I guarantee that you'll have fun along the way.

The two main areas to troll for unique home accessories are **Magazine Street** in the uptown area and **Royal Street** in the French Quarter.

Savvy Sister

The term "shabby chic" was coined in the 1980s by the U.K. magazine *The World of Interiors* and was later popularized by Rachel Ashwell, who literally wrote the book on shabby chic. For Rachel Ashwell home merchandise, style books, and how-to DVDs, visit www.shabbychic.com.

Named for a "magazin," a warehouse that was built in the late 1700s to house products awaiting export, Magazine Street is now a hotbed for trendy shops, hip eateries, and antique shops galore. Be sure to make time for a stop at shabby chic central, **Pied Nu (504-899-4118,** www. piednuneworleans.com). Located at 5521 Magazine Street, Pied Nu (pronounced *pea-YAY new*) means "barefoot"—and the store specializes in timeless, elegant furnishings and accents that define the shabby chic look. Started in 1993 by two friends—one with a background in fine arts and the other with a knowledge of history—Pied Nu offers a carefully culled section of furnishings, home accessories, jewelry, and clothing.

For more information on Magazine Street, including a list of merchants, visit www.magazinestreet.com.

Royal Street, in the heart of the French Quarter, is blanketed in a rich, historic air and is a delight of centuries-old iron-laced balconies, sculptured fountains, and block after block of storefronts and eateries. Royal Street is just a block from bustling Bourbon Street and is defined by a mix of upscale retail shops, galleries, and arguably some of the best antique stores in the country. On any given day, you might happen upon street musicians or local artists displaying their works.

Definitely carve out an hour or two to troll **M. S. Rau Antiques (504-523-5660,** www.rauantiques.com), a Quarter landmark for nearly a century. The two-story, 30,000-square-foot showroom spans nearly a block. Known primarily for its extraordinary eighteenth- and nineteenth-century furniture and fine art and silver collections, the store also has a beguiling collection of walking canes and sticks. This is the place to find that one amazing piece (or just enjoy browsing).

For more information on the French Quarter, including downloadable maps of shops and antique stores on Royal Street and beyond, visit www.frenchquarter.com.

Where to Stop

From Creole to Cajun, the cuisine of New Orleans can be sampled from the more than 3,000 restaurants that beckon you from just about every corner of the city. But be warned: New Orleans is no place for diets, so dig in!

In the French Quarter, **Johnny's Po-Boys (504-524-8129)** on St. Louis Street is the place to binge on the city's famed po' boy sandwiches, which are served from a busy, crammed lunch counter. Choose from more than 45 variations of po' boys along with other regional favorites such as shrimp creole and red beans. Prices are about the only lean thing on the menu, and you'll likely want to return more than once during your visit.

For upscale dining in the Quarter, **Brennan's Restaurant (504-525-9711,** www.brennansneworleans.com) on Royal Street is an absolute must. The spirit of the menu is Creole fare with rich sauces and prime meats and seafood. Breakfast at Brennan's is an elegant affair with succulent dishes such as Eggs Bayou Lafourche (poached eggs over Cajun andouille sausage topped with Hollandaise sauce)—just beckoning to be chased with a Creole Bloody Mary. A rich and colorful history, the restaurant was also the birthplace of Bananas Foster, created in 1951 when owner Owen Edward Brennan challenged his chef Paul Blangé to create a dish with bananas. The dish was named after a local commissioner and regular Richard Foster. Thirty-five thousand pounds of bananas are flamed each year at Brennan's for its world-famous dessert.

Located in the uptown district near Magazine Street and easily accessible by streetcar, **Dante's Kitchen (504-861-3121,** www.danteskitchen. com) is a low-profile, local favorite. Set in a lively old house, the fare is Louisiana cuisine with a contemporary twist. They serve brunch on Saturdays and Sundays.

It's likely you'll find yourselves at some point on **Bourbon Street**—and if you do, **Galatoire's (504-525-2021,** www.galatoires.com) is the place to stop for fare wrapped in four generations of French Louisiana cuisine. While Galatoire's calling card was once not taking reservations, they now accept them for dining in the newly remodeled second-floor dining room.

You'll definitely want to plan a girls' night out at the **Chris Owens Club & Balcony (504-523-6400,** www.chrisowensclub.net). The high-energy song and dance cabaret show is performed by Louisiana legend and club owner Chris Owens and her band. This spitfire of a lady has been a French Quarter fixture and celebrity since the 1960s, and although her age is "unlisted" (as is her phone number, I was told), her revealing get-ups and boundless energy definitely confirm the old aphorism that age is just a state of mind. The club is located smack dab in the center of the French Quarter at 500 Bourbon Street. Reservations are not required most evenings, and a dirt-cheap cover charge of $11 gets you into the show and includes your first drink.

Chick Wit

Try local favorites wherever you are. On a trip to Biloxi, Mississippi, my friends and I were invited by the owner of a popular seafood joint to try his special alligator sausage. Although I wanted to stick to my fried shrimp platter, I took a bite … and *wow*, it was awesome! It also swelled the owner with pride, and we had a wonderful experience meeting him. When in Rome …

—Maja, social worker

Where to Stay

Wrapped in a warm and accommodating atmosphere, **Hotel St. Marie** is an affordable option in the French Quarter and is within easy walking distance to Royal and Bourbon Streets. Rooms feature reproduction antique furnishings that speak to an authentic New Orleans décor and have coffee makers, Internet access, hair dryers, and bath amenities. Many rooms feature balconies overlooking the street scene on Dauphine and Toulouse and the historic vistas of the Quarter, while other guest rooms overlook the hotel's tropical courtyard and pool area. The hotel offers 24-hour concierge and baggage service, valet parking, and in-room spa services. Rates vary seasonally, but you can book rooms as low as $89 during the week. *504-561-8951. www.hotelstmarie.com.*

The **Royal Sonesta Hotel New Orleans** is among the most elegant choices in the bustling Bourbon Street district. The landmark hotel is built in a traditional style, with gabled windows, French doors, and wrought-iron lace balconies. The 500 guest rooms and suites offer a mini-bar, flat-screen TVs, and wired and wireless high-speed Internet access. The exclusive seventh-floor **Rclub** is serviced by private elevators and features a luxury club lounge, concierge services, special food and beverage amenities, and upgraded bath products. On-site dining includes two restaurants: **Begue's** for French and Creole specialties and **Desire Oyster Bar,** a lively street-side bistro. Cafés and bars are sprinkled throughout the resort, and full room service is available.

Rooms start at $249, but check the website for packages such as the Just Us Girls—which, for $349 per person (double occupancy), includes a two-night stay, limo transportation to and from the airport, European turndown service, Hurricane cocktails and photographs at **Pat O'Brien's,** coffee and breakfast breads from **Coffee and Champagne,** and lunch at Desire Oyster Bar. Takers of this perfect girl-getaway package also receive a welcome kit complete with masks, feather boas, a directory of Magazine Street and Royal Street Shopping, and a Quarter Fling Coupon book. *1-800-SONESTA or 504-586-0300. www.sonesta.com/RoyalNewOrleans.*

Note that the Royal's sister hotel, **Chateau Sonesta,** is also in the French Quarter and offers more affordable rates starting at $99. Packages are also available. *1-800-SONESTA or 504-586-0800. www. sonesta.com/ChateauNewOrleans.*

You also can't go wrong with the **W New Orleans French Quarter** on Chartres Street, where a sleek décor is complemented by playful accessories such as gumball machines, game tables, and fluffy pillow-top beds. Enjoy the courtyard and dine at **Bacco** restaurant. Rates start at $179, and packages are available. *1-800-522-6963 or 504-581-1200. www.starwoodhotels.com.*

Powder Room

Girls, take time out. You're working way too hard! Stop by **Belladonna Day Spa & Retail Therapy** (2900 Magazine Street, **504-891-4393**, www.belladonnadayspa.com) for a Cinderella Pedicure. It's like a facial for your feet with a purifying tea tree soak, a callus-banishing alpha-hydroxy acid sugar scrub, a hydrating shea-clay mask, deep-penetrating massage cream, and a final buff and polish (90 minutes for $95). The indoor-outdoor day spa also features a boutique featuring everything from bath and body products to tableware and linens.

More Home Décor Destinations

If you're pining for a collectible piece of artwork—especially one with dreamy visions of the Southwest—head to the awe-inspiring town of **Santa Fe, New Mexico.** More than just an epicenter for Native American art (which is among the best in the world), you'll find an amazing array of styles and mediums—from contemporary art and photography to sculpture and modern mixed media. The main gallery drag is Canyon Road—an entire mile of art showplaces such as the world-renowned **Gerald Peters Gallery.** Visit www.santafegalleries.net for a full list of galleries. Stay at the peaceful **Sunrise Springs** (**1-800-955-0028** or **505-471-3600**, www.sunrisesprings.com), an artful eco-resort with a spa and Japanese tea house.

For an offbeat antique and vintage shopping jaunt, plan a getaway to the charming town of **Mount Dora, Florida.** Located about 30 minutes northwest of Orlando, this quaint lake-speckled town hosts several antique events annually—namely, the **Village Antiques Festival** in the spring and the **Renninger's Antique Extravaganza** held three weekends during the winter months. Stay in any number of the city's bed and breakfast inns to experience the laid-back pace of small-town life. For more information, contact the Mount Dora Area Chamber of Commerce (**352-383-2165,** www.mountdora.com).

New England is also a haven for antique enthusiasts, and your best bet is to follow the trail of the **New England Antique Shows.** Dealers hit the road for a series of shows from **Boston, Massachusetts,** to **Essex Junction, Vermont.** The **Champlain Valley Antiques Festival** in Essex coincides with the fall foliage season in early October. For more information, call **781-862-4039** or visit www.neantiqueshows.com.

In **Vancouver, British Columbia,** you have two equally entertaining choices for home décor shopping: **Antique Row** and **Gallery Row.** Antique Row on Main Street, between 16th and 25th Avenues, features traditional antiques and twentieth-century nostalgia—ranging from Art Deco accessories to kitschy retro items. Gallery Row, along Granville Street from the Granville Bridge to Broadway, boasts more than 20 art galleries and antique dealers. Add spice to your visit with a side trip to **The Punjabi Market** or the **Little India District,** where you'll find stores with exotic foods, spices, and a huge selection of 24-karat gold jewelry. For more information, visit www.vancouver.com.

Thrift Seekers

In This Chapter

* Hitting the world's largest outlet complex in south Florida
* Strolling through the factory outlets in New England
* Exploring the old-world treasures of Ohio's Amish country
* Desert thrifts and thrills in Palm Springs
* A few more thrifty destinations

I don't know about you, but I love a good bargain—one where you unearth that amazing designer short-sleeved shrug that goes brilliantly with your new cropped jeans. In your size. Marked down to pennies. Oh, girlfriend! It sets off a surge of happy chemicals in my overloaded brain that equates to sniffing the head of a puppy. Obviously, I'm a simple girl. But I know many of you swing on the same monkey bars that I do.

Most of us, however, cannot afford the time nor were endowed with the patience required to go digging through piles of junk for that one trophy piece. Unless, of course, you make a long weekend of it with the girls. In this chapter, I've dug up places where discriminating bargain hunters flock to shop. And as always, these trips come with a side salad peppered with tastes of local culture and cuisine.

Sawgrass Mills and The Colonnade Outlets

South Florida is teeming with more than just wild alligators, palm trees, and breezy shorelines. With some 28 million visitors per year, **Sawgrass Mills** and the adjacent **Colonnade Outlets** make up the largest retail and entertainment shopping complex in the state of Florida and the world's largest outlet mall. The center is approximately 10 miles west of the Fort Lauderdale/Hollywood International Airport and 30 miles from Miami.

Among the more than 400 stores that make up this bargain beat are high-clout anchor stores such as **Off 5th Saks Fifth Avenue Outlet, Nordstrom Rack, Neiman Marcus Last Call, Burlington Coat Factory, J. C. Penney Outlet, VF Outlet, BrandsMart USA, Marshalls, Bed Bath & Beyond,** and others. Sprinkled among the biggies are retailers such as **Calvin Klein Company Store, Furla, Polo Ralph Lauren Factory Store, Salvatore Ferragamo Company Store, Lacoste, Cole Haan, Nine West Outlet, Timberland, Tommy Hilfiger Company Store, Escada Company Store, Hugo Boss Factory Store,** and the **Nautica Factory Store.**

The **Colonnade Outlets** are a relatively new addition adjacent to Sawgrass Mills and feature an exclusive, upscale collection of style-defining stores. The foliaged, open-air promenade is blanketed in a Mediterranean style that makes you forget that you're in an outlet market (except, of course, for the discounted prices). The **Féraud/Rösch, David Yurman, Fitelle, and Vilebrequin** stores are among the first outlets of their kind in the country. You'll also find outlet boutiques for **Salvatore Ferragamo Company Store, Burberry, Coach Factory, Crate & Barrel Outlet, Kate Spade, Malo, Stuart Weitzman,**

Barneys New York Outlet, and **Valentino.** *12801 West Sunrise Boulevard, Sunrise, FL 33323.* **954-846-2350.** *www.simon.com.*

Where to Stop

Sawgrass Mills and The Colonnade Outlets have no shortage of places to stop and refuel. Two sprawling food courts offer more than 20 places to eat. You'll also find higher-end, full-service chain restaurants such as **The Cheesecake Factory, Empire Pizza Café, Legal Sea Foods, P. F. Chang's China Bistro, Rainforest Café, Paul Maison de Qualité, Grand Lux Café,** and their newest addition, **Villagio.**

But when you're ready to venture outside the Sawgrass area, southwest Florida has loads of activities, restaurants, and miles of shoreline to explore. The heart of **Fort Lauderdale Beach** is a straight 30- to 45-minute shot down Oakland Park Boulevard. Once you hit the beach, a scenic drive north or south along State Road A1A offers miles of options and beaches plus great people-watching.

As a native Floridian, I couldn't have you visit my old stomping grounds without experiencing the **Rustic Inn** (**954-584-1637,** www.rusticinn. com) in Fort Lauderdale. About a 30-minute drive from Sawgrass Mills, this seafood restaurant is located along a sleepy canal seemingly in the middle of nowhere. The dress is Florida casual (in other words, wear your "nice" flip-flops), and be prepared for a wait because reservations are not accepted. Tables are lined with newspapers, and your major eating utensil is a wooden mallet. Slap on that plastic bib if you opt for a bucket of the inn's famous garlic crabs. The lively menu includes everything from Key West-style conch fritters and deep-fried gator and frog legs to surf-and-turf meals, whole lobsters, and Florida stone crab claws (available only in season October–May).

Powder Room

If you're itching for deep discounts on a bargain-basement level, head to the infamous **Swap Shop** (954-791-7927, www. floridaswapshop.com). Open seven days a week, this sprawling 88-acre flea market is less than 30 minutes from Sawgrass Mills. By day, the Swap Shop is a circus of vendors, food courts, and local produce markets; by night, the grounds transform into a 14-screen drive-in movie complex.

Where to Stay

You'll find a handful of reliable chain hotels within a five-mile radius of Sawgrass—most in the nearby city of **Plantation.** The **Holiday Inn Express Plantation** provides a great value for the price. Start your day with a complimentary breakfast, and hitch a ride to the mall on the free shuttle. Rates start at $138, but you can usually find a better price at sites such as www.priceline.com. *954-472-5600. www.expressplantation.com.*

Located directly across from Sawgrass Mills, **The Crowne Plaza Hotel** is about as close as you can get to shopping central. This 10-story building features a fitness center, outdoor heated pool and Jacuzzi, restaurant, cocktail lounge, room service, and a free shuttle to anywhere within three miles of the hotel. Rooms come with a microwave, mini refrigerator, coffee maker, high-speed Internet access, and the hotel's signature sleep amenities, such as eye masks and relaxation CDs. Rates start at $129, but check the website for packages and promos. *954-851-1020. www.sawgrasshotel.com.*

Just under four miles from the mall, **The Hyatt Regency Bonaventure Conference Center & Spa** offers a luxurious resting place after long days of outlet strolling. Rooms are decked in a British Colonial décor accented with subtle tropical colors and feature plush bedding, flat-screen or LCD TVs, spacious bathrooms with marble tubs and walk-in showers, MP3 docking stations, microwave ovens, mini refrigerators, and Internet access. Hotel amenities include two restaurants, several cafés and bars (such as the chic **Bar ZEN**), and a full-service **Red Door Lifestyle Spa.** Rates vary by season, but you can usually catch a package deal or special offer on the website. If you can bear the heat, rates are lowest in the summer months. *954-616-1234. www.bonaventure.hyatt.com.*

The Kittery Outlets

Known as the Gateway to Maine, **Kittery** is a quaint seaport village just an hour north of Boston and easily accessible via Interstate 95. Settled in the early 1600s, Kittery bills itself as Maine's oldest incorporated community and is perched on the Atlantic shores, where miles of islands and inlets, beaches, and bays give it its seaside charm. Fishing, shipbuilding, and other marine-related industries have been the center of its economy and history. And then, there's the shopping.

On each side of Coastal Route 1 is the **Kittery Outlets** shopping village, where you'll find a mile of some 120 outlet stores. The dozen or so clusters of outlets and restaurants make up a village setting for apparel stores such as **Anne Klein, Banana Republic, Brooks Brothers, Calvin Klein, Coldwater Creek, Dana Buchman/Ellen Tracy, Eddie Bauer, Izod, J. Crew, J. Jill, Liz Claiborne, Lucky Brand Jeans, Old Navy, Ralph Lauren, Puma, Van Heusen,** and **Wilson's Leather.** More than 20 home stores such as **Calphalon, Crate & Barrel, Le Creuset,** and **Pfaltzgraff** are there for the browsing—as is **The Cosmetics Company Store** for Estée Lauder-owned brand closeouts. *375 U.S. Route 1, Kittery, Maine 03904, 1-888-548-8379. www. thekitteryoutlets.com.*

One unique stop is **The Kittery Trading Post (1-888-587-6246,** www.kitterytradingpost.com). The KTP is a definite place to stop for outdoor enthusiasts. A sportswear and supply destination since 1938, the two-story retail center offers clothing, outerwear, accessories, and footwear as well as a gift section with unique Maine-made gifts for home and hearth.

 *Powder Room*

Kittery isn't the only outlet beat in town. About an hour north is **Freeport, Maine,** which boasts more than 170 upscale outlets including an expansive **L. L. Bean Outlet.** Call **1-800-865-1994** or visit www.freeportusa.org for a free visitor's guide.

Where to Stop

The Kittery Outlets are sprinkled with fast-food haunts, coffee shops, and the **Weathervane Seafood Restaurant (207-439-0330)**—a comfy place for hearty portions of seafood and American favorites. You can grab a classic Maine lobster roll or "Fish Chowda" next door at **The Shack (207-439-0316,** www.weathervaneseafoods.com), Weathervane's original joint for fresh, fried seafood served in an informal, friendly setting.

Definitely save room, though, for a trip to **Bob's Clam Hut (207-439-4233,** www.bobsclamhut.com), just a quick skip down the road on the west side of Route 1. What literally started as a hut opened in 1956 by Bob Kraft is now a long-standing Kittery tradition. New owners took over in 1986, and a few new coats of paint and one charming white picket fence later, Bob's is still the go-to joint for fried clam baskets, clam chowder, fish and chips, and lobster rolls (served hot or cold—your choice).

When you've had your fill of fried and battered comfort foods, make dinner reservations for an exquisite dining experience at **Black Trumpet (603-431-0887,** www.blacktrumpetbistro.com) in **Portsmouth.** The two-story bistro and wine bar is in Portsmouth's historic old port, just 10 minutes from the outlets. Both floors offer views of the Piscataqua River, and you'll often spy tugboats escorting enormous tankers into the harbor. The first-floor dining room offers a cozy setting while the upstairs wine bar is a more intimate space, where tables are first-come, first-served. The menu changes every six weeks to make use of fresh seasonal ingredients.

Speaking of Portsmouth, plan a day trip to the history-rich city that sits near the mouth of the Piscataqua River—a short, wide waterway that divides New Hampshire and Maine. Following the **Harbor Trail** is the best way to dip your toes into Portsmouth's fascinating history. The Harbor Trail passes more than 70 points of scenic and historic city sites. Along the way are 10 buildings listed on the National Register of Historic Buildings, 10 National Historic Landmarks, and 3 homes maintained by the Society for the Preservation of New England Antiquities. Guided walking tours are available throughout the summer and fall, or you can request a map for a self-guided tour. *603-436-3988. www.portsmouthnh.com.*

Where to Stay

With rates starting in the $80 range, the **Best Western York Inn** is a pocketbook-friendly option. The hotel is located in the town of York, about three miles from the outlets and close to other area attractions such as Old York village and the Cape Neddick "Nubble" Lighthouse. Perks include complimentary breakfast, an indoor swimming pool, workout area, and in-room wi-fi Internet access. Ask about their Shopping Package, which comes with all the perks plus 10 percent off standard rates. *207-363-8903. www.yorkinnmaine.com.*

How could you resist staying at a hotel that overlooks Chick's Cove? If you're willing to make the 30- to 40-minute drive outside the outlets, **Village Cove Inn** in **Kennebunkport** is also a good value for the area. Guest rooms are dressed with Maine maple furniture and have either two queen beds or one king bed with a sitting area and pull-out couch with modern conveniences such as coffee makers and refrigerators. Some rooms have private decks and microwaves. The hotel boasts indoor and outdoor heated pools, a fitness facility, a spa treatment room, and two restaurants. Rates can fluctuate from $79 to $229 depending on the season ("supervalue" season is late October through mid-May), but check the website for value packages. They currently offer a Girlfriend Getaway package with perks such as a morning breakfast basket, dining certificates, and discount coupons to Kittery Outlets starting at $189 per person for double occupancy. *1-800-879-5778 or 207-967-3993. www.villagecoveinn.com.*

For a luxury oceanside getaway, book your stay at **The Cliff House Resort & Spa** (**207-361-1000,** www.cliffhousemaine.com) in **Ogunquit** about 20 minutes away from the outlets. A family-owned business welcoming guests since 1872, The Cliff House sits on 70 acres of oceanfront, high above Bald Head Cliff. Sounds of the ocean will lull you to sleep as every room has a balcony with an ocean view, affording sunrise and sunset landscapes against the distant horizon. Rooms feature picture windows, coffee makers, and Internet access (for a fee). Rates start at $175 for the European plan (meals not included), or add $63 per day for the American plan (breakfast and dinner included). Many package options are offered, such as The Seaside Shopper, all inclusive with three nights lodging, a welcome cocktail, breakfast, a three-course meal one night of your choice, a Cliff House tote bag, Kittery Outlet coupons, and sales tax and service charges starting at $416 per person for double occupancy.

Amish Country, Ohio

Since the early 1800s, the Amish community has flourished in the **Holmes County/Amish Country** region of northeast-central Ohio. The largest Amish community in the world, the region is equal distance from Pittsburgh, Columbus, and Cleveland—all of which are a little less than a two-hour drive away (by car, not carriage, that is).

Centered in Holmes County, Amish Country extends into each of the five surrounding counties where some four million visitors flock each year in search of the country-life experience, unspoiled scenery, home cooking, and of course, beautifully crafted home wares and accessories that don't come with big-city price tags. Amish Country is well-known for its many talented artists working in crafts—especially quilts, furniture, and baskets.

For hunting down quality handicrafts at old-world prices, the place to head is **Walnut Creek**—home of the weekly **Holmes County Amish Flea Market (330-893-2442,** www.amishfleamarket.com). This Amish market offers more than 100,000 square feet of up to 500 booths with bargains ranging from practical buys to countless handicrafts. This is the real thing. Clothes are hand-sewn, foods are homemade, and home wares are carefully handcrafted. You'll find home décor, collectibles, crafts, antiques, primitive folk art, wood products, clothing, furniture, produce, candles, toys, and quilts. And you won't go hungry, either, with meats, cheeses, candy, jams, jellies, and made-on-premises fudge to sample. They're open Thursdays, Fridays, and Saturdays, 9 A.M.–5 P.M., early April through mid-December.

Berlin is among the most popular destinations for visitors because of the vast number and variety of retailers. More than 60 stores are located within two miles in Berlin, making it a place to spend a day strolling through town. Make a stop at the **Berlin Village Gift Barn (330-893-2648,** www.oldeberlinvillage.com), a restored dairy barn with a delightful mishmash of furniture, garden accessories, quilts, dinnerware, pottery, candles, luggage, and handbags—all tastefully and artfully displayed.

Savvy Sister

Lancaster County, Pennsylvania, is home to a thriving Amish community and many stores with locally made handicrafts. **Dutch Haven** in Ronks, Pennsylvania, is among the most well-known. For more information on the Pennsylvania Amish country, visit www.800padutch.com.

You'll also want to make time to hit historic downtown **Millersburg,** the seat of Holmes County. The town is best known for its rich past, highlighted by the grand **Millersburg Courthouse** and **Victorian House Museum.** The Historic Downtown Millersburg shopping district is the place to head for artisan shops, antiques, vintage home accessories, handmade pewter tableware and jewelry, furniture, and quilts. Duck into **MinMar Quilt Shoppe (330-674-4800,** www.minmarquiltbarn.com) for gorgeous handmade quilts in every size, baskets, and gifts.

Where to Stop

Ohio's Amish Country is sprinkled with a bevy of charming places to immerse yourself in warm hospitality and country cooking. Among the most famous is the **Amish Door Restaurant and Village (1-888-264-7436,** www.amishdoor.com) in Wilmot. The restaurant features "Amish-Kitchen Cooking" for breakfast, lunch, and dinner. The restaurant boasts generous family-style meals piled with real mashed potatoes, broasted chicken, slow-cooked roast beef, home-baked bread, and country fresh produce from the salad bar. You may want to save room for a stop at the bakery, where you'll find freshly made pies, cakes, cookies, and traditional Amish baked goods such as snitz pie (dried apple pie), date-nut pudding, and apple dumplings.

Also in Wilmot, **Grandma's Alpine Homestead (330-359-5454,** www.grandmashomestead.com) is a local favorite for the all-you-can-eat buffet of homemade Amish cooking. Pile your plate with fried chicken, mashed potatoes, noodles, gravy, stuffing, pulled pork, red-skinned potatoes, knockwurst and sauerkraut, sweet potatoes, and meatballs. If that doesn't get your taste buds tingling, stop by for dessert and coffee just to marvel at the restaurant's famous cuckoo clock—the world's largest, as featured in the *Guinness Book of World Records.*

A family-owned business since 1938, **Boyd & Wurthmann Restaurant (330-893-3287)** in Berlin has earned its reputation as the place "Where the Locals Eat" for its delicious, homemade, Amish-style breakfasts, lunches, and dinners. There are more than 20 kinds of pie, from standards such as

STOP *Bad Trip*
Take heed, all you type-A multitaskers. In accordance with tradition, Amish-owned businesses are generally closed on Sundays. Use this golden opportunity to pack a lunch and explore the scenic countryside, or take a quiet day of rest.

Dutch apple, cherry, and blueberry to delicate creations such as peanut butter, chocolate, graham cracker cream, black raspberry cream, and seasonal surprises.

Where to Stay

If you're truly caught up in the spirit of returning to a simpler time, cuddle up at night to the sounds of crickets and ... well, not much else. The **Amish Country Campsites (330-359-5226,** www. amishcountrycampsites.com) offer 50 recreational vehicle and 10 tent sites where you can set up camp and enjoy evenings of fireside conversations. The campsite offers restrooms with warm showers, public telephones, free wi-fi access (yes, really!), complimentary firewood for campfires, 20- and 30-amp electrical hookups, and water at each site. Free back-road driving maps are available. You can't beat the rates, which start at $21 per night or $125 per week for two people.

Perched on 70 acres of lush countryside, **The Inn & Spa at Honey Run (1-800-708-9394** or **330-674-0011,** www.innathoneyrun.com) in **Millersburg** offers a peaceful, nature-inspired atmosphere with elegant dining, blissful spa services, and warm hospitality. The well-appointed rooms and cottages are sprinkled throughout the property and come with coffee makers, private baths with Natura amenities and luxury bathrobes, and personal items. Rates include a continental breakfast, 24-hour concierge and baggage service, and access to all common areas and inn activities. Rates start at $119 for standard lodge rooms.

For a group of three or four, consider booking the Woods or Cardinal Cottage, which have two bedrooms, studio kitchens, and fireplaces and start at $239. The inn often runs all-inclusive specials such as the Girlfriends Getaway Package, inclusive of accommodations, a gourmet four-course dinner at the inn's dining room (excludes alcohol), a welcome reception of hot spiced cider and cookies, unlimited movie rentals with popcorn, a Facial Party at the Spa at Honey Run, and all the other perks that the inn offers. You can even saunter to breakfast in your PJs—no questions asked. The package starts at $225 per person double occupancy.

For more information about Ohio's Amish Country, visit www. visitamishcountry.com.

Palm Springs, California

You might not think at first that bargains would top the list of **Palm Springs** attractions. Maybe tanned and chiseled retirees, manicured palm trees, and golf courses set against a hazy mountain backdrop are the first images to pop in your head when you think of Palm Springs. Well, they're all there—but so are the bargains! This retro-glam desert community is home to two outlet centers as well as a few hidden gems for hunting down vintage items and local art and handicrafts.

Desert Hills Premium Outlets (951-849-6641, www.premiumoutlets. com) in **Cabazon** (about 20 minutes west of Palm Springs) offers some 130 outlet stores **including Coach, Dior, Dolce & Gabbana, Elie Tahari, Giorgio Armani, Gucci, Lacoste, J. Crew, Loro Piana, MaxMara, Polo Ralph Lauren, Space (Prada, Miu Miu), Salvatore Ferragamo, Tod's, Yves Saint Laurent, Zegna,** and many more. More than 10 cafés and quick bites are also available.

Directly next door to Desert Hills, the **Carbazon Outlets (951-922-3000,** www.cabazonoutlets.com) are smaller but have a diverse offering of retail haunts such as **Couture New York, Crate & Barrel Outlet, Greg Norman, Karen Kane, Le Creuset, Marciano,** and **Rip Curl.**

Chick Wit

My girlfriends and I plan annual trips to the outlet mall and IKEA near Washington, D.C. The first time we went, one of the gals bought a cheap, fake crystal star paperweight and deemed it the "Shopping Star Award." Every year, the gal who spends the most money wins the Shopping Star Award. My husband is grateful that I have not yet had the pleasure of being awarded this honor.

—Marci, project manager

Once you've had your fill of factory outlets, head to the northern section of Palm Canyon Drive, known as the **Antique and Heritage Gallery District.** Stop by **111 Antique Mall (760-864-9390,** www. info111mall.com), where you'll find retro vintage furnishings, art, and lighting.

Also pop into the **Angel View Prestige Boutique** (760-322-2440, www.angelview.org). The thrift shop features high-quality women's and men's apparel and collectibles. Proceeds from the Angel View thrift shops (several more are spread throughout neighboring cities) support the Angel View Crippled Children's Foundation.

For a full list of shops and businesses on Palm Canyon, visit www.palmcanyondrive.org.

Where to Stop

Many of the best restaurants in Palm Springs are found in **The Loop**, an area formed by North Palm Canyon Drive and Indian Canyon Drive. Everything from landmark dining destinations to trendy hot spots are all within walking distance. Among the many casual eateries and restaurants, a long-time favorite is **Los Casuelas Terraza** (760-325-2794, www.lascasuelas.com) on Palm Canyon. Flavorful authentic Mexican dishes and an extensive tequila list are complemented with live music throughout most of the day. The festivities begin in the morning with table-strolling mariachis and carry on until late at night in the bar, which features a heated dance floor.

Top-rated, award-winning, and much loved by locals and visitors alike, **Le Vallauris** (1-888-525-5852 or 760-325-5059, www.levallauris.com) features Mediterranean French California cuisine. Located in a restored historical landmark, Le Vallauris is decorated with tapestries, Louis XV furniture, and colorful flowerbeds that surround an idyllic tree-lined, temperature-controlled patio. Frequented by the upper crust of Hollywood celebrities, fashion innovators, and politicians, Le Vallauris creates a culinary experience from popular entrées such as roasted rack of lamb with thyme and garlic, Maine lobster ravioli with basil cream, tender grilled veal chops with Calvados sauce—or the most popular dish, the stunning seared Lake Superior whitefish with mustard sauce. The restaurant is open for lunch, dinner, and Sunday brunch.

Perhaps it's the crisp desert air or the endless sunny skies, but the Palm Springs community likes to take its party outside and offers several street fairs and festivals. One not to miss is **Village Fest** (760-320-3781, www.palmspringsvillagefest.com), held every Thursday evening (except for holidays) along Palm Canyon Drive. Shops keep their doors open late, and you'll find booths with food vendors, locally grown produce, crafts, and artisans. Street entertainers charm the crowd with magic, music, and costumes. Best of all, admission is free.

Where to Stay

The **Wyndham Palm Springs** is home to a 5,000-square-foot swimming pool (the largest in Palm Springs). With colorful interiors and rewarding views of the San Jacinto desert mountains, the guest rooms at Wyndham Palm Springs include wireless Internet access, coffee makers, and work desks. Rates start at $129, but check the website for current promos and packages. One usually offered is the Girlfriends Getaway, which is a Stay Two Nights and Get the Third Night Free offer and includes overnight accommodations, a welcome cocktail for two, breakfast each morning for two, a spa discount, and one VIP coupon booklet to the Desert Hills Prime Outlets per person. Stay Sunday through Thursday and get a free upgrade to a pool view (based on availability). Rates start at $99. *760-322-6000. www.wyndham.com.*

Just a 15-minute shot from the Desert Hills outlets, the **Doral Desert Princess Palm Springs** is a classic choice mixing golf, tennis, and spa treatments into your shopping excursion. This four-star Palm Springs golf resort offers 285 elegant guest rooms and suites with golf course, pool, or mountain views and complete with amenities such as private balconies, refrigerators, and Internet access. The **Fairway Café** is open for breakfast, lunch, and dinner, and the **Cabana Bar** is a fun place to sip a smoothie or cocktail poolside. Opt for the Shop 'Til You Drop package, which comes with a spacious room for two for one night, a full American breakfast for two, a VIP coupon book for Desert Hills Premium Outlets—all for rates at $229 double occupancy. *760-322-7000. www.doralpalmsprings.com.*

Get your free guide to Palm Springs by calling **760-778-8418** or visiting www.palm-springs.org.

More Thrifty Destinations

For one weekend each month, the quiet town of **Canton, Texas,** stakes its claim as home to one of the largest open-air flea markets in the country. The **First Monday Trade Days** market is a tradition that, according to legend, dates back to the 1850s when the first Monday of each month was the day people made the trip into town to watch court proceedings (Canton's designated day for a stop by the circuit judge was the first Monday of the month), conduct business, and stock their pantries. First Monday Trade Days takes place Thursday–Sunday before the first Monday of every month. About an hour outside Dallas, a trip to the area is worthy of a getaway not only for the bargains but also for the scenic countryside and charming inns and B&Bs that dot the area. *903-567-6556. www.firstmondaycanton.com.*

Two outlet centers just 20 minutes apart—each with more than 100 brand-name manufacturers and designer outlet stores—are as good a reason as any to head to sunny **Myrtle Beach, South Carolina,** for a getaway. Both the **Tanger Outlet Centers** off Highway 17 and the 501 are just minutes from the beaches and plenty of lodging and eating options. Stay at one of the many resorts or condos in the nearby **Kingston Plantation.** *843-449-0491 (Highway 17 location) or 843-236-5100 (Highway 501 location). www.tangeroutlet.com.*

San Diego, California, is also home to several outlet centers worthy of a getaway. **Las Americas Premium Outlets (619-934-8400,** www.premiumoutlets.com) boasts 125 stores for savings on favorite brand and department store names such as **Banana Republic, BCBG Max Azria, Bebe, Calvin Klein, Coach, GUESS, J. Crew, Kenneth Cole,** and **Neiman Marcus Last Call.** The **Viejas Outlet Center (619-659-2070,** www.shopviejas.com) is located adjacent to the Viejas Casino and entertainment complex and offers more than 60 outlet stores in an open-air Spanish-style plaza. Stay at the nearby **Ayres Inn Alpine (1-800-446-0935,** www.ayreshotel.com).

Part **3**

Head Trips: Mind and Body Retreats

While we all need alone time, we often gain the deepest insights about ourselves from the reflections of our friends. In the chapters that follow, we share quality "me time" at destinations that focus on the mind, body, and spirit. We travel to relaxation and fitness spas that tune up your inner core and outer shell, and explore beautiful beaches where sand and ocean clear our noggins of static and stress.

(Photo courtesy of Lake Austin Spa Resort.)

Relaxing the day away at Lake Austin Spa Resort's LakeHouse Spa in Austin, Texas.

Spa Escapes

In This Chapter

* ❊ Almost heaven: Mayflower Inn, Connecticut

* ❊ Beach bliss at Naples Grande Golden Door Spa, Florida

* ❊ Splash therapy at Lake Austin Spa Resort, Texas

* ❊ Red rock visions of Mii Amo spa in Enchantment, Arizona

* ❊ East meets West Coast Zen in La Costa, California

* ❊ More relaxing spa destinations

Caught ya! If you flipped past the shopping excursions and adventure trips only to make a beeline to this chapter, then you're a girl after my own heart. Spa vacations are on the rise, and for good reason. Where else are you forced to trade your cell phone and frenzied pace for a pair of comfy slippers, a soft terry robe, and a lazy itinerary laced with massages, facials, and navel gazing?

And, sharing the experience with like-minded girlfriends is the icing on the gluten-free cake. Can I get an ahh-men?

Advice and Etiquette

But first, here are a few ground rules:

* **Homework:** Study the spa menu before your visit and if you have questions about a treatment, call the spa and ask for details. If you're pregnant and decide on a massage, tell the receptionist at the time you book your appointment. Not all therapists are trained in maternity massage, and a special therapy table is required. If you do have a baby bump—or any health issues, for that matter—you may want to check with your physician before scheduling a treatment.

* **Arrival:** Plan to arrive at the spa at least 30 minutes before your appointment to change and unwind. Better yet, check in a few hours early to take advantage of amenities such as steam rooms, saunas, whirlpools, and showers.

* **Etiquette:** Cell phones, mobile devices, and other gadgets are simply not appropriate at the spa. You know that, and I know that—but people still sneak them in like contraband. Being plugged in 24/7 is a powerful addiction—but it's also part of the reason you and the gals chose a spa getaway. If you must bring your gizmos (why?), be sure to power them down completely so they don't go off in your locker and disturb other guests.

* **Cancellation:** Heaven forbid if you have to cancel a spa appointment. But if you do, call and cancel at least 24 hours in advance. You may be charged for your service otherwise.

* **Disrobing:** Therapists learn some nifty towel tricks in their training that keep your private parts under wraps throughout the treatment. But always disrobe to your level of comfort. I usually stash a two-piece bathing suit in my spa tote in case I'm overcome by a flash of modesty come treatment time.

* **Communicating:** Let your therapist know about any injuries, allergies, or sensitivities before your treatment, including preferences to touch, music, aromas, or lighting. If the pressure during

a massage gets too intense, give the therapist a heads up. A good grunt usually does the trick.

❋ **Tipping:** Plan to tip your therapist between 18 and 20 percent of the regular treatment price. If you book a spa package that includes multiple services, the gratuity may already be included—but if not, ask for a tip envelope at the reception desk, and tip each therapist accordingly. I usually precalculate the tip before my service because of that post-treatment wooziness (and so I don't have to count on my fingers in public).

Powder Room

Spa vacations can be pricy. Trim the fat from your trip by 1) booking your stay off-season, 2) calling the spa or checking the website for seasonal promotions or special packages, and 3) joining the spa's e-mail list (if available) to get notified of offers and promos. Another advantage of off-season travel is that while the weather might not be optimal, the waiting areas and locker rooms will be less crowded.

Indulgence Inn: Mayflower Inn & Spa

118 Woodbury Road, Route 47, Washington, CT 06793. **860-868-9466.** *www.mayflowerinn.com.*

Just a two-hour car trek from Manhattan lies a haven so nurturing and peaceful you'll think you've stumbled upon an undiscovered land when you arrive at this New England oasis. Family owned and managed, the historic country house inn and spa is perched on a lush 58-acre estate flourishing with vibrant gardens and specimen trees. Walks through the thought-provoking Shakespeare Garden and American Poetry Maze invite unhurried meandering. For the more athletic types, the adjacent Steeprock Reserve allows for seasonal recreational options such as hiking, cycling, fishing, horseback riding, skiing, and snowshoeing.

Dining at the **Mayflower Inn & Spa** is a culinary treat alive with the fresh flavors of what the inn has dubbed "Connecticut Cuisine." Meals feature local organic ingredients from the state's coast and country-side in masterful creations. Inn guests eat in the elegant Main Dining Room, the Shakespeare Garden (weather permitting), or the informal Tap Room.

But it's the spa that has racked up a long list of accolades owing to a deep-seated commitment to bridging luxury and personal well-being.

The Spa House

Built to capture the spirit of the original inn, the 20,000-square-foot Spa House is a standalone cottage with an air of intimacy and serenity. Overlooking the Blue Heron Pond, the central Garden Room is guarded by a Willem de Kooning painting that sets the cool and contemplative mood of the experience. The eight candlelit treatment rooms are complemented by a warming thermal sanctuary, a heated indoor pool, two scented steam rooms, a shimmering domed whirlpool, four exercise studios, a yoga garden, and a labyrinth.

The Mayflower's Active Body programs will keep you and the girls on the move. Start the day with the Mayflower Rise & Shine class, a gently invigorating morning sequence that prepares your mind and body for the day ahead. Yoga flow, stretch and release, ballet, and even cardio-dance fusion classes grace the list of choices. A handful of al fresco activities are also available, such as tai chi, qi gong, and Zen fly fishing in the Blue Heron Pond.

Spa guests eat breakfast and dinner in the spa Dining Room, adjacent but separate from the Main Dining Room, and lunch in the Loggia in the Spa House. While lighter and healthier than the inn's guest menus, the spa cuisine menu marries nutrition with explosive flavor.

Spa and Salon Treatments

Spa services range from balancing facials and massage therapies to soul-reviving rituals and soaks (hour-long massages start at $165; facials start at $180). Nourishing nail therapies, scalp treatments, and gentle waxing services are also on tap starting at $65.

The treatment of the house is the Mayflower Smooth-as-Silk Scrub—the ultimate in all-natural exfoliation. The scrub is a seasonally adjusted selection of three sugar and sea salt scrubs created exclusively for the Mayflower Spa. You can choose the essential oil blend that suits your mood: purify, energize, or relax. The super-energizing body polish is followed by an application of rich, smoothing shea butter and a massage (60 minutes for $165 or 90 minutes for $245).

Package Options

Mayflower offers three ways to enjoy the spa. From Sunday through Friday, weekend inn guests can use spa amenities, participate in fitness classes, and purchase à la carte spa services. Between the main house and 3 cottages, the Mayflower offers 21 rooms and 9 suites—each individually appointed with elegant furnishings and eighteenth- and nineteenth-century artwork. Rooms start at $520.

Also offered Sunday through Friday, the Mini-Luxe Experiences are short stays inclusive of accommodations, unlimited fitness classes, three spa cuisine meals daily, gratuities, and spa treatments à la carte. Two-night stays start at $1,750, and three-night stays start at $1,950.

The Above and Beyond Experience is the ultimate way to go. And on first blush, the price tag may seem exorbitant. But get this: the rate includes *unlimited* spa treatments. Layer your days with specialty facials, detoxifying body wraps, massages, or treatment rituals. Besides unlimited spa and salon services, the destination experience also includes accommodations, three spa cuisine meals daily, unlimited access to classes, and gratuities. You are also provided with workout clothes, spa robes and slippers, outdoor gear such as rain jackets and boots, heart-rate monitors, pedometers, and MP3 players with personalized music selections based on information collected by your personal spa advisor.

Three-night stays start at $4,800, four-night stays start at $5,750, and five-night stays start at $6,700.

> **Savvy Sister**
>
> When the same ol' massage just isn't cutting it, try something really old. Many spas, Mayflower included, offer treatments steeped in Eastern-based energy therapies. Thai massage (60 minutes for $165 or 90 minutes for $245) combines yoga-like stretches and rhythmic compression with gentle rocking to move toward a state of calmness and spiritual well-being.

Beach Bliss: Golden Door Spa at Naples Grande Resort & Club

475 Seagate Drive, Naples, FL 34103. **239-594-6321** *or* **1-888-422-6177.** *www.goldendoor.com or www.naplesgranderesort.com.*

While Naples Grande Beach Resort has been a happening beach destination for more than 20 years, the addition of the famed **Golden Door Spa** in March 2007 upped its appeal as an idyllic escape. Bordering the resort is the protected mangrove forest of **Clam Pass Park,** where just beyond lies the powdery sand and tranquil waters of the Gulf Coast. Green certified by the Florida Department of Environmental Protection, the property maintains its commitment to protecting the delicate ecology of southwest Florida without detracting from luxurious amenities and accommodations.

Besides beachcombing and water sports galore, the resort has 15 Har-Tri clay tennis courts, three swimming pools, and a new, high-performance fitness center where you can work with specialists on customized programs that include body analysis and strength training.

Resort Rates and Dining Options

City or gulf views are framed from most of the rooms and suites, which were recently renovated to reverberate a more refined, contemporary vibe underlined by Florida's casual style. The bungalows, located separately from the main resort, are blanketed in an Asian-inspired simplicity that reflects the Golden Door Spa aesthetics. Fully furnished terraces, sitting areas, and a queen Murphy bed make a bungalow room a good choice for a girlfriends' trip. The expansive bathrooms mark the high point, where after a shower under a rain-head fixture, you can slip into a plush spa robe. Rates fluctuate seasonally. Peak season is January through April, and you'll get the best rates from May through December. Off-season, expect double rooms to start at around $160, suites at $205, and bungalows at $299. During high-season, rooms jump to $395, suites to $460, and bungalows to $349.

Dining choices abound with two high-end restaurants along with a poolside bar and grill and two other options for casual fare. **Aura Restaurant & Bar** serves familiar favorites with a clever and flavorful twist. The seafood dishes are primo, and the Sunday brunch is a feast not to be missed. Adjacent to Aura, the **Chill Out Bar** offers a futuristic backlit bar where you can sip on pomegranate cosmos and nibble on complimentary upscale hors d'oeuvres during weekday happy hours. Famous for its steaks, **The Strip House** is blanketed in an all-red interior where rosy lighting and walls hung with photos of vintage burlesque stars create a vibrant backdrop.

The Golden Door Spa

Since opening in 1958 in its original Southern California location, the Golden Door name is synonymous with elevating the spa experience to a personal journey toward enhanced well-being. As the spa brand has expanded across the United States, that layered, whole-body experience has been turned up by integrating the natural landscape that surrounds each location (for example, the spas in Telluride, Colorado, and Carefree, Arizona). The newest Golden Door Spa at the Naples Grande Resort is no exception—and is, in fact, a harmonious homage to the spa's philosophy and the pristine beaches and mangrove estuary that guard it (but with a more timely, modern twist).

An intermingling of Japanese architecture and contemporary design, the spa aesthetics lean on outdoor elements and natural materials to set the tone for the experience. The 16,000-square-foot, indoor-outdoor spa village encompasses four linked pavilions that echo the style of a Japanese temple. Among the 12 spacious, clean-lined treatment rooms is a Golden Door Villa suite complete with a private whirlpool, wading pool, soaking tub, and sundeck. The nail and hair spa seems to float on the turquoise water that surrounds it and features a four-station Golden Door "buff bar" (a pedicure banquette of sorts) and a master hairstyling station that overlooks the pool.

Petite Zen gardens dot the al fresco amenities, which beg for calm, unhurried lounging. The outdoor courtyards offer whirlpools, sauna and steam chambers, rain showers, a meditation labyrinth, and a cozy day bed flanked by breezy curtains and plush pillows. The meditation areas both indoors and out feature chaise lounges equipped with pre-programmed iPods.

Spa and Salon Treatments

Tucked among the tantalizing treatment options are signature luxuries such as the Tsah-Tee Oho-Nee Restorative Facial, a cleansing ritual inspired by the Seminole tribe native to south Florida. A rhodochrosite stone is used during the treatment to recall the restorative power of the "red stone" or Tsah-Tee Oho-Nee that was believed to heal the spirit, transform emotions, and guide the heart toward new love and happiness. Natural poppy flower seeds are used to exfoliate while extracts of delicate tropical hibiscus extracts nourish (80 minutes for $175).

> ### Powder Room
> If you plan to book more than one treatment at a spa separate from the resort (such as the Golden Door), consider a spa package. Usually, the package price includes a discount and/or the gratuity. With tips at an average of 18 percent of the treatment price, an included gratuity makes a big difference in the total cost.

Signature facials start at $120, massages start at $120 for 50 minutes, manicures start at $60, and pedicures start at $80.

Aqua Therapy: Lake Austin Spa Resort

Just 30 minutes from downtown Austin, **Lake Austin Spa Resort** nests on 19 lakefront acres in Texas Hill Country. A relaxed, friendly atmosphere radiates throughout the peaceful grounds set against the cool blue water of **Lake Austin.** Embracing the charming Hill Country of the region and reflecting the colors and textures of the natural landscape, the property echoes the surroundings in architecture by generous use of Texas limestone, garden beds, fireplaces, cedar posts, and tin roofs. The award-winning property has climbed to the top of the destination spa must-see list because of its commitment to innovative wellness and discovery programs.

You won't get bored at Lake Austin, where creative fitness classes abound. The resort's signature BodyFlow class is a flowing fusion of tai chi, yoga, and pilates. The high-intensity Trek & Spin class pairs a treadmill workout with a group cycling session. Other offerings include canoeing, hydro-biking (yes, cycling in the water), kayaking, sculling, hiking, meditation, and dance. Aquatic aerobics and swimming classes take place in one of three pools. The training center overlooks Lake Austin and features state-of-the-art cardiovascular, circuit, and free weight training equipment. Private sessions with certified fitness professionals are available.

Discovery classes in healthy cooking, nutrition, communication skills, body image, relationships and sexuality, journaling, crafts, gardening, and other subjects are offered regularly. Special weeks and seasonal topics include programs such as Mother/Daughter, the Culinary Experience, Urban Cowgirl, Yoga for Everybody, Gotta Dance, For the Love of Books author series, and the Gathering of Wise Women. Special events are also planned around the holiday season.

Encouraging relaxation, the 40 lakeside guest rooms offer a casually elegant décor and furnishings crafted by local artisans. All rooms have plush linens, Kohler steeping/soaking tubs, signature lavender spa amenities, and cotton spa robes—and some suites have private wildflower gardens. The Lady Bird Suite honors former U.S. first lady Lady Bird Johnson and includes a sitting room, fireplace, private wildflower garden, and hot tub. *1705 South Quinlan Park Road, Austin, TX 78732. 1-800-847-5637 or 512-372-7300. www.lakeaustin.com.*

The LakeHouse Spa

Showered in prestigious accolades since opening in 2004, the 25,000-square-foot **LakeHouse Spa** is a destination begging for a girlfriend getaway. A destination unto itself, the two-storied facility has 30 treatment areas all equipped with showers, a customized sound system, and outdoor treatment porches. Indoor treatment rooms are sound-proofed while outdoors, the spa offers private garden courtyards for men and women with tented treatment areas, tandem spa suites, and poolside cabanas where you can indulge in an al fresco massage or other bodywork.

The LakeHouse Spa is also home to **Iris Salon** for hair, makeup, and nail treatments. A spacious relaxation area dubbed the Blue Room for its majestic blue ceiling offers a place to kick up your feet before and after a treatment. Fresh, healthy cuisine is served at **The Aster Café** in an intimate dining room atmosphere. Outdoors, the Palm Pool is perfect for lounging while the 4,000-square-foot Pool Barn houses an open-air, junior Olympic-size indoor pool.

Spa and Salon Treatments

The LakeHouse Spa boasts a spa treatment menu overflowing with tempting options. The staff consists of more than 80 highly trained therapists and technicians who offer more than 100 types of therapeutic massages, body scrubs and wraps, baths, facials, healing therapies, and salon treatments.

If the treatment choices become overwhelming, look no further than the spa's signature treatments. Texas Starry Night will gently rock you to sleep with a gentle lavender oil application, massage, and body wrap (50 minutes for $140 or 80 minutes for $190). The Gifts of Our Garden is a home-grown treatment that draws on the therapeutic herbs cultivated onsite in the Healing Gardens and includes a relaxing exfoliation, shower, massage, body wrap, plus a fresh herbal elixir. In an outdoor cabana close to the gardens themselves, you will choose an herb to be integrated into your treatment (100 minutes for $295).

Massage therapies start at $120 for 50 minutes, decadent body treatments such as the Seaweed Sensation hover around the $135 mark for 50 minutes, and facials start at $150. In the salon, pedis start at $70 and manis at $60.

Rates and Packages

Lake Austin Spa Resort offers a variety of three-night or longer packages for groups and individuals. Vacation packages include accommodations in one of the lakeside guest rooms, three gourmet meals daily, unlimited indoor and outdoor fitness activities and discovery classes, gratuities, and a selection of luxurious spa treatments based on packages selected and the length of stay.

The packages are further classified by room type and the amount of spa treatments and activities you want to squeeze into your trip. The most affordable option is the double occupancy Signature Room, where spa and fitness classes are à la carte for $1,555. Upgrade your stay to include a $330 spa and fitness allowance, and the same room jumps to $1,830. Add a $645 spa and fitness allowance, and you're at $2,070. You get the picture. The higher the allowance, the more you save. This allows each girl to customize her experience even when sharing accommodations.

The spa is very accommodating for groups, so be sure to check the website or call for current girlfriend getaway packages and group discounts.

Powder Room

Bring a slice of Lake Austin's culinary program home with you by picking up a copy of *FRESH: Healthy Cooking and Living from Lake Austin Spa Resort* (Favorite Recipes Press, 2002). Written by Lake Austin Spa Resort's award-winning chef Terry Conlan, the cookbook is filled with decadent quick meals that don't sound as healthy as they are. It's also available by calling **1-800-847-5637** or by visiting www.lakeaustin.com.

Red Rock Zen: Mii Amo at Enchantment Resort

525 Boynton Canyon Road, Sedona, AZ 86336. **1-800-826-4180** *or* **928-282-2900.** *www.miiamo.com or www.enchantment.com.*

You may have heard about an enchanting spa retreat hidden deep in the belly of a winding canyon, where life-changing dreams of mind and body transformations really do come true. Well it's no fairytale. Echoed in the Native American language of northern Arizona, **Mii Amo** (roughly translated as "journey") is counted among the world's top spas not only for its life-affirming wellness programs but also for its organic melding with the mouth-dropping beauty that engulfs the 70-acre property.

Tucked in the red rocks of **Boynton Canyon,** Mii Amo weaves the mind and body connection into a setting harmoniously in tune with its surroundings. The 24,000-square-foot Zen-style retreat spans two stories and houses 19 treatment rooms, 5 private outdoor treatment areas, indoor and outdoor pools, an 80-seat bistro, library, boutique, relaxation nooks, a movement studio, and expansive windows throughout with sweeping views of the canyon.

The transcendental heart of Mii Amo is the Crystal Grotto, a circular room with an earthen floor and an aperture in the domed ceiling carefully positioned so that during the summer solstice, the sun's rays fall onto a central fountain. Each morning, guests and staff gather in the Grotto to set daily intentions—while each evening, guests can join in a closing-day meditation.

Spa and Salon Treatments

Pretty nails and glowing skin aside, Mii Amo offers several signature treatments that travel far below the surface. The Soul Seeker treatment seeks to deepen your awareness and connection with your authentic self (90 minutes for $260) while the Aura-Soma Color Readings reveal your true self and invite you to reconnect with your innate talents and gifts. The 90-minute version of this journey includes a gentle color-balancing massage (60 minutes for $205 and 90 minutes for $260).

> **STOP** **Bad Trip**
>
> Granted, the stress released by a good massage is enough to make you burst into song—but out of courtesy to other spa goers, cackling and chatting above a hushed tone is a no-no in the confines of a spa. Wait until you're back to your room to raise the roof.

Signature facials and massages start at $145 for 60 minutes while Ayurvedic Balancing rituals for hands and feet are $65 to $80.

Package Options

Inherent in the definition of a destination spa, adult guests are generally required to stay in onsite accommodations and take part in custom or predetermined programs. But because Mii Amo shares the property with the family-friendly **Enchantment Resort,** resort guests are welcome to schedule a spa treatment and enjoy the amenities or take part in specially designed day packages.

If you opt to stay at the Enchantment Resort, the Casita Junior Suites start at $450 double occupancy and have fireplaces, a separate living room area, kitchenettes, and spa robes. The larger Casa Suites and Haciendas start at $850 and have full kitchens and one or two bedrooms, depending on your needs. All rooms are wrapped in an elegant Southwest décor with rich woods and plush linens and are an easy walk to the spa, tennis courts, and the restaurant.

If you decide on the three-, four-, or seven-night programs at Mii Amo, you'll stay in one of the 16 casitas or suites within a stone's throw of the spa. Each of you will choose among one of five journeys depending on your goals: Healthy Lifestyle, Rejuvenation, De-Stress Mind & Body, Spiritual Exploration, and Ayurvedic Balance. Prices are all inclusive, and each program comes with a predetermined number of spa treatments and three meals daily at the **Mii Amo café,** where eclectic spa cuisine is served onsite from an exhibition-style kitchen with community and private seating.

The 3-night package includes 6 spa treatments and starts at $2,178 per person. The 4-night package comes with 8 treatments and starts at $2,456 per person. The 7-night package includes 2 spa treatments daily and starts at $3,892 per person. Rates vary by season and room choice (the best rates are available in December and January).

The Feng Shui Way: La Costa Resort & Spa

*2100 Costa Del Mar Road, Carlsbad, CA 92009. **1-800-854-5000** or **760-438-9111**. www.lacosta.com.*

Located just north of San Diego in the coastal foothills of Carlsbad, this distinctly SoCal property is marked by clusters of white-washed buildings with red tile roofs, streets lined with rows of perfectly manicured palm trees flanked by colorful flower beds, and mature Bird of Paradise plants. Built in 1965, **La Costa Resort & Spa** is legendary for being the first resort in the United States to open with a full-service spa and for becoming the headquarters for the world-renowned Chopra Center (which I'll tell you about in a moment).

The Mediterranean-style resort village spans some 400 rolling acres and boasts two 18-hole golf courses, 17 tennis courts, 7 heated pools, 5 dining choices (including the acclaimed **BlueFire Grill**), an athletic club and fitness complex, 4 heated swimming pools, and programs for little ones and teens.

Room choices are extensive, from the Plaza Rooms (starting at $375) central to the resort activities to spacious suites and villas (starting at $650). The Spa Rooms (starting at $525) feature expansive bathrooms with deep soaking tubs. All rooms include flat-screen TVs, high-speed Internet access, plush robes, personal items, and myriad services upon request. Be sure to check the website for seasonal packages that include discounted room rates plus spa treatments and breakfast.

The Spa at La Costa

Central to the sprawling property is **The Spa at La Costa.** Spanning 43,000 square feet of indoor and outdoor space, the California Colonial style is felt throughout—with smooth stucco walls, terra-cotta tile work, cathedral ceilings, and a magnificent central 25-foot bell tower. The atmosphere is balanced by Feng Shui principles adhered to throughout the interior and outdoor spaces.

You enter the spa through a spacious reception area, which also serves as a tasteful boutique beautifully arranged with mindful gifts and skin-care items. The entrance trails off on one side into the spa lounge areas and at the other side into the attached **Yamaguchi Salon,** where Feng Shui philosophies are woven into the hair and nail services.

An impressive 42 treatment rooms are hidden among the lush land-scaping, including two VIP spa suites with side-by-side massage tables, shower, bathroom, fireplace, and outdoor garden patio with a whirl-pool tub. Indoor amenities include private women's wet areas with steam, sauna, whirlpool, cold plunge, showers, and lounges. Colorful flower beds and gardens set the backdrop of the outdoor spa courtyard, where you'll find a lounge pool, sunbathing nooks, and an invigorating Roman waterfall pool. A spa bistro, co-ed spa lounge, and movement studio round out the amenities.

Spa and Salon Treatments

Spa therapies include exotic massages, herbal wraps, scrubs, and facials that start in the $160 price range for 50 minutes. The La Costa defining treatment is the Indochine Indulgence, a 100-minute journey that calls on ingredients derived from the Indian Ocean to coax silky-soft skin to the surface. The service starts with a brown sugar and Dead Sea salt scrub, followed by an Egyptian milk bath, then a massage with Ayurvedic oils, and finally a lotus body wrap—all for $295.

In the salon, Feng Shui haircuts (a technique that harmonizes your style and personality with the five energy elements of Feng Shui) with a senior designer start at $125 while the signature Yin Yang Pedicure is $80. The ultimate experience is the Shogun Makeover with celebrity stylist Billy Yamaguchi, which includes a consultation, haircut and color, and a custom makeup program for $600.

Chopra Center for Well Being

A must for introspective relaxation seekers, the **Chopra Center for Well Being** (**1-888-424-6772**, www.chopra.com) was founded by Dr. Deepak Chopra and Dr. David Simon, who chose La Costa as the center's official headquarters and flagship location in 2002. The center offers alternative healing therapies that combine traditional medicine with Ayurvedic principles for medical consultations, body treatments, health and wellness workshops, meditation instruction, and yoga classes.

A short walk from the spa, the center houses a small boutique overflowing with books and Ayurvedic oils and supplements. Beyond that, yoga and meditation rooms are positioned along a hallway that ends with three private treatment rooms, where practitioners offer services based on your *dosha* and personal needs. Of the more popular treatments, Pizichilli is a gentle and rhythmic therapy where a continuous stream of warm, herbal oils is applied by two therapists to eliminate toxins from your body (70 minutes for $395). More affordable therapies are also offered, and a trip to the center includes unlimited organic teas, meditation and yoga classes, and access to The Spa at La Costa amenities.

More Spa Destinations

The 30,000-square-foot **Springs Eternal Spa at Bedford Springs Resort** is among the few spas in the country to use natural spring water in all of its treatments. The historic Bedford Springs Resort is an elegant Colonial resort in the Allegheny Mountains of south-central Pennsylvania. Ask about the popular Eternal Indulgence Package, which includes a luxurious guest room, breakfast buffet and dinner in the Crystal Dining Room, $100 spa credit per person, a spa take-home gift, and use of the Bedford Bath—the Bedford Springs signature bathing ritual the day of your treatment. Rates are from $280 per person weekdays, based on double occupancy. *2138 Business Route 220, Bedford, PA 15522.* ***814-623-8100.*** *www.bedfordspringsresort.com.*

A place where loafing around in your spa robe all day is strongly encouraged, **Sundara Inn & Spa** offers spa-inspired suites that sleep up to 5, villas that sleep up to 8, an intimate spa with 14 treatment rooms, a central bathhouse, an infinity-edge pool, and organic spa cuisine. Ask about their Girlfriend Spa Retreat package, which bundles two-night accommodations for two, $200 in spa credits per person, one $50 food and beverage credit per suite, and a breakfast buffet each morning for $454 per person. *920 Canyon Rd., Wisconsin Dells, WI 53965.* ***1-888-735-8181*** *or* ***608-253-9200.*** *www.sundaraspa.com.*

Located 13 miles from Palm Springs, the expansive **Desert Springs J. W. Marriott Resort & Spa** boasts one of the largest spas in southern California. The spa houses 48 treatment rooms, a salon, bistro, yoga studio and fitness facilities, a heated outdoor lap pool, and a 600-square-foot VIP suite with a personal butler. For groups, the spa offers a private wing with its own lounge, treatment rooms, and showers. Ask about the Escape Relaxation Package, which includes accommodations, spa treatments, and daily spa access (rates varies seasonally). *74855 Country Club Drive, Palm Desert, CA 92260.* ***1-888-538-9459*** *or* ***760-341-2211.*** *www. spaatdesertsprings.com.*

Project Weight Loss

In This Chapter

* Tear up the trails (and the scales) with a trek to Red Mountain Spa in southwestern Utah

* Munch, move, and spa away the pounds at Cal-a-Vie in California

* Immerse yourselves in the healthy side of life at Canyon Ranch in the Berkshires of Massachusetts

* Get serious about weight loss at Hilton Head Health Institute in South Carolina

* More weight-loss destinations

It's a sensitive subject for just about every woman I know: the weight game. Here's a funny story. My husband once signed me up with a personal fitness trainer as a surprise gift. "Oh, uh, thanks. Why?" I remember saying as he announced my present just as I was about to tear into a plateful of cheese-smothered enchiladas at our favorite Mexican hangout. His response went a little something like this: "Well … your butt's gotten … well, eh, kind of … big." Oh no he didn't (yes, he did). Although we no longer patronize that Mexican restaurant (I caused a slight scene) and I did forgive him for his act of generous idiocy, I do admit that sometimes it takes a dramatic jolt to set the fork down and go for a hike.

But what if the dramatic kick in the enchiladas was to take shape as a vacation? And what if you got to drag along your closest friends for mutual moral support? Is this situation sounding better? In this chapter, I promise not to comment on the size of your butt and instead explore a few well-trodden trails that lead down the road toward a better self-image and possibly the elimination of a pound or two (or four or more). A vacation focused on your mutual well-being? Sounds like the ultimate getaway to me.

Red Mountain Spa

1275 East Red Mountain Circle, Ivins, UT 84738. **1-877-246-HIKE** *or* **435-673-4905.** *www.redmountainspa.com.*

One of the few resorts to boast its own adventure concierge, **Red Mountain Spa** looks to its majestic surroundings to act as the focal point for fitness. The property is about a two-hour drive from **Las Vegas** and is nestled in the red rock bluffs of **Snow Canyon State Park** in southwest Utah, near **Zion National Park, Bryce Canyon,** and the north rim of the **Grand Canyon.** Red Mountain is a fitness and health destination where adventurous outdoor programs for all levels are tempered by a blissful menu of spa treatments, luxury accommodations, and savory cuisine.

Activities

Red Mountain Spa not only encourages guests to take a hike but also boasts a hiking program that rivals any adventure resort in the country. From novice to expert, sandstone to lava rock, and science to spirituality, more than 30 hikes led by an expert crew of some 40 guides keep guests of all fitness levels and interests on the move. Hikers are treated to an amazing array of desert animal life, plants, and rock formations that vary from twisting spires of Navajo sandstone, carved canyons, lava flows, and lava caves.

And you don't have to worry about finding yourself on a trail that exceeds your abilities. Hikes are rated for length, pace, and elevation gain, and guests are encouraged to hike at their current fitness level with daily treks from beginner to advanced levels. A self-guided hiking assessment is available to all guests.

Besides trekking the trails, Red Mountain boasts a bounty of innovative multilevel outdoor sports, including rock climbing, kayaking, guided bike rides, horseback riding, orienteering, tai chi, national park excursions, and back-country wilderness trips.

A breadth of introspective journeys round out the offerings, such as wellness and mind/body classes, spirit hikes, geology and archeology walks, stargazing, breath work, meditation, nutrition classes, self-awareness workshops, cooking classes, and art and creative expression classes. And if you're still bored—although that's unlikely—the property features three swimming pools (one indoor and two seasonal outdoor) and golf at any of the 15 nearby courses.

Cuisine also reigns supreme at Red Mountain, where three health-infused gourmet meals are served each day in the Canyon Breeze Restaurant. The Southwest-inspired menu is collectively known as "Adventure Cuisine" and includes four categories of choices: Green Cuisine (vegetarian), Power Fuel (sports nutrition), Detox (anti-inflammatory), and Call of the Wild (palate expanding).

The day starts with a breakfast buffet featuring hot and cold dishes, a fresh fruit bar, and juices. Lunch satiates your hunger with gourmet buffet items as well as a fresh salad and fruit bar. At dinner, you can choose from an array of selections and featured chef's specials.

When it's time to chill, **Sagestone Spa** offers a relaxing time out. The spa is located within a geodesic dome where chocolate, lime, and moss-green hues create a blissful, contemporary vibe. You'll arrive via the top floor of the spa, which also houses a full-service salon and boutique. Embraced by breathtaking vistas, the second floor consists of a relaxation area as well as the men's and women's changing rooms. The ground floor hides 14 treatment rooms including one spacious couples suite, two outdoor cabanas, and meditation nooks. The spa treatment menu features more than 50 services crafted from freshly harvested desert botanicals; mineral-rich muds, clays, and salts; and handcrafted essential oils. Á la carte spa and salon services start at $110 for facials and massages, $45 for manicures, and $55 for pedicures.

> *Powder Room*
>
> Lock in your hard work with the spa's signature Ocean Within Reshaping Body Mask treatment (50 minutes for $115). This body mask was designed to work in conjunction with a body contouring or weight-loss program. The refreshing aroma and soothing texture envelopes your body in the best of sea and science. By stimulating the metabolic processes, the mask boosts the natural processes of lypolysis (fat burning).

Rooms and Packages

Red Mountain houses up to 210 visitors in guest rooms that blend flawlessly with the surroundings. With a décor awash in earth and desert tones and natural fabrics that complement the red-rock vistas, king or double queen rooms feature oversized soaking bathtubs, spa robes, coffee makers, TVs, and Internet access.

Villa suites offer more space to spread out and can accommodate up to six guests. The suites offer king or double queen bedrooms, bedrooms with adjoining suites, or two-bedroom suites. Rooms and villas are surrounded by indigenous desert landscapes combined with manicured lawns and gardens and are convenient to the Canyon Breeze Restaurant, Sagestone Spa, fitness center, and swimming pools.

Rates range from $349 to $709 per person, per night—inclusive of three healthy meals daily, guided morning hikes, awareness walks, tai chi, unlimited fitness classes, cooking demos, nutrition classes, healthy living classes and events, and full use of spa and resort amenities.

I'm a package girl myself. I say, "Plan it out for me, and I'll show up." Red Mountain speaks to gals like me with tons of fitness, weight-loss, spa, detox, and seasonal packages. Of those, the seven-night Fitness Boot Camp package is a great way to jump-start a fitness regimen. Starting at $455 per person per night (based on double occupancy), the package includes all the regular rate inclusions along with a private nutritional consultation, a fitness consultation, two personal training sessions, a heart rate workshop with take-home heart monitor, a METAbeat Cardio-Metabolic Assessment (heart fitness screening), REE testing (resting energy expenditure analysis), boot camp classes, a choice of two Sagestone Spa treatments, a welcome gift, a healthy dose of motivational coaching, and other take-home aids.

New to the package lineup is Red Mountain's seven-night Re-Energizing Weight-Loss package, starting at $415 per person, per night (based on double occupancy). The program includes fitness testing, private nutritional and fitness consultations, a personal trainer, smart shopping/mindful dining consults, a heart rate monitor, take-home supplements, a contouring body wrap, and a firming body wrap.

Savvy Sister

Don't shun the spud! According to Dr. Ralph Ofcarcik, Ph.D., director of nutrition services at Red Mountain Spa, research has found that the potato is a champ at naturally suppressing hunger. Other appetite-suppressing foods include fish, beef, apples, oranges, brown pasta, and oatmeal. You'll find out more fascinating food facts through the health and fitness services offered as part of the Red Mountain experience.

Among the less-ambitious but crowd-pleasing packages, the Girls Getaway package allows your entourage to conquer mountains by day and revisit those good ol' days of pajama parties by night. Rates start at $525 per person, per night (for groups of four, based on double occupancy for the three-night package) and include one treatment per person, a welcome gift, and upgraded accommodations in a two-bedroom Villa Suite for three nights (sleeps three to four).

Cal-a-Vie

29402 Spa Havens Way, Vista, CA 92084. **1-866-772-4283.** *www.cal-a-vie. com.*

Secluded, exclusive, and a respite for many a celebrity, **Cal-a-Vie** specializes in the art of reshaping the bodies of its guests while showering them in a no-worries, just-relax environment. Hidden on 200 private acres in **Vista,** 40 miles north of **San Diego,** Cal-a-Vie is a European-inspired health spa resort with room for just 24 weekly guests. With a four-to-one staff-to-guest ratio, the boutique retreat offers the utmost in personalized attention. The name, created from the words "California" and "vie" (French for "life"), embodies its philosophy by combining luxurious European spa traditions with the California concepts of fitness, health, and nutrition.

Activities

The transformation takes place as soon as you arrive with an individual fitness assessment. A custom schedule is prepared for you with body and skincare programs, activities, and nutritionally balanced gourmet meals.

Every day is a little different, so boredom is never an issue. Tuck yourselves in early, because mornings start at the crack of dawn with a vigorous walk into the surrounding hills, where panoramic sunrise views cheer you on. After a nourishing breakfast, it's off to a stretch class, a weight workout, a private tennis lesson, an indoor cycling class, a round of boxing, or possibly a game of water volleyball. Classes are assigned according to your fitness level and goals, and although they vary by day, you'll generally get a mix of aerobic exercise, strength training, and stretching.

Flushed from all the exercise, afternoons allow time for a therapeutic soak in the hydrotherapy tub, lounging by the heated pool, taking a thoughtful walk around the labyrinth, or relaxing with a scheduled spa treatment. Evenings are spent either in the comfort and privacy of your villa or attending one of the educational lectures available before falling into bed.

Just like your daily itinerary, the food menu is always a happy surprise—and you'll never know what the chef might serve up. Healthful dishes tempt the palate with garden-fresh herbs and veggies that maximize the benefits of your fitness and beauty program. The menu features regional produce selected at its seasonal peak, unprocessed whole grains, essential fatty acids, and lean proteins. Ingredients are carefully prepared and artfully woven into mouthwatering masterpieces. A weekly cooking class led by Cal-a-Vie's award-winning culinary staff is part of the package and is a fun, interactive way to learn how to energize and balance your body while sticking to your weight-loss goals at home.

Did I mention that this place is full of surprises? The luxurious guest rooms are no exception. Complete with fine linens and handcrafted furniture, each of the 25 Mediterranean-style villas has its own distinctive touches and accent furniture pieces. All have magnificent views from private balconies. Step out of a soothing bathtub and into a plush robe and spa slippers, which you'll find in each room. The resort also provides a continuous supply of workout shorts, T-shirts, sweatpants, and sweatshirts. A complimentary laundry service picks up your dirty clothes after breakfast and returns them on the same day. Each villa is also equipped with wireless Internet access.

Rates and Packages

Cal-a-Vie offers three-, four-, and seven-night vacation packages that include gourmet spa cuisine, fitness classes, hiking, beauty and spa treatments, lectures on health and nutrition, accommodations, and workout clothes (this is one trip that will be easy to pack for). Rates also include transportation to and from San Diego International Airport.

Beginning on Sunday afternoon and ending the following Sunday morning, the recommended seven-day programs are tailored to your fitness level (with intensity increasing gradually through the week). The European Plan includes three meals daily, accommodations, sixteen therapeutic spa treatments, and all fitness classes starting at $7,395. The California Plan is the same except that it includes six spa treatments and starts at $6,895.

The La Petite Week packages are structured for three or four nights. The three-night program starts at $3,595 and comes with three meals a day, accommodations, six spa treatments, fitness classes, a nutritional lecture, and a cooking demonstration. The four-night program is the same except that it includes nine spa treatments and starts at $4,695.

Be sure to check the website for special rate weeks and seasonally priced options. Also, ask about the all-women's weeks, which are scheduled throughout the year.

Canyon Ranch Resort

165 Kemble Street, Lenox, MA 01240. **1-800-742-9000.** *www.canyonranch. com.*

When it comes to life-altering mind and body retreats, Canyon Ranch Health Resort is the mother of all health destinations. It was 1979 when visionaries Mel and Enid Zuckerman acquired Tucson's Double U Ranch in Tucson, Arizona, and shaped the site into the now world-renowned Canyon Ranch.

With the success of its first location, the Zuckermans opened the doors of the **Lenox, Massachusetts,** retreat in 1989. Guarding 120 woodland acres, the **Canyon Ranch Resort** in Lenox is smack between New York City and Boston (about 150 miles from each). The unhurried tempo of New England meets the energizing atmosphere of Canyon Ranch in this spectacular Berkshire setting. The architectural focal point of Canyon Ranch is the historic marble and brick Bellefontaine Mansion. Built in 1897, the mansion is a replica of Louis XIV's Petit Trianon and was built by the architects who designed the New York City Public Library. The main buildings are the inn, spa, and mansion—all connected by climate-controlled, glass-enclosed walkways and arranged around the reflecting pool and formal gardens. Sweeping views of rolling lawns and the surrounding woods set the serene vibe.

> (STOP) **Bad Trip**
>
> Don't even think about lighting up or getting lit. Smoking is permitted only in designated outdoor areas but is strongly discouraged. You are at a *health* resort, after all. Alcohol is not served or permitted in any public area at Canyon Ranch and is not available for purchase.

Activities

At the core of the Ranch experience is the comprehensive menu of life-enhancement programs, mind/body classes, and seriously soothing spa treatments. Because of the extensive activities and programs offered at Canyon Ranch, the first step in defining your experience is to peruse the comprehensive 70-page Lenox Guide to Services. An amazing array of programs, from weight management to spiritual wellness to dealing with specific ailments such as diabetes or arthritis—as well as health services and luxury spa services—are yours for the mixing. A personal program advisor will help you custom-design your stay.

The heart of Ranch activities is the 100,000-square-foot spa complex with exercise, weight training, and cycling gyms; yoga and pilates studios; indoor tennis, racquetball, basketball, and squash courts; an indoor swimming pool; an indoor running track; massage and body-work rooms; and skincare and beauty salons. Men's and women's locker rooms feature saunas, steam, and inhalation rooms; whirlpools; and a cushy relaxation lounge.

Canyon Ranch offers more than 50 fitness classes and activities daily, including an extensive outdoor sports program that features group hiking, biking, tennis, canoeing, kayaking, sculling, snowshoeing, and downhill and cross-country skiing. A variety of spiritual fitness classes, such as yoga, tai chi, chi gong, and meditation are also offered daily.

Outdoor facilities include a 50-foot swimming pool, tennis courts, and a ropes challenge course. Miles of walking, hiking, biking, and cross-country ski trails are available both on Canyon Ranch grounds and in surrounding areas.

Meals are meant to nourish both mind and body—and a shot of wheat-grass and a heap of bean sprouts no longer constitutes spa cuisine, thanks in part to the forward-thinking creative chefs of Canyon Ranch. Besides savoring the flavors of the delicately prepared meals, learn the secrets of how to prepare your own tasty, low-fuss meals at the daily Lunch & Learn classes. Led by executive Canyon Ranch chefs, the interactive and engaging demos are complimentary to all guests. Enjoy the flavorful creations in the demonstration kitchen while you learn tips and tricks for creating light, healthy dishes.

At the end of the day, you'll hit the sack in elegant New England-style rooms. Located in the two-story inn, the newly remodeled guest rooms have a king or two queen beds, a sitting area, and a vanity. Spacious executive rooms and luxury suites are also available.

Powder Room —

Keep up the good eats with a copy of *The LPGA Cooks with Canyon Ranch*, a collection of personal recipes from the Ladies Professional Golf Association made extra healthy by Canyon Ranch chefs. Recipes such as Karrie Webb's Avocado, Mango, and Walnut Salad and Nancy Lopez's Turkey Chili are complemented by best-loved dishes from the Ranch kitchens. All proceeds from the cookbook go to Shape Up America!, a not-for-profit organization committed to raising awareness of obesity as a health issue. For more information, visit www.shapeup.org. Order the cookbook at www.canyonranch.com.

Rates and Packages

Canyon Ranch stays are all-inclusive, and rates include transportation to and from Hartford (Connecticut) or Albany (New York) airports or the Albany (Rensselaer) train station, accommodations, three gourmet meals daily, unlimited fitness classes, a generous allowance toward spa services, taxes, resort amenities fees, access to tons of classes and demos, and personalized programs and services.

Packages revolve around individual needs and goals. Ideal for first-time guests, the Life Enhancement Program is the defining Canyon Ranch experience. The structured, seven-day program allows guests to focus on a particular life area from stress reduction to medical transitions in a nurturing group atmosphere. Outside the regular inclusions, the program comes with individual services and consultations with Canyon Ranch health professionals, group discussions, in-depth blood work, and a follow-up consultation with a Canyon Ranch physician to review results and make recommendations.

The ranch also offers an impressive array of health packages. The New Approaches to Weight Loss package requires a three night or longer stay and goes beyond the frenzy of fad diets to unlock what's keeping you from reaching a healthy weight. An experienced team of Canyon Ranch specialists guides you through new approaches to diagnosis and treatment of weight challenges. The latest clinical advances are available to help you balance the hormones, behavior, and brain chemistry that govern your eating patterns and weight loss. This package includes a comprehensive health assessment and numerous consultations and follow-ups with health-care and nutritional professionals.

Stays are three, four, five, and seven nights with rates starting at $2,040 (depending on the season and accommodations). For double occupancy in a deluxe room, three-night stays start at $2,040 per person and include $360 allowance for services; four nights at $2,770 with $600 allowance for services; five nights at $3,550 with $720 allowance for services; and seven nights at $5,130 with $1,200 allowance for services.

Check the website for seasonal packages, discounts, and special events.

Hilton Head Health Institute (H3I)

*14 Valencia Road, Hilton Head Island, SC 29928. **1-800-292-2440** or **843-785-7292**. www.hhhealth.com.*

Founded in 1976 as a weight-loss retreat center, the **Hilton Head Health Institute** has established a worldwide reputation as a leader in health and fitness—primarily for its pioneering weight-control program. If the words "fat farm" have fluttered into your head, you can rest assured that while H3I is serious about getting its guests on the fast track toward health, the great food, friendly staff, and charming southern beach-side setting culminates in a fun and functional getaway. The H3I program is built on a foundation of core principles, lifestyle management, nutrition, fitness, and behavior modification to help you lose weight, be as healthy as you can, and maintain those healthy habits for a lifetime.

The institute is located in the gated community of **Shipyard Plantation** near the south end of **Hilton Head Island.** A barrier island off the coast of South Carolina, Hilton Head is just north of **Savannah, Georgia,** in the heart of the Low Country.

Activities

While the oceanside location makes for a scenic backdrop, a visit to H3I is no day at the beach. The mantra at H3I is "get serious about weight loss," and this theme is threaded throughout your daily activities. Your day starts early with a sunrise beach walk. A light but filling breakfast is followed by a "thermal walk"—a leisurely 20-minute walk that keeps your metabolism elevated. Guests will next listen in on one of three daily healthy lifestyle lectures that range from breaking unhealthy eating patterns to planning nutritious meals.

A snack break or "metabomeal" (a fruit, vegetable, juice, or nuts) is followed by activities such as pilates, yoga, water aerobics, or tai chi. Lunch is followed by the second thermal walk, another fitness option, and another metabomeal. The third lecture of the day is followed by free time, dinner, and the final thermal walk. The day ends with a stretch class or a group outing. Are you exhausted yet?

The experienced culinary team creates superb, low-fat cuisine that averages 1,200 calories per day for most guests. Meals are served in a sunny dining room that overlooks a lagoon and the fairways that run through the Shipyard Plantation. Cooking classes take place in a state-of-the-art demonstration kitchen to seal in the philosophy that nutritious, low-calorie food is easy to prepare and integrate into your lifestyle.

Savvy Sister

The swimming pool at H3I is set to between 83 and 88 degrees, which is the temperature recommended by the Arthritis Foundation as the optimal temp for healthy joints. Who knew? For more joint tips, visit www.arthritis.org.

The fitness studio complex also offers treatment rooms for hot stone and therapeutic massage services.

At the end of the day, you'll appreciate the comfy accommodations located in condominium-style buildings within a short walk from the main campus. Guests stay in one-, two-, or three-bedroom fully furnished villas that encourage relaxation and reflection.

Rates

The rates at H3I include accommodations, nutritious meals and snacks, lectures, demonstrations, classes, individual lifestyle assessments (including blood screening and nutrition), fitness and behavior components, the use of all fitness and recreation facilities, taxes, and gratuities.

Your stay at H3I will run between $2,495 and $5,970 for semiprivate accommodations and $3,570 to $7,970 for a private room. A minimum stay of seven nights is required.

More Weight-Loss and Fitness Destinations

Perched on the shores of a private spring-fed lake and surrounded by miles of forest, the **Grail Springs Health & Wellness Spa** accommodates just 26 guests at a time. You can choose spa services à la carte or take part in one of several specialized programs: Cellular Detox, Holistic Detox, Health Rejuvenation, Juice Fasting Retreat, or Weight Loss. All-inclusive, five-night program rates start at $2,519. *2004 Bay Lake Road, Bancroft, Ontario.* *1-877-553-5772.* *www.grailsprings.com.*

As the name implies, **New Life Hiking Spa at The Inn of the Six Mountains** is renowned for its extensive hiking programs and offers diverse terrain for every fitness level. Guests choose from three different programs. The Mini Vacations are two to four days of low-stress workouts that include rooms, meals, and the hiking spa program for $229. The Jump Start Getaways are five to ten days of focusing on weight loss and building the foundation of a healthy lifestyle, starting at $219. The Weight Loss Retreat lasts 11 days or longer and invites participants to make drastic changes in their eating habits and lifestyles and starts at $209. *PO Box 395, Killington, VT 05751.* *1-866-298-5433 or 802-422-4302.* *www.newlifehikingspa.com.*

Located in the southwestern corner of Utah, the 30,000-square foot **Fitness Ridge Resort & Spa** offers a one-week minimum, results-oriented program for health, fitness, and weight loss. The program includes guided hikes, unlimited fitness classes, cycling, three calorie-checked and portion-controlled meals a day, cooking demonstrations, and classes in nutrition and stress management. One-week double occupancy starts at $1,295. *760 South 200W, Ivins, UT 84738.* *1-888-870-2639.* *www.fitnessridge.com.*

Committed to helping its participants create healthier lifestyles, the **Cooper Wellness Program** is located on the 30-acre campus of **The Cooper Aerobics Center.** Guests stay at Cooper Guest Lodge in rooms designed to calm and relax the senses. The center of the action is the 40,000-square-foot fitness center, where participants get personalized plans for fitness and exercise, nutrition and weight loss, and stress management. The all-inclusive programs include a fitness assessment, workshops, personal training, and three balanced meals daily—plus snacks and tools to get you on track to a fit, stress-free lifestyle. The 4-day Wellness Program starts at $2,295, the 6-day starts at $2,895, and the 13-day program starts at $4,795. *12200 Preston Road, Dallas, TX 75230.* **972-239-7223.** *www.cooperaerobics.com.*

Nothing but Beach

In This Chapter

* Exploring the pristine shores of New England's Cape Cod
* Sunning off the coast of Sarasota's barrier islands
* Hanging 10 on Hawaii's Garden Isle
* More beachy destinations

When I was first given the task of hunting down places to go for this book, I was so excited by the endless adventures that women could experience together (paragliding, shopping, spa pampering, flying down a ski slope, and so on) that I completely forgot the one type of getaway that nearly all of us crave: a super-relaxing jaunt to the beach, where the smells of seafood, suntan lotion, and briny ocean air lull you into midmorning naps and long, lazy, and wonderful afternoons. Well, the fine editors of *The Complete Idiot's Guide* team are clearly no idiots—and they were quick to

point out that they wanted some beach action. Of course! What was
I thinking?

A fabulous beach getaway is just the thing to bring you together with
the girls while framing your days with visions of crashing waves and
gorgeous sunsets. In this chapter, we'll dig our toes into sand, surf, and
the local tastes and diversions of our seaside excursions.

Cape Cod, Massachusetts

For those of us raised in metropolitan cities anywhere outside New
England, **Cape Cod** is a place so unique and breathtakingly beautiful
that a visit can border on a mystical experience. The pristine, unspoiled
beaches of the Cape are considered to be among the world's best—
especially along the 40-mile stretch of the **Cape Cod National
Seashore.** About an hour's drive from Boston's Logan International
Airport, the Cape boasts 559.6 miles of seashore scattered with light-
houses, bike trails, shopping, galleries, and restaurants galore.

Where to Plop

More than 100 beaches dot the coastline, each with various facilities
and activities among the 15 towns that make up the Cape. Here's how it
breaks down:

* The **Upper Cape** is closest to the mainland and includes the
  towns of **Bourne, Sandwich, Falmouth,** and **Mashpee.** Plan to
  spend a few days exploring the area's quaint fishing villages (such
  as **Woods Hole**) and catching a ferry to **Martha's Vineyard.**
  For the warmest waters in the Cape, plant your beach chairs in
  the Buzzards Bay area, home to **Old Silver Beach, Chappaquoit
  Beach,** and **Woodneck Beach.** Shared by the towns of
  Barnstable and **Sandwich, Sandy Neck Beach** on the Cape
  Cod side is another gorgeous stretch of coastline with hiking
  trails through the dunes. Get a map and more information about
  Falmouth at www.falmouthchamber.com.

* The **Mid-Cape** towns are **Barnstable, Yarmouth,** and **Dennis.**
  Sprinkled throughout the area are villages such as **Hyannis** and
  even smaller hamlets such as **Hyannisport**—two areas where
  you'll definitely want to spend a day or two. Make your way to

Kalmus Beach in Barnstable or West Dennis Beach in Dennis, both of which are on Nantucket Sound. Get maps and lists of beaches with facilities for Dennis beaches at www.dennischamber. com, and get more information about Hyannis at www.hyannis. com.

* The Lower Cape is the narrower portion of the Cape and includes the towns of Harwich, Brewster, Chatham, and Orleans. Make time to explore the resort town of Chatham, where you'll find posh shops and eateries along the pedestrian-friendly Main Street and historical landmarks such as the Chatham Lighthouse. The quaint town of Orleans is sandwiched between tranquil Skaket Beach on the Cape Cod Bay side and Nauset Beach on the Atlantic side—both splendid shores to spend a day. Request a Chatham visitor's guide at www.chathaminfo.com.

* The Outer Cape is home to Eastham, Wellfleet, Truro, and Provincetown. Among the most notable beaches are Coast Guard Beach, Nauset Light Beach, and Marconi Beach, which are part of the Cape Cod National Seashore (a $15 day pass per car is required June–September when lifeguards are on duty). The National Seashore comprises 43,604 acres of shoreline and upland landscapes. You'll definitely want to take a day or two to explore the colorful shops, art galleries, and restaurants of Provincetown. Print a map, a hiking trail guide, and learn more about the Cape Cod National Seashore at www.nps.gov/caco. For more P-Town information, call 508-487-3424 or visit www.ptownchamber.com.

Where to Stop

As you make your way up or down the Cape, you'll find a multitude of places to eat, from beachside clam shacks to fine restaurants that celebrate local flavors.

If you find yourselves in the Woods Hole village of Falmouth, make a stop at Captain Kidd Restaurant & Bar (508-548-8563, www. thecaptainkidd.com)—one of many friendly watering holes that dot the Cape. The Kidd is a casual spot to grab a bite or brew if you're waiting to catch the ferry to Martha's Vineyard.

In Barnstable, the chic yet relaxed **Naked Oyster Bistro & Raw Bar** (508-778-6500, www.nakedoyster.com) in Hyannis serves New England fare with a modern kick. Order champagne by the glass, and share a chilled seafood tower from the raw bar with littlenecks, oysters, jumbo shrimp, tuna sashimi, and chilled lobster tails.

The **Ocean House** (508-394-0700, www.oceanhouserestaurant.com) in Dennisport overlooks Nantucket Sound and serves simple yet artfully presented food. Contemporary dishes infuse traditional Cape Cod tastes with exotic twists, which are complemented by an extensive wine list, specialty martinis, and live jazz.

Provincetown has too many good eats to mention, but locals will insist that you make time for **The Mews Restaurant & Café** (508-487-1500, www.mews.com). Boasting a huge selection of vodkas (which, rumor has it, were sampled by celebrity cook Rachael Ray when she was in the neighborhood for a TV shoot). First-rate seafood, a seaside location, and hospitable service make The Mews an easy choice.

Finally (are you full yet?), another culinary P-Town outing where the view alone scores high is **The red Inn** (1-866-473-3466, www.theredinn.com), which overlooks the very spot where the pilgrims first came ashore in 1620 (making their more public landing in Plymouth Rock a month later). Offering a menu that changes with the season, The red Inn has racked up accolades for its succulent seafood (such as local pan-roasted cod and grilled fresh lobster). Reservations are strongly recommended and are taken up to six weeks in advance.

Among the many Cape diversions, a whale-watching cruise is a must. For a scenic shoreline and whale-watching tour, the **Hyannis Whale Watcher Cruises** (1-888-942-5392 or **508-362-6088**, www.whales.net) set sail from Barnstable Harbor and shoot up through Cape Cod Bay. The Whale Watcher Cruise is three-and-a-half to four hours and is $40 per person. Tickets are sold first-come, first-served daily at the harbor. Catch a spectacular sunset on the Clambake Cruise, a two-and-a-half to three-hour tour that for $60 per person includes a clambake dinner with lobster, cash bar, and live entertainment. Reservations a few days in advance for the dinner cruise are recommended. In the unlikely event that you don't spot a whale on your tour, the company will happily issue you a rain check for a future tour.

The Seal Cruise on the **Monomoy Island Ferry (508-945-5450,** www.
monomoyislandferry.com) is another unique diversion for wildlife
lovers. A twin-engine boat takes you on a 90-minute tour along the
entire west side of the **Monomoy Islands,** where the seals sun on the
shore. Cruises are $25 per person.

Powder Room

Between Memorial Day and Labor Day, the Cape is hopping
with summer revelers. If splashing in the waves and lying half naked
on a beach isn't your major priority, head to the area in late spring
or early fall when the towns are less crowded and lodging prices
are lower. Visit www.capecodtravelguide.com for seasonal special
offers, travel deals, and packages.

Where to Stay

The **Lamb and Lion Inn (1-800-909-6923** or **508-362-6823,** www.
lambandlion.com) in Barnstable offers moderate pricing and a relaxed,
fun atmosphere where the innkeepers include the cutest crew of half-
pint pups (two Yorkies and two pocket Pomeranians). The pet-friendly
inn offers a handful of outstanding deals popular for girlfriend getaways,
all of which are customized to your preferences. The Party-at-Our-
Place package features a three-course "girl's dinner" served poolside, in
a private dining room in front of a roaring fire, or at your place (provided you are booked in the Barn or Lamb's Retreat cottages). You'll
get a one-hour in-room massage, plus you can choose either a casual
culinary class or a wine tasting with cheese and chocolate pairings.
Rates start at $225 per person based on a party of four, exclusive of
room cost. The rooms all have their own personalities, and if you plan
to share lodging, consider one of the larger ones such as the Lamb's
Retreat (nicknamed "The Cottage"). A horse stable back in the 1700s,
The Cottage features French doors that open into a bedroom, a loft
sleeping area with a double bed, a spacious living room area with sofa
bed, dining area, and full kitchen. "Lairs" (the smaller rooms) start
at $145 during low season and $189 during high season. The Lamb's
Retreat is $180 during low season and $250 during high season.

Charming B&Bs and inns abound on the Cape but tend to fill up
fast in the summer, so be sure to book your stay early. In Falmouth,

the **Inn on the Sound (1-800-564-9668** or **508-457-9666,** www. innonthesound.com) offers 10 tranquil rooms and sits high on a bluff, with panoramic ocean and Martha's Vineyard views. In Sandwich, the stately **Annabelle Bed & Breakfast (508-833-1419,** www. annabellebedandbreakfast.com) offers six elegant rooms, personable service, and a heavenly breakfast. In Yarmouth, **The Captain Farris House Bed & Breakfast (508-760-2818,** www.captainfarris.com) is an elegant resort home built in 1845 with lovely gardens and 10 luxury rooms. In Chatham, the **Captain's House Bed & Breakfast (1-877-625-7678** or **978-546-3825,** www.captainshouse.com) sits majestically on the shoreline and offers five breezy rooms (all with sea views). And in P-Town, the **Brass Key Guesthouse B&B (1-800-842-9858** or **508-487-9005,** www.brasskey.com) offers 42 rooms tucked in the historical buildings that guard a pool and terrace. B&B rates vary dramatically by season, but check websites for specials.

If you decide to revel in the luxury Chatham experience, then **Chatham Bars Inn (1-800-527-4884** or **508-945-0096,** www. chathambarsinn.com) is your top choice. A beloved Cape Cod landmark since its opening in 1914, the oceanfront resort is perched on 25 acres of beautifully landscaped grounds on the Atlantic Ocean and offers an interior marked by Cape Cod's casual elegance. If self-indulgence is your goal, check into the resort's spa suites, each complete with a Jacuzzi tub, plasma television, and space for private in-room massages. Rates vary seasonally and start at $425 during the summer. Check the website for special offers.

In P-Town, the **Crowne Pointe Historic Inn & Spa (1-877-276-9631** or **508-487-6767,** www.crownepointe.com) is a plush hotel convenient to the heart of the action. The restored main mansion and historical buildings are guarded by meticulously manicured grounds, a heated outdoor pool, the acclaimed on-site bistro, and the new full-service Shui Spa. Rates can range dramatically from $99 to $672 per night depending on the season and include a gourmet breakfast, afternoon tea, and wine-and-cheese social hour. Watch for specials and packages on the website.

For more information on Cape Cod or to request a travel guide, contact the **Cape Cod Chamber of Commerce** at **1-888-332-2732** or visit www.capecodchamber.org. Another good source on Cape Cod is the **Massachusetts Office of Travel & Tourism** at **1-800-227-MASS** or www.mass-vacation.com.

Sarasota, Florida

While sand and surf might be its greatest draw, the southern Gulf Coast town of **Sarasota** has a fascinating history that has led to its crowning as Florida's cultural hub for performing arts and theater. In 1927, circus magnate John Ringling named Sarasota as the headquarters for "The Greatest Show on Earth" and provided a fanciful escape that lasted through the Great Depression. Today, the Ringling name graces the causeway that takes you to the area's sparkling beaches and is woven into the fabric of the city's culture and traditions.

Sarasota and its outlying beaches are about an hour south of Tampa International Airport, or you can fly directly into the Sarasota Bradenton International Airport. The string of barrier islands between **Sarasota Bay** and the **Gulf of Mexico** boasts some of the most gorgeous coastlines because of their powder-white sands, incredible Gulf sunsets, and tranquil waters.

Where to Plop

Longboat Key to the North, **Lido Key,** and **Siesta Key** are the primary beach haunts of Sarasota. Here's the breakdown:

* Longboat Key is a quiet island retreat marked by miles of well-manicured resorts and charming cottages framed by colorful impatiens and oleanders. This 10-mile-long paradise is the least crowded of the three keys. You won't find much public parking here, and beach facilities are sparse—but if you stay at one of the many resorts or cottages, you'll have your own chunk of beach.

* Lido Key is home to Sarasota's famed **St. Armand's Circle,** which was originally designed by John Ringling and is home to sidewalk cafés and upscale eateries, boutique shopping,

Savvy Sister

For nearly 20 years, Longboat Key has been the site of Sarasota's annual **Stone Crab, Seafood, & Wine Festival,** which marks the opening of Florida's stone crab season in late October. Florida stone crab season runs from October 15 to May 15. If you're a crab lover, that's the time to go!

and galleries that invite strolling. North Lido Beach is the most secluded but is easy to get to and convenient to the Circle. Lido Beach is the central stretch, is staffed with lifeguards, and offers concessions and amenities. **South Lido Beach Park** is at the southern tip of the key and is marked by skyline views of downtown Sarasota, picnic areas, and a nature trail with scenic overlooks and boardwalks.

* Siesta Key tends to draw a livelier crowd, but don't let this scare you off if you're just looking to chill. Just south of all the action is **Crescent Beach,** which has been dubbed by locals as Siesta Key's best "nonprivate private" beach. Crescent offers the same lush, white sands as Siesta Beach—but it's relatively secluded and quiet, with a limited public access road. At the southern tip of Crescent is the **Point of Rocks,** an excellent spot for snorkeling. At the southern end of Siesta Key is **Turtle Beach,** a family-oriented area with picnic tables and sand recreation. Siesta Key is also home to **Siesta Village,** an eclectic collection of shops, restaurants, and watering holes perfect for an afternoon daiquiri. The village is famous for its **Siesta Key Drum Circle,** where almost every Sunday evening a spontaneous rhythm of drums, bongos, and maracas fill the evening air. Bring your drum sticks, because everyone is invited to join the ruckus.

Chick Wit

For beach trips, I always bring a couple of hats along with a soft collapsible cooler that I can fit into my luggage. Always buy sunscreen at your local drugstore at home before you go, because you'll have fewer and more costly choices once you hit the beach. I go with nothing less than 30 SPF for the face and 15 for the body. Believe me, you'll still tan if that's what you want. Nothing is more unattractive (or painful) than looking like the shrimp and lobster that you'll be having for dinner!

—J. J., publishing executive

Where to Stop

On Lido Key, make your way to St. Armand's Circle to refuel. **Hemingway's Retreat Restaurant & Bar (941-388-3948,** www.hemingwaysretreat.com) is Circle-central and offers a casual place to grab a Rum Runner and beach-inspired fare, such as beer-battered coconut fried shrimp or broiled Florida lobster tails. **Columbia Restaurant (941-388-3987,** www.columbiarestaurant.com) is a popular spot for its famous 1905 Salad, inventive tapas, and homemade sangria as well as for its **Patio Lounge**—where live music most nights makes it one of the liveliest joints on the Circle.

Siesta Key has a little bit of everything. **The Broken Egg Restaurant (941-346-2750,** www.thebrokenegg.com) is a classic place to start your day with homey breakfast and lunch dishes. For kicking it casual in Siesta Village, **The Old Salty Dog (941-349-0158,** www.theoldsaltydog.com) is a fun place to sling back a cold one during happy hour, while nearby **Blasé Café & Martini Bar (941-349-9822,** www.theblasecafe.com) has a more refined appeal.

The path to stellar seafood dishes on Siesta Key leads to **Ophelia's on the Bay (1-877-229-9601** or **941-349-2212,** www.opheliasonthebay. net) on the Bay and **Turtles (941-346-2207,** www.turtlesrestaurant. com) of Little Sarasota Bay. Ophelia's boasts eclectic upscale dishes that borrow tastes from American, Asian, Italian, and Floridian flavors. Turtles offers a much more casual atmosphere, but the menu has a creative flair that keeps it a favorite among locals. Both restaurants offer views of tranquil Little Sarasota Bay.

A visit to Sarasota wouldn't be complete without a trip to the **John and Mable Ringling Museum of Art (941-359-5700,** www.ringling. org). Located on a 66-acre estate on Sarasota Bay, The John and Mable Ringling Museum of Art was established in 1927 as the legacy of John Ringling (1866–1936) and his wife, Mable (1875–1929), and is the **State Art Museum of Florida.** Also on the grounds are the **Museum of the Circus** and John Ringling's winter home on the bay, Cà d'Zan (House of John), a beautifully restored mansion. The $19 general admission fee includes access to

Powder Room

Florida's Gulf Coast peak season starts in February and continues through Easter, when accommodation reservations are strongly recommended. While value season is June through September, temperatures are moderate and hover around the 90°F mark during the hottest months.

the Museum of Art, Cà d'Zan mansion, Circus Museum, Mable's rose garden, and manicured grounds. Several food options are also available. It's open seven days a week except holidays.

Where to Stay

On Longboat Key, you'll have many options—from grand hotels to condos to beachside bungalows. The **Longboat Key Club & Resort** (**1-888-237-5545** or **941-383-8821**, www.longboatkeyclub.com) is an easy choice, though, because of its onsite dining options, full-service spa and fitness center, Gulf-side pool, tennis courts, golf course, water sports and recreational equipment, and private beach. Rooms and suites feature balconies with beach, lagoon, or golf course views along with amenities such as coffee makers, microwaves, refrigerators with ice makers, plasma or LCD TVs, bathrobes, and Internet access. Rooms start at $199 per night off season and increase to about $209 high season, but check the website for packages and promos. The Girlfriend Getaways package includes three nights in a two-bedroom beach-view suite, eight 50-minute spa treatments, daily breakfast, a gentle yoga class, a complimentary shuttle to St. Armand's Circle, a beachside portrait, and a welcome amenity starting at $270 per person per night.

For vacation rentals on Longboat and Lido Key, call **1-877-702-9981** or visit www.flvacationconnection.com.

If you decide to stay on Lido Beach, the **Lido Beach Resort** (**1-800-441-2113** or **941-388-2161**, www.lidobeachresort.com) has garnered high marks for its oceanfront location, tropical atmosphere, and friendly service. The one- and two-bedroom suites all have kitchenettes (most have full kitchens), free Internet access, plush bedding, and personal amenities. The resort has two beachfront heated pools (one for families and one for adults only), three poolside Jacuzzis, a free on-call shuttle to and from St. Armand's Circle, a beachside Tiki bar, and two casual onsite restaurants. Rates start at $169, but check the website for offers and online specials.

On Siesta Key, **Captiva Beach Resort** (**1-800-349-4131** or **941-349-4131**, www.captivabeachresort.com) offers competitive rates and is just a half block from Crescent Beach. Furnishings are nothing fancy, but all 20 rooms and suites have comfy beds with pillow-top mattresses, private baths, fully equipped kitchens, and seating areas. Rooms start at $115, but check the website for several budget-friendly packages.

For a more unique and secluded experience, **Turtle Beach Resort Cottages & Inn (941-349-4554,** www.turtlebeachresort.com) is tucked away at the south end of Siesta Key and is shrouded by banyan trees, palms, and lush tropical gardens. The inn has an old Florida feel with wooden walkways that wind through paths leading to the waterfront pool. Use of hammocks, fishing piers, canoes, kayaks, and paddle boats is complimentary. Guests are often treated to a visit by Charlie the blue heron and his entourage of dolphins, ospreys, bald eagles, pelicans, wild parrots, and manatees. Each of the studios, cottages, and suites have their own lively design theme, and all have private hot tubs and full kitchens. Turtle Beach is a five-minute walk from the inn, and the gourmet waterfront seafood restaurant Ophelia's on the Bay is next door. Rates start at $250.

For more information on Sarasota and the island communities, contact the **Sarasota Convention and Visitors Bureau** at **1-800-522-9799** or **941-957-1877,** or visit www.sarasotafl.org.

Kauai, Hawaii

Beware of chickens crossing the road and frequent rainbow sightings. Oh, and a cornucopia of beautiful flora and fauna and beach scenes that seem plunked from fairytales. With more than 40 exotic beaches, the island of **Kauai, Hawaii,** is about as breathtaking as you can get. Kauai is Hawaii's fourth largest island and is aptly dubbed the Garden Isle for its lush tropical greenery and sand beaches. The tropical climate provides just the right amount of sun and rain to nurture exotic trees and flowers (such as plumeria, the scent of which perfumes the air around its delicate blooms). Besides

STOP *Bad Trip*

Some of the largest waves on the planet break on the shores of Kauai, and it's strongly recommended that you swim only at beaches with lifeguards on duty (which include **Hanalei Beach Park, Waioli, Anahola, Wailua, Lydgate, Poipu, Salt Pond,** and **Kekaha**). For daily ocean conditions, advisories, and more beach safety tips, visit www.kauaiexplorer.com.

the spirited roosters that strut through the towns, island birds such as the nene goose (the state bird) and egrets are often seen enjoying their island paradise.

Where to Plop

The island of Kauai has four main areas, each with its own wonders:

* The **North Shore** is characterized by rugged mountains, spectacular sea cliffs, and breathtaking beaches—the most famous of which is **Hanalei Bay.** The legendary Hanalei coastline offers a two-mile-long, half-moon bay with white sand and majestic mountain backdrops. The best area to swim is in the center of the bay at Hanalei Beach Park, which has restrooms, a pavilion, and is watched over by a lifeguard. The **Napali Coast State Park** takes up 17 miles of the northwest coastline and can only be seen via the sea, the air, or by hiking.

* The east side of the island, aptly dubbed the **"Coconut Coast,"** is dotted with clusters of coconut trees and golden sand beaches. **Kealia Beach** is the place to head to watch surfers and boogie boarders ride the waves. **Lydgate Beach Park** is an inviting spot for first-time snorkelers because of the two tranquil lava-rock-enclosed ocean pools. The eastern side of the island is also the best area to pick up your souvenirs with shopping haunts such as **Kapaa Town,** the **Coconut Marketplace,** and other shopping plazas.

* Just south of the Lihue and Kalapaki areas—home to the airport and considered the gateway to Kauai—is the **South Shore** and **Poipu Resort** area. The south coast is considered the sunny, hopping side of the island and is home to famous Poipu Beach. **Poipu Beach Park** is a long stretch of sandy shoreline with lifeguards and amenities such as showers, picnic tables, and pavilions. Poipu can get crowded during the busy summer season, so if privacy is what you want, head to **Maha'ulepu**—a rugged and remote beach that is also a research site and habitat for endangered plants and animals as well as a sacred area for native Hawaiians. The beach does not have facilities or a lifeguard, though, so swim at your own risk. Other areas to mark on your map are the **Salt**

Pond Beach, the **Spouting Horn,** and the historical **McBryde Garden.**

✳ The west side, best known as the spot where Captain James Cook set foot when he first sighted the Hawaiian Islands, is marked by plantation-style towns that formerly dominated the islands. The two main beaches here are **Kekaha Beach Park** and **Lucy Wright Beach Park,** both near the two roads leading into **Waimea Canyon** (in other words, the Grand Canyon of the Pacific).

Where to Stop

No beach rendezvous would be complete without a sweet, cold stop along the way. Hawaii will satisfy your sweet tooth with its own answer to the snow cone: shave ice (not "shaved" ice). You'll find shave ice stops in places ranging from stores to trucks on the side of the road—and especially in populated beach areas, where you'll find **Jo Jo's Shave Ice** (808-635-7615) in Waimea. No worries, though, ice cream fans: Kauai-created Lappert's Ice Creams are served in soda shops and restaurants throughout the island (the Kauai Pie flavor is heavenly— trust me on that).

On the North Shore, the **Kilauea Fish Market** (808-828-6244) might be tiny—but you'll likely hit it up a couple times for its fresh and affordable plate lunches and dinners. The **Princeville Resort** (1-866-716-8110, www.princevillehotelhawaii.com) is another place to head for Sunday brunch at **Café Hanalei,** pupus and cocktails at **The Living Room,** or a traditional beachside luau with a Polynesian buffet and show.

○⚢ *Savvy Sister*
> The Hawaiian language is both rhythmic and colorful. Here are a few words to help you blend in: *aloha* (a fond greeting or farewell and the spirit of Kauai), *huhu* (angry or agitated), *lolo* (feeble minded), mahalo (thank you), *mana* (spiritual power), *nani* (beautiful), *pupu* (appetizer or snack), *wahine* (woman), and *wikiwiki* (quickly).

The South Shore and Poipu areas are teeming with many savory dining options. For the tastes of Hawaiian regional cuisine, **Plantation Gardens Restaurant and Bar (808-742-2121,** www.pgrestaurant.com) in the **Kiahuna Plantation Resort** offers a garden setting as a backdrop for traditional dishes and tropical cocktails. The restaurant is a restored plantation manor where you can linger outdoors on the breezy lanai or in the dining room with sweeping views of the Moir Gardens.

As for diversions, you'll want to catch a view of the mystical shores and cascading waterfalls of the Na Pali Coast. The best way is by water, and *Na Pali Explorer* (**1-877-335-9909,** www.napali-explorer.com) offers boat excursions narrated by marine naturalists and Hawaiian cultural specialists. The Scenic Sightseeing Expedition is a three-and-a-half-hour cruise up the coast that for $89 per person includes pupus platters of fruit, veggies, and Hawaiian-style chips and dips. The Snorkel Expedition is five hours and for $135 per person includes a continental breakfast, a deli lunch and beverages, and complimentary use of snorkel gear and flotation devices for a snorkeling stop in the pristine waters of Nualolo Kai.

You can hike Waimea Canyon or peer down onto its breathtaking expanse from the air. **Blue Hawaiian Helicopters (808-245-5800,** www.bluehawaiian.com) boasts the most luxurious and environmentally responsible helicopters in the touring biz. The Kauai tour takes you above **Hanapepe Valley, Mana Waiapuna** (home of the "Jurassic Park Falls"), **Olokele Canyon,** and then onto Waimea Canyon. You'll also fly over the Na Pali Coast, the **Bali Hai Cliffs,** the waters of **Hanalei Bay, Wailua Falls,** and (weather permitting) **Mount Waialeale,** the heart of the ancient volcano. Tours last just under an hour and are $251 per person. Book your flight online for a discount.

A beach trip to Hawaii isn't complete without a luau and hula dancing, and the **Smith Family Garden Luau (808-821-6895,** www.smithskauai.com) offers the full package. Evenings start with a welcome reception followed by cocktails and live music, a traditional Luau feast, and a final Rhythm of Aloha show with authentic Polynesian dancing. It's held three to five days weekly (depending on the season). Adults are $75 per person, but buy tickets online for discounts.

Chick Wit

Be flexible. I once went on a trip with four headstrong 30-some-thing females, and no one wanted to compromise. We spent more time planning the day's agenda than sight-seeing. It's so much more fun to let everyone go their own way, then meet up for happy hour later.

—Dana, magazine publishing executive

Where to Stay

On the North Shore, **Hanalei Colony Resort and Spa** is among the most picturesque places to perch and offers two-bedroom, two-bath condominium-style rooms furnished in contemporary island décor. Rates start at $240 and include fully equipped kitchens, a private lanai, laundry facilities, and access to swimming pool and Jacuzzi areas. The Girlfriends Package includes a day for two at the Hanalei Day Spa, an in-room manicure or pedicure for two, a *Na Pali* boat or horseback ride for two, a wine-tasting dinner for two, and all beach supplies (beach towels, sunscreen, and after-sun lotion) for two. Ocean-view rooms for a five-night stay start at $3,290. *1-800-628-3004 or 808-826-6235. www.hcr.com.*

If you plan to set up camp on the South Shore, you'll have plenty of choices. The **Bamboo Jungle House** is a charming B&B where beds are decked in breezy netting and all three rooms have French doors opening onto a private lanai with an ocean view. The house has an out-door pool, Jacuzzi, and lush gardens but no air conditioning or in-room phones. Rates start at $130 and include breakfast. *1-888-332-5115 or 808-332-5515. www.kauai-bedandbreakfast.com.*

The **Kiahuna Plantation & The Beach Bungalows** is also a good choice for girlfriend getaways because of its proximity to restau-rants and shops and its beachfront location. Set on 35 acres, the plantation-style accommodations offer plenty of room choices,

Powder Room

For more on Kauai and Hawaii's other idyllic islands, pick up *The Complete Idiot's Guide to Hawaii* by Corey Sandler and Michael Roney (Alpha Books, 2007).

from one-bedroom garden-view rooms to spacious suites and bunga-lows (each with various amenities). The resort has a swimming pool, easy beach access, sun decks, tennis courts, and the on-site **Plantation Garden Restaurant** for dinner and cocktails. Rates start at $240, but check the website for packages, promotions, and special rates. *808-742-2200. www.castleresorts.com.*

To find many other vacation rental companies as well as Kauai maps and a free travel planner, call the **Kauai Visitors Bureau** at **1-800-262-1400** or visit www.kauaidiscovery.com.

More Beach Destinations

Midway between Los Angeles and San Diego, the Orange County village of **Laguna Beach** is home to a stretch of Pacific coastline with tons to do—from shopping to gallery browsing and wine tasting. You'll find dozens of hotels, B&Bs, seaside villas, and dining options. Consider a stay at the **Surf & Sand Resort** (**1-888-869-7569,** www. surfandsandresort.com), an oceanfront resort central to the action and with great packages. Download a virtual visitor's guide at www. lagunabeachinfo.com.

The **Outer Banks** region of North Carolina boasts more than 100 miles of unspoiled coastline and is the place to go for a quiet, peaceful getaway. From the northernmost town of **Duck** to the tip of **Hatteras Island,** North Carolina's barrier islands are dotted with historical stops and miles of national parks and wildlife refuges. This is the place to rent a beach-front house and enjoy the quiet sounds of sea grasses swaying and waves gently breaking ashore. For more information, call the **Outer Banks Visitors Bureau** at **1-877-629-4386** or visit www.outerbanks.org.

If dipping your toes into the warm waters of the Caribbean is beckoning you and the girls, **Puerto Rico** offers everything you could want in an island getaway but with more bang for your buck than some of the more remote islands. Plus, because it's a commonwealth of the United States, Puerto Rico is the only Caribbean destination that doesn't require a passport (with the exception of the U.S. Virgin Islands). With its rich history and diverse culture, Puerto Rico offers some 270 miles of sandy beaches with plenty of upscale resorts, hotels, private villas, and lively dining options. For more information, visit www.gotopuertorico.com to research your trip.

Part 4

Culture Club: Excursions That Feed Your Mind and Appetite

For most of us, good taste and creative skill is acquired, not granted by birth. In the chapters ahead, you'll find destinations that fuel your creative and inquisitive sides. We visit places where you can sharpen your cooking skills, unleash your hidden desire to paint, or begin writing that piece of poetry that's sitting patiently at the forefront of your brain. We refine your taste for good food and wine. And we wrap up with historical trips to cities defined by their rich pasts.

(Photo courtesy of Mark LaPolla, Hudson River Valley Art Workshops.)

A typical day of creative inspiration at the Hudson River Valley Art Workshops studio in Greenville, New York.

The Joy of Learning

In This Chapter

* Cooking delicious dishes in Calistoga
* Painting pretty pictures in the Catskills
* Focusing your lens on the Grand Tetons in Wyoming
* Putting pen to paper in the mountains of North Carolina
* A few more learning destinations

The science of happiness is a complex business, but the latest buzz indicates that the pursuit of hedonistic pleasures can only get you so far up the stairway to bliss. Tapping into your own latent talents and stimulating that gray matter of yours can be a much more satisfying path toward joy and well-being. Another well-documented component of happiness is spending quality time with friends. Hmmm ... sounds like the ingredients of a learning getaway with your closest friends.

In this chapter, we'll get your creative juices flowing, sharpen a skill, and expand your minds and friendships. (See *O, The Oprah Magazine*'s March 2008 "Happiness" issue to read the full article, or search for "Five Things Happy People Do" on www.oprah.com.)

Get Cooking: Gourmet Retreats at CasaLana

1316 South Oak Street, Calistoga, CA 94515. **1-877-968-2665** *or* **707-942-0615.** *www.casalana.com.*

What's the difference between braising and roasting? And which knife do you use to chop an onion versus dismembering an entire chicken? Don your chef's apron and learn the basics of fine cooking or enhance your already-honed skills with a culinary retreat. Gourmet Retreats at **CasaLana** in the heart of Napa Valley wine country offer hands-on cooking classes in the professionally equipped kitchen of **CasaLana Bed and Breakfast** in **Calistoga.** Located in the heart of Napa Valley, Calistoga is a wellness destination renowned as the "Hot Springs of the West" and offers a walkable historic downtown, boutique shops, and world-class restaurants.

Chick Wit

When doing anything with your girlfriends, always remember your camera. If you forget it, buy a disposable one in a pinch. The one and only thing I'm looking forward to in old age is being able to look back at photo albums and remember the events, laughter, and tears shared with my best girlfriends. Then, I will know how complete my life was.

—Joanne, executive assistant

The Gourmet Retreats at CasaLana offer a range of options, from relaxed weekend classes to five-day boot camps—all geared toward avid home cooks and food enthusiasts at every level. The intimate class sizes of up to 12 students allow direct interaction with the chefs and personal instruction. The lush gardens of CasaLana also offer you the opportunity

to pick fresh herbs, vine-ripe vegetables, and fruits to use in your masterful creations. Accommodations are available at CasaLana Bed and
Breakfast, or you can choose among the many B&Bs, resorts, and hotels
sprinkled throughout the area.

You can choose among the following retreat options:

* The Culinary Learning Vacations focus on essential skills that
  promise to boost your kitchen confidence. Both the three-day and
  five-day Culinary Learning Vacations cover topics ranging from
  pantry essentials, stocks, soups, and sauces to cooking techniques
  for various cuts of meats, fish, and vegetables. Each day, your class
  will prepare dishes that incorporate a variety of cooking methods,
  such as sautéing, roasting, broiling, and poaching. Along the way,
  you'll learn basic knife skills, how to choose the right tool for the
  task, and how to properly care for your cutlery. You'll study flavor
  dynamics and balance as you learn to enhance flavors while adding your own style and flair to the dishes that you create. Besides
  a head swimming with new culinary inspirations, you'll leave with
  a detailed reference manual complete with recipes and a souvenir
  chef's apron. The three-day course is $650 per person, and the
  five-day course is $1,100 per person. Both include meals prepared
  in class served with wine.

* Boot Camp for Cooks is a five-day course for confident cooks
  who want to take their skills to the next level. Building on your
  culinary expertise, you'll learn techniques that inspire you to
  approach cooking with more creativity. Topics include sauces,
  bread baking, pastries, ingredient selection and storage, pantry
  essentials, menu planning, and entertaining. You'll harvest your
  own herbs, vegetables, and fruits from the CasaLana gardens to
  use in your recipes. On top of all that, your group will visit local
  culinary points of interest (such as a winery or farmers' market)
  to learn about food at the source, how to select the season's best
  picks, and pairing food and wine when planning menus. Evenings
  offer free time for you to explore Napa Valley on your own. The
  five-day course is $1,100 per person and includes a reference man-
  ual with recipes, an apron, and meals prepared in class served with
  wine.

* Gourmet Weekend classes offer a recreational cooking experience where you learn a variety of recipes and techniques at a relaxed pace. Your retreat begins on Friday with the preparation of a multicourse meal that incorporates various cooking methods. Saturday morning will be spent making a delicious brunch to enjoy before your departure in the afternoon. Weekend retreat menus are planned to take advantage of seasonal produce or to focus on a particular ethnic cuisine or style of cooking. As part of the weekend, you'll receive recipe handouts and indulge in meals prepared by your class (served with wine). The two-day course is $350 per person.

* Wine Country classes are a one-day immersion into regional or seasonal cuisine. Courses last about five hours and start at $160 per person. You'll receive printed recipe handouts and enjoy a delicious meal served with wine.

Where to Stay

Your best bet is to stay onsite at CasaLana, where the tranquil river setting and lush gardens create a naturally relaxing atmosphere. Nestled on an acre of land that borders the Napa River, CasaLana is marked by Mediterranean architecture, a central courtyard, aromatic herb gardens, and two spacious guest rooms.

The Arbor Room has a four-poster queen bed with luxury linens, a plush down comforter, and antique furnishings that speak of an Old World style. The Palisades Room has an ultra-comfy, pillow-top king-size bed and a private patio and is blanketed in warm, inviting hues that merge with the garden setting. Both rooms offer large sky-lit bathrooms with oversized showers and separate soaking tubs, in-room coffee and tea service, refrigerators with complimentary beverages, TVs, and a phone. Stays include a sumptuous continental breakfast served on the patio overlooking the river. Rooms start at $189.

If accommodations at CasaLana are booked or you're looking for more space to spread out, Gourmet Retreats will make reservations for you at one of the nearby Bed and Breakfasts in Calistoga. Of the many options, the Cottage Grove Inn is a good choice for girlfriends. The inn is central to the downtown Calistoga district and offers quaint cottages with plush amenities scattered among a grove of elms with rates starting at $250. Other B&Bs in the area range from $155 to $350.

Delicious Diversions

Make time for a side trip to **COPIA (1-888-512-6742** or **707-259-1600,** www.copia.org) in Napa. The American Center for Wine, Food, and the Arts, COPIA is a nonprofit discovery center with a mission to explore, celebrate, and share the pleasures and benefits of wine, its relationship with food, and its significance to our culture. Food classes are offered daily that celebrate the season—from cooking with artisan cheeses to summer grilling techniques—all with a tasting component and a side of food appreciation for $15 (45 minutes). General admission to the center is free and includes daily wine tastings and introductory wine, food, and garden experiences.

The **Culinary Institute of America**'s California campus in nearby **St. Helena** also offers cooking demonstrations ($15) as well as heavenly multicourse, wine-pairing dinners at their **Wine Spectator Greystone Restaurant.** For cooking demo reservations, call **707-967-2320.** For dinner reservations, call **707-967-1010.** For more information, visit www.ciachef.edu/california.

Powder Room

Calistoga is well known for its therapeutic mud baths and geo-thermal spring waters. The **Spa Solage** at the boutique hotel **Solage Calistoga** (1-866-942-7442, www.solagecalistoga.com) takes mud slinging to a new level with its Mud Bar & Bathhouse. The spa's 60-minute, three-part circuit Mudslide Experience starts with a self-applied mud cocktail, a soak in the natural spring waters, and winds up with a nap in futuristic sound chairs. The experience is $95 per person plus another $25 day pass fee for nonresort guests.

Brush Up: Artistic Painting Classes at Hudson River Valley Art Workshops

PO Box 659, Greenville, NY 12083. **1-888-665-0044** *or* **518-966-5219.** *www.artworkshops.com or www.greenvillearms.com.*

Dust off those artist brushes you've been hanging onto for "someday" and head to the **Catskills,** where you and the girls can unleash your creativity onto a willing canvas. Since 1982, the **Hudson River Valley Art Workshops** has offered classes in watercolor painting, oil painting, acrylic painting, pastels, drawing, and collage at a scenic inn in upstate New York's Hudson Valley. The workshops are open to fledgling and practiced artists alike and unite participants with top teaching artists in workshops held throughout the year. With a rotating cast of award-winning instructors, you may even get the chance to cull your skills under the tutelage of a favorite painter.

The all-inclusive workshops include art instruction, meals, and accommodations at the **Greenville Arms, 1889 Inn**—an historic and quaint B&B framed by the natural beauty of the Catskill Mountains. Art classes take place inside the **Carriage House Studio** (a spacious indoor facility) or outdoors with the surrounding landscape of the mountains and the Hudson River as your muses.

Class sizes are limited to 20 students, ensuring you'll get the attention you need. Although some workshops are geared toward intermediate or advanced artists, most are open to all levels. At various dates throughout the year, the Hudson River Valley Art Workshops also host Artist's Retreats that invite free expression with no set program. While painting pretty pictures is definitely high on the to-do list for all the retreats and workshops, the staff encourages artists to relax, focus on their creativity, and embrace artistic camaraderie.

Choose among the following packages:

* The Three-Day Weekend Workshop Package includes tuition for one evening and three full days of classes, three nights of lodging, breakfast and dinner daily, and refreshments for $715 per person double occupancy. If you prefer your own room, single occupancy is $825.

* The Week-Long Workshop Package includes tuition for evening presentations, five full days of classes, six nights of lodging, breakfast and dinner daily, refreshments, and a welcoming wine and cheese reception for $1,160 per person double occupancy ($1,320 for single occupancy).

* The Artist's Retreats are six-night or three-night packages and include lodging, breakfast and dinner daily, refreshments, maps and directions to painting sites, and indoor setups. The six-night package is $630 per person double occupancy ($790 single occupancy), and the three-night package is $365 per person double occupancy ($475 single occupancy).

Nonpainting guests are welcome for lower rates. Some workshops may have an additional model fee.

Once your deposit and enrollment forms are received, you will receive a supply list and detailed travel information. Supplies might include a folding stool, a field easel, and whatever else the instructor deems necessary. Remember to bring "play" clothes and comfortable shoes that are appropriate for working in the great outdoors.

The Greenville Arms, 1889 Inn has 16 unique guest rooms, each with various amenities but all with the charm of a warm Victorian inn. All rooms have private bathrooms, air conditioning, and a mini refrigerator. Some have fireplaces and porches, and most have handmade quilts and elegant antique furnishings. Inn amenities include a picturesque front porch, intimate parlors, the Carriage House living room, lush lawns and gardens, a lazy hammock, and an outdoor pool.

Healthful, delicious meals that emphasize fresh ingredients are served in the charming dining rooms of the inn. At breakfast, you'll have a wide choice from a full menu. At dinner, guests are served the same three-course meal, different each night (special diets can be accommodated with advance notice). And

Powder Room

Quilting caught your fancy? The Hudson River Valley Art Workshops also offers all-inclusive fiber art and quilt art classes for similar pricing as the painting retreats. Learn how to create gorgeous designs in contemporary and classic patterns.

if the mood strikes for a sweet treat, the inn is also home to **Life by Chocolate,** an artisan chocolates and confections boutique that sells molded chocolates, dipped chocolates, truffles, nougats, and other candies—all made on the premises.

Take a Picture: The Great American Photography Workshops

Grand Tetons National Park, Wyoming. **1-866-747-4279.** *www. gaphotoworks.com.*

With the advent of camera-equipped cell phones, the art of photography has been watered down to snapping shots of random, everyday scenes that certainly capture a moment but lack artful appreciation. A great picture takes a keen eye, a sense for lighting, and an understanding of your photography equipment—and it doesn't hurt to have amazing scenery for inspiration. The **Great American Photography Workshops** mixes art with pleasure on photography learning trips that capture images from every scenic corner of the country.

The **Grand Tetons** trip in northwest **Wyoming** is just one of the 20 or more trips planned throughout the year that explore breathtaking landscapes through a lens. Home to one of the most recognizable mountain vistas in the world, the jagged vertical lines of the Teton Range contrast with the green valley and crystal lakes that make a camera sing.

The workshops are led by a rotating crew of passionate, professional photographers. Participants vary from amateur to advanced, so don't be intimidated if you're a novice. For all photo tours, topics include equipment use and maintenance, field techniques, and composition and critiques of your past or current work. On most days, you'll set out early for hands-on outdoor work and then spend the afternoons inside for "class" work.

With a few exceptions, all workshops—including the Grand Tetons trip—are priced at $795 per person. The fee includes a set of workshop notes compiled from the key points from trip leaders. Tuition includes all lectures, field work, and critiques of your slides in general sessions.

Travel costs, film processing, lodging, entrance fees, and meals are not included. Trips are limited to 15 people. Photography workshops start on Wednesday evenings with a social hour followed by an evening of instruction and conclude around noon on the following Sunday.

(STOP) **Bad Trip**

Equipment failure or missing parts can easily ruin a trip. For digital camera users, don't forget your memory card, battery charger, and laptop. For 35 mm users, bring lots and lots of film. You can always pick up film on the road, but it's cheaper to stock up at home. Bring along spare batteries and your camera manual, too, in case of technical issues.

Where to Stay

Photographers on the Grand Tetons trip will have a block of rooms reserved for their stay at **Cowboy Village Resort** in the western town of **Jackson Hole.** You should book a room once you've reserved your workshop spot. Cowboy Village offers individual cabins with kitchenettes, full baths, covered decks with barbecue grills, and access to a covered swimming pool and hot tub. The cozy cabin village is a brisk walk or quick bus ride away from the Town Square, where you'll find restaurants, galleries, and shops. Special rates with the photography tour are $100 (normally, summer rates start at $120). *1-800-962-4988. www.townsquareinns.com.*

Where to Stop

You'll have plenty of eating options—the **Snake River Grill** (307-733-0557, www.snakerivergrill.com/), **Sweetwater Restaurant** (307-733-3553), and **Bubba's Barb-B-Que** (307-733-2288) to name a few—or kick up your boots one night with a Western show or hoedown. **Bar J** (307-733-3370 or 1-800-905-2275, www.barjchuckwagon.com) serves a mean all-you-can-eat chuckwagon supper complemented by a Western show while **Bar T 5** (307-773-5386 or 1-800-772-5386, www.bart5.com) whoops it up with a covered wagon ride to a creekside canyon with a Dutch-oven dinner and live Western music. Download a dining guide, town and area maps, and get more information on Jackson Hole at www.jacksonholenet.com.

Free Expression: Fearless Writing Retreat for Women

Lake Logan, North Carolina. **828-298-3863.** *www.clarityworksonline.com.*

The act of writing from your heart is a powerful art form that allows creative expression to bubble up from beneath layers of fear and emotion. **Fearless Writing Retreats** offer a safe, supportive, and fun atmosphere for you to allow those words to surface while sharing the experience with scenic Lake Logan in the **Blue Ridge Mountains** as a backdrop. Show up with a blank journal or a piece you've been working on for years. Women from all walks of life and experience are welcome at the retreat. The common thread is a simple desire to write.

Fearless Writing Retreats are led by published author and writing coach Peggy Tabor Millin, who started the retreats as a way to explore how the writing process nurtures the inner life and transforms the outer world of the writer. She creates an environment that gives women a voice and inspires them to speak their own truths through words. Groups are limited to 12. The three-day or seven-day retreats have a flexible itinerary of silent times, group times, and afternoons of reflection or exploring the natural beauty of the majestic location.

The three-day program is $647 per person and includes a private room for three nights, all meals, and the program. The seven-day retreat is $1,689 per person and includes a private room with bath for seven nights, all meals, and the program.

Where to Stay

Retreats take place 30 miles outside the mountain town of **Asheville** at the **Lake Logan Conference Center** in **Canton, North Carolina.** Operated by the Episcopal Diocese of Western North Carolina (who saved the land from development, but that's another story), Lake Logan is nestled at the foot of **Cold Mountain** in a peaceful valley between the **Pisgah National Forest** and the **Shining Rock Wilderness** in the Blue Ridge Mountains.

You'll stay in one of the six rustic, cozy cabins. Each has four bedrooms, a private bath, and a common space with a microwave, refrigerator, and coffee maker. Although rooms have two beds, Peggy encourages that you each have your own room for the retreat so that you have a private space to write.

Buffet-style meals are served in the dining hall—a stone and cedar lodge that overlooks the **Pigeon River.** A typical meal might include country biscuits made from scratch, a crisp garden salad, fresh trout, steaming in-season vegetables, and blackberry cobbler.

A seven-day retreat is also held on **Seabrook Island, South Carolina.** Custom group retreats are available.

Where to Stop

Make a side trip before or after your retreat to the grand **Biltmore Estate (1-800-411-3812** or **828-225-1333,** www.biltmore.com). Located three miles south of downtown Asheville in the **Biltmore Village,** the 8,000-acre estate is home to the 250-room Biltmore House, the Biltmore Winery, and more than 75 acres of meticulously manicured gardens.

If quiet inspiration is more your thing, take a drive to **Pisgah National Forest,** home of **Looking Glass Falls** and **Mount Pisgah.** Just a short drive from the retreat area in Canton, stop at **Pisgah Inn (828-235-8228,** www.pisgahinn.com) in **Waynesville** for gorgeous sweeping vistas.

Savvy Sister

A Room of Her Own Foundation is a nonprofit organization with a mission to further the vision of writer Virginia Woolf and bridge the gap between a woman's economic reality and her artistic creation. Through support, grants, and an annual writer's retreat in New Mexico, the foundation embraces the notion that the future can be changed by the artistic perspectives of women in the written arts. Find out more at www.aroomofherown.org.

More Learning Destinations

Chef, teacher, and author of 16 cookbooks with several in the works, Hugh Carpenter leads cooking vacations through the high desert country of **San Miguel** in central **Mexico. Camp San Miguel** (www. hughcarpenter.com/schools/camp-san-miguel/) culinary classes are created for travelers looking to combine a cooking vacation with plenty of free time to explore the territory. The $1,900 per-person price tag includes six days of cooking instruction, activities, lunches, receptions, and dinners. A six-day Napa Valley program is also available. For more information, call **1-888-999-4844** or **707-252-9773** or visit www. hughcarpenter.com.

Group opportunities to peer at the world through a photo lens are plenty. **Horizon Photography Workshops (410-885-2433,** www. horizonworkshops.com), based in northeast **Maryland,** combines lectures and photo critiques with field work and hands-on activity starting at $325. **Wilderness Photography Expedition Tours (406-222-2986,** www.tmurphywild.com) arranges custom adventures for groups (rates are custom per group) to photograph areas such as Costa Rica, Alaska, the desert Southwest, the prairie of South Dakota, Antarctica, and Africa. **Exposure36 Photography (1-866-368-6736,** www.exposure36. com) offers workshops throughout the year that capture the best scenes of the seasons, from the Canadian Rockies and Pacific Northwest in the summer to the Smoky Mountains of Tennessee in the fall starting at $525.

The **Summer Arts Workshops (1-888-682-3601,** www.cloudcroftart. com) in the mountain village of **Cloudcroft, New Mexico,** range from watercolor and oil painting to woodcarving, ceramics, and photography. The five-day workshops are held from mid-June to mid-August. Rates start at $325 per person and include tuition, five full days of classes, a reception, and refreshments. Stay at the **Burro Street Boardinghouse,** a log cabin with cozy bedrooms, a wood-burning stove, and old-time charm.

Good Taste

In This Chapter

* ✳ Savoring the flavors of the Pacific Northwest
* ✳ Curbing your sweet tooth with a trip to Hershey, Pennsylvania
* ✳ Toasting and tasting in Temecula Valley wine country
* ✳ Breaking bread over farm-fresh dinners in Vermont
* ✳ More destinations in good taste

As a kid, I actually believed that chickens where raised under fluorescent lighting in grocery stores and that green gelatin counted as a vegetable. We all have weird ideas as children, but as rational adults, the truth can be messy and complicated—especially when it comes to food. Is it organic? Is it locally sourced? Is it sustainable? Was the meat source raised humanely and fed foods that didn't stunt its growth (and therefore mine and my family's)?

In this chapter, we'll explore epicurean getaways where the chicken was clearly not raised in a grocery store but ran free and wild on a farm until meeting its fate on a plate—where the seafood is as fresh as the briny air, where the produce was hand-picked that morning by a local farmer, where the wine sings of the local soil, and where the cocoa beans used to make that gooey wonderful chocolate dessert sustain the economical and social survival of Third World cultures. These are getaways that pair great food with cherished friendships, and every morsel and sip brings about a shared appreciation for good taste. Bon appétit!

Foodie Paradise: Seattle, Washington

Expand your culinary palate with a trip to **Seattle,** where the cuisine is the stuff of a foodie's dream. From Pacific Northwest fare to an eclectic array of culturally diverse dishes, Seattle is alive with tastes and creative flair. Plus, what better way to see a city so rich in history than by eating your way through its streets?

Food Finds

Among the many sights and things to do in Seattle, here are some gastronomical options.

First, **Pike Place Market (206-682-7453,** www.pikeplacemarket.org) tops the must-see list for foodies. The market has a colorful history that dates back to the early 1900s, when the cost of onions increased to phenomenal proportions. In response to outraged locals, the city councilperson at the time proposed a public street market that would connect farmers directly with consumers. Customers would "meet the producer" directly—a philosophy that is still the foundation of Pike Place Market businesses. Spanning nine acres, the market is the oldest continually operating farmers' market in the United States and is a lively gathering place for farmers, craftspeople, and artists to sell their goods. You can grab a map at the market's information booth or take a free one-hour tour on Saturdays. Weekday tours are offered Wednesday through Friday and are $10 per person.

You can take on the hustle and bustle of Pike Place Market yourselves or get acquainted with the celebrated landmark through an interactive tour. The **Savor Seattle Food Tours (1-800-838-3006** or **206-898-4418,** www.savorseattletours.com) offers two-hour guided walks through the market sprinkled with tales, culture, and tastings. You'll strap on audio devices so you don't have to strain to hear the guide (or in case wanderlust takes you off course). Along the way, you'll sample locally made and harvested foods such as artisan cheeses, smoked salmon, and homemade pastries. Daily tours are $39, and you'll walk away with a better understanding of the market and a local dining guide and seasonal recipes.

As tempting as it may be to cart off bagfuls of fresh seafood and produce from the market, it won't do you much good back at the hotel. The next best thing to an impromptu dinner party is a cooking adventure with **Diane's Market Kitchen (1-877-624-6114** or **206-624-6114,** www. dianesmarketkitchen.com). Your personable and knowledgeable host, Diane LaVonne, will walk you and a group of up to 12 through a culinary learning experience that starts with a visit to Pike Place. She'll lead you through the market as you handpick artisan cheeses, locally sourced meats, produce, and fresh herbs. After a quick walk to her bright and spacious kitchen, you'll tie on your apron and get to the business of cooking under her engaging instruction. Chatting, laughing, and eating along the way are encouraged as you prepare your Northwest bistro-style meal. The three-hour classes are $104 per person and include follow-up recipes and notes. Select Washington State wines and microbrews are available for purchase. Winemaker dinners, special tasting events, and private classes are also available.

On first blush, the **Tillicum Village Salmon Bake Tour (1-800-426-1205** or **206-933-8600,** www.tillicumvillage.com) might sound a bit touristy—but even locals will tell you that the experience is not to be missed. Board a boat to **Blake Island State Park** and feast on king salmon baked to perfection on cedar stakes in traditional Northwest Coast Native American style. The salmon pits are fired up on the island just as your boat leaves the pier. Onboard, you'll sample steamed clams before disembarking at **Tillicum Village Longhouse** for the salmon dinner, which includes a salad bar, wild rice, new potatoes, warm brown bread, and a salmon-shaped chocolate dessert. Specially bottled Washington State wines are available to sample for additional cost. The evening concludes with a Native American dance performance and a demonstration on how the salmon are laced onto the cedar cooking stakes. The four-hour dinner experience leaves from Pier 55 and is $79.95 per person.

Where to Stop

For a shopping and tasting detour with a cultural edge, head to the **International District** for a colorful sprinkling of import shops, markets, and diverse restaurants. Sometimes called Chinatown—although the area is home to a diverse mix of Asian cultures—the area is also referred to as the "ID" by locals and spans eight city blocks just south of Pioneer Square. **Uwajimaya Asian Food & Gift Market** is at the center of everything. Stop by **The Wing Luke Asian Museum** for a walking map. For a list of the many Asian bistros and dim-sum cafés in the ID (as well as in other Seattle 'hoods), visit www.urbanspoon. com.

Powder Room

Cheese lovers, unite in your passion with the **Seattle Cheese Festival** (www.seattlecheesefestival. com) held annually in mid-May. Attend a seminar, watch live chef demos, or simply nibble your way along the cobblestones of Pike Place Market.

And for something completely nonfood related, take a Seattle ghost tour led by "Jake," a local ghost enthusiast of Private Eye Tours (**206-365-3739**, www.privateeyetours.com), who leads you on a three-hour excursion—in a ghostly white van, no less—to some of Seattle's creepiest and haunted locations. The tour is $25 per person.

Seattle Underground Tours (206-682-4646 ext. 202, www. undergroundtour.com) are an interesting diversion, too, if you've never experienced them. Bill Speidel's Underground Tours offer guided walks in the rugged pathways beneath Seattle's streets for $14 per person (or with advance notice, you can book a private tour). The Underworld Tour is for adults only and explores the more seedy side of the underground.

Where to Stay

For bed and breakfast lodging, start your search at the **Bed & Break-fast Association of Seattle (1-800-348-5630** or **206-547-1020,** www.lodginginseattle.com), offering independently owned accommodations at every price range throughout Seattle. **A Pacific Reservation Service (1-800-684-2932** or **206-439-7677,** www.seattlebedandbreakfast.com) can help you find B&Bs, inns, condos, guest houses, hotels, motels, apartments, cottages, and even houseboats throughout the Pacific coast. You can also download a Lodging Directory from the **Washington Bed and Breakfast Guild (1-800-647-2918,** www.wbbg.com) or peruse its members by region or special offers.

If the comforts of a luxurious resort are more your style, the 16-story **Hotel Deca** fits the bill with its smart and stylish Art Deco style. Located in the university district, the boutique-style hotel is about four miles from **Pioneer Square** and **Pike Place Market.** Rooms and suites have a rich elegance with amenities such as plush bedding, microwaves, refrigerators, wireless Internet access, and flat-screen TVs. Rates start at $119, but the hotel offers several value-packed packages. The Get Nailed Seattle Spa Package comes with accommodations in a sky-level premium room, two manicure and pedicure vouchers at a nearby spa, two $25 gift certificates to Victoria's Secret, champagne and chocolates, turndown service, and an express continental breakfast for $395 for two for one night (additional nights are discounted). *206-634-2000. www. hoteldeca.com.*

Located on Pier 67, the **Edgewater Hotel** is Seattle's only luxury waterfront hotel with dramatic views of **Elliott Bay,** the **Olympic Mountains,** and the downtown skyline. Plus, the onsite **Six Seven** restaurant makes the resort perfect for foodies on a mission—not only for its award-winning New American cuisine but for the breathtaking floor-to-ceiling views across the bay. Guest rooms have an upscale lodge feel with plenty of extras, such as plush bedding and bath ameni-ties complete with a rubber ducky. Book the Girls on the Edge package complete with accommodations for two, pedicure sets, nail polishes, magazines, two in-room movies, girly cocktails, and breakfast for two at Six Seven with optional in-room delivery. Package rates vary, but rooms generally start at the $269 per night mark. *1-800-624-0670 or 206-728-7000. www.edgewaterhotel.com.*

Sweet Tooth Fantasy: Hershey, Pennsylvania

You call yourselves chocolate lovers, but you've never been to the land of milk and cocoa? Well then, off we go to **Hershey, Pennsylvania,** where Chocolate Avenue and Cocoa Street are lined with Hershey's Kisses–shaped street lamps and the sights and sounds of an idyllic town built by chocolate. The town's reputation for being "the sweetest place on Earth" dates back to 1907, when Milton S. Hershey opened Hersheypark as a retreat for his chocolate factory workers. Now, "Chocolate Town U.S.A." is among America's sweetest vacation spots. Located in the rolling hills of central Pennsylvania's Derry Township, Hershey is a 90-minute drive from Philadelphia and a quick 15 minutes from Harrisburg International Airport.

Sweet Visits

Start your excursion at **Chocolate World,** the official visitor's center of the Hershey Company. Book your spot on the Trolley Works tour first—a round-trip ride through town where a singing conductor points out historical and cultural landmarks such as the real factory and the family homestead along the way. Then, strap yourselves in for The Great American Chocolate Tour, which takes you through the chocolate-making process from bean to bar. A handful of other entertaining options are available, but don't miss "Chocolate, the Experience," where a chocolatier guides you through the art of chocolate tasting with samples ranging from creamy milk chocolate to robust dark chocolates. Stock up on candy at the **Hershey Market Place Shops,** or stop for a bite at one of the two cafés, confections store, or milkshake shop. *Admission: Chocolate World free, trolley ride*

Savvy Sister

It's true, it's true! Chocolate really can be good for you! Research has proven that chocolate, primarily the dark varieties, is packed with antioxidants (translation: anti-aging properties) and may improve heart health. For more cocoa facts, recipes, and chocolate-covered inspirations, visit www.allchocolate.com.

$12.95, and the chocolate tasting experience $9.95. **717-534-4900.** *www. hersheys.com/chocolateworld.*

Make time to duck into the **Hershey Museum** located next to the Hersheypark main entrance. The museum offers a fascinating peek into the life of Milton S. Hershey, the candy empire he founded, and the model town he created. Among the exhibits, the "Kisstory" is a fun and nostalgic look at one of Hershey's most treasured treats. *Admission: $7.* **717-534-3439.** *www.hersheymuseum.org.*

Finally, chocolate tasting can take its toll—and for a candy-coated experience of a more refined kind, book yourselves a treatment at **The Spa at The Hotel Hershey** (also dubbed "The Chocolate Spa"). The 30,000-square-foot European-style spa was built in 2001 to mimic the design of Hershey's High Point mansion. Start with a Whipped Cocoa Bath (15 minutes for $40) followed by a Chocolate Bean Polish (30 minutes for $65) or a Cocoa Massage (50 minutes for $160). You'll find other lush experiences on the menu as well as salon services and fitness classes. **1-877-772-9988** *or* **717-520-5888.** *www.hersheypa.com.*

Where to Stop

If you don't stay at the historic Hotel Hershey, be sure to plan a stop at one of its restaurants. The **Circular Dining Room** is among the most famous for its many accolades and sweeping property views. The menu plays on the chocolate theme throughout, with sophisticated yet playful dishes (and the desserts are, of course, heavenly creations). The buffet-style Sunday brunch is a favorite affair followed by a stroll through the gardens. **717-534-8800.** *www.thehotelhershey.com.*

Yet another remarkable work of Milton Hershey's dedication to the community, the **Hershey Gardens** started out as a simple rose garden in 1937 and now offer 23 acres of spectacular seasonal blooms, theme gardens, and the always colorful Butterfly House. *Admission: $10.* **717-534-3492.** *www.hersheygardens.com.*

Keep an eye out for **The Hershey Story, The Museum on Chocolate Avenue**—which, by the time this book hits the shelves, should just have opened its grand doors. Located in downtown Hershey across from Chocolatetown Square, the two-storied living Hershey history promises to celebrate the life and legacy of Milton S. Hershey in an engaging and vivid experience that includes a café with a special area for chocolate tasting and an interactive Chocolate Lab. *717-534-3439. www. hersheystory.org.*

Where to Stay

The two Hershey properties central to the action are the elegant and timeless Hotel Hershey and the more budget-friendly Hershey Lodge. Guests of the Hershey Resorts (including the nearby Hershey Highmeadow Campground) get the best prices on Hersheypark tickets, early access to select rides and attractions, complimentary Hersheypark shuttle service, access to Hershey Country Club's golf courses, admission to Hershey Gardens and Hershey Museum, and exclusive opportunities for packages and special passes.

The **Hershey Lodge** offers post-and-beam ceilings, exposed stonework, and comfortable furniture—all of which pay homage to Hershey's rural Pennsylvania Dutch heritage. The lodge has three swimming pools, a fitness center, tennis courts, and a miniature golf course. Rates vary, but visit the website for seasonal packages. *717-533-3311. www.hersheylodge. com.*

The **Hotel Hershey** is a Mobil Four-Star, AAA Four-Diamond Hotel, Virtuoso-exclusive property and member of the National Trust Historic Hotels of America. The grand hotel offers 230 deluxe guest rooms and 29 suites, each elegantly appointed in a Mediterranean theme with views of the formal gardens, the lushly planted front terrace, or the town of Hershey in the valley below. The resort is home to the famed spa, two swimming pools (indoor and outdoor), a fitness center, tennis and bocce ball courts, bicycle rental, and nature trails. Rates vary, but check the website for seasonal packages. *717-533-2171. www.thehotelhershey.com.*

For more about Hershey or to request a free visitor's guide, call **1-800-437-7439** or visit www.hersheypa.com.

Wine Country: Temecula, California

Certainly lesser known than the Napa and Sonoma regions (but every bit as gracious), **Temecula Valley** offers a wine country immersion on a boutique, unhurried scale. Just an hour from San Diego and 90 minutes from Los Angeles, the area is a secret haven for burned-out L.A. denizens. A clean coastal breeze blows in through a pass in the mountains, creating a unique microclimate that has given birth to more than 20 wineries producing award-winning premium wines. The friendly mountain town of Temecula sits at 1,100-foot elevation, which gives way to cool summer nights rare in the southern California climate.

Grapevines

Start your path to grape-ness with a wine tour so that you can get familiar with the lay of the land. Among the many tour companies, **The Grapeline** offers a couple good options. The Grapeline Wine Shuttle offers all-day transportation to four or five wineries with a stop for lunch at your choice of restaurant or deli. Tasting tickets are not included with the shuttle tour, but you'll get coupons for discounted tastings (tastings normally run between $8 and $12 per person). The all-inclusive Vineyard Picnic Tour offers hosted transportation with four winery stops, a gourmet picnic lunch in a scenic vineyard setting, and all tasting tickets. Both tours include a coupon book with winery discounts and are scheduled from 10:30 A.M. to 4:30 P.M. daily. The Wine Shuttle tour starts at $42 per person, and the Vineyard Picnic tour starts at $88 per person (more on weekends). *1-888-894-6379 or 951-538-2093*. *www.gogrape.com*.

> **Chick Wit**
>
> Wine-tasting tours are such a fun way to bond with friends and gain insight into their personalities while also meeting new people. You learn about the local wines, get to chat with the vintners, and by the end the day, your tour group is one big, happy (and slightly tipsy) family!
>
> —Anita, media director

After a tour, you can spend the rest of your getaway exploring the wineries on your own. Most of the vineyards are located on the main drag of Rancho California Road, but download a wine country map at www.temeculamapguide.com so you don't miss any. For profiles and contact information of Temecula Valley vineyards and wineries, visit www.temeculawines.org.

Where to Stop

Spend a day wandering through the **Old Town Temecula District** (www.oldtowntemecula.biz). Among the quaint and historic storefronts reminiscent of the Old West, you'll find antique stores, friendly eateries, and a farmers' market held most Saturdays. Pop into the **Temecula Valley Cheese Company** (**951-693-9500**, www.tvcheese.com) for a nibble on artisan cheeses, meats, and breads and also into the **Temecula Olive Oil Company** (**951-693-0607**, www.temeculaoliveoil.com) for the wonderful tastes and smells of 100 percent California olive oil products, including gourmet foods and bath and body potions.

Soar above the vineyards and then enjoy a champagne breakfast with **A Grape Escape Hot Air Balloon Adventures** (**1-800-965-2122** or **951-699-9987**, www.hotairtours.com). Watch the sun rise over the pristine landscape during the one-hour flight. Once back on the ground, you'll toast your flight with champagne and a continental breakfast served picnic style in the gardens at **Wilson Creek Winery** (**951-699-9463**, www.wilsoncreekwinery.com). The $134 per person outing includes a souvenir snapshot.

Besides tours and tastings, the wineries offer plenty of other entertaining possibilities. Enjoy a wine country dinner at **The Pinnacle Restaurant** at **Falkner Winery** (**951-676-8231**, www.falknerwinery.com), a lazy Sunday afternoon of live music and champagne cocktails at the **Baily Winery** (**951-676-9463**, www.bailywinery.com), or a champagne and jazz session at the **Thornton Winery** (**951-699-0099**, www.thorntonwine.com).

Where to Stay

Temecula Creek Inn has been a part of the wine valley history since its opening in 1969. The landmark inn has continually upgraded its accommodations and grounds and offers first-rate dining, championship golf, tennis courts, a heated outdoor pool, a fitness center, and a central lounge with a cozy stone fireplace. Rooms and suites have a warm interior marked by touches of Native American and Western accents, and all have wireless Internet, and refrigerators while most have balconies that overlook the golf course, creek, or mountains. Rooms start at $149 or you can opt for a package. The Wine Country Getaway includes deluxe accommodations, a select bottle of Temecula Valley wine upon arrival, breakfast, a picnic lunch, tour and tasting tickets to select Temecula Valley wineries, and a wine dinner at the **Temet Grill** (featuring cuisine expertly paired with regional wines), starting at $335 per night for two. *1-877-517-1823. www.temeculacreekinn.com.*

For a more personal experience, book your stay at the **Loma Vista Bed & Breakfast.** The Old Mission–style home has 10 wine-themed rooms, an outdoor hot tub, and an inviting patio that overlooks the vineyards. Besides preparing a fresh morning meal, the convivial innkeepers will arrange your wine tours, scoop on their favorite local eateries, schedule an onsite massage, or prepare an afternoon cheese platter to accompany a wine you bought that day. *1-877-676-7047 or 951-676-7047. www. lomavistabb.com.*

If you want to play vintner and wake up surrounded by vineyard views, stay at one of the luxury villas at **South Coast Winery Resort & Spa.** The resort offers several pampering packages such as the Spa-Tacular Getaway, which includes accommodations in a villa with a Jacuzzi tub, a bottle of sparkling wine on arrival, a massage or facial at the GrapeSeed Spa, and two complimentary tickets to the wine-tasting room. Cost is just $290 per person based on double occupancy. *1-866-994-6379 or 951-587-9463. www.wineresort.com.*

For more information on visiting the area, call the **Temecula County Visitors Bureau** at **1-888-363-2852** or **951-676-5090,** or visit www. temeculacvb.com.

Powder Room

If all things wine are your passion, check out the Women & Wine website—a lifestyle company that creates signature experiences for savvy women who love wine, food, travel, and living well. The company offers wine trips, a wine club, and tons of information for developing a confident tasting palate. For more information, visit www.womenwine.com.

Farmhouse Dinners: Inn at Baldwin Creek in Vermont

1868 North Route 116, Bristol, VT 05443. **1-888-424-2432.** *www.innatbaldwincreek.com.*

The **Inn at Baldwin Creek** and **Mary's Restaurant** rest peacefully on 25 picturesque acres framed by six charming red barns, perennial flower and herb gardens, manicured lawns, and lush woodlands. A restored 1797 Vermont farmhouse, this bed and breakfast inn is midway between **Burlington** and **Middlebury** at the base of the **Green Mountains**—an area dubbed the "land of milk and honey" because of the fertile soil and the many small farms that dot the landscape. For more than 25 years, innkeepers and owners Linda Harmon and Chef Douglas Mack have welcomed guests to enjoy their quiet pastoral setting and to connect heart to palate with their celebrated farmhouse dinners and culinary events.

The Farmhouse Dinner Series was born from the owners' desire to bring the farmers—most of them close friends—into the fold of their epicurean operations. The dinner series is held every Wednesday evening in July and August and allows guests to meet their local farm partners. You'll sample their fare with a complimentary appetizer table and then enjoy a multicourse dinner composed exclusively of local, farm-fresh ingredients. The grand finale of the Farmhouse Dinner Series is the Feast of the Farms Harvest Celebration thrown annually in September. Held in the big red barn and spilling outdoors under a white peaked tent, the event is a lively celebration that features a silent auction supporting the farm community, live bluegrass tunes, and of course, amazing seasonal fare. This event sells out each year, so make your plans early.

If you miss out on the Farmhouse Dinners, no worries—the inn offers a calendar full of events that celebrate local tastes, from a chocolate fest in January and garlic celebration in August to a fall apple blowout and special gardening and handicraft getaways. The monthly Table Talks Series gets you up close and personal with local food experts. Held on Friday evenings, the lively discussions cover a variety of topics—from current food trends to food politics. Table Talks are free, or you can enjoy them over a farm-fresh, three-course dinner designed around the evening's topic. Dinners are $25 per person, or you can enjoy dessert and coffee for $10 per person during the discussion portion of the evening. Stay at the inn during a Table Talk weekend and receive 15 percent off your Saturday and Sunday lodging rate—plus a gift to remember your tableside chats.

You can also get in on some kitchen action with hands-on cooking classes held throughout the year—each themed to culinary style, regional cuisine, or season. Dabble in French bistro cooking, or take a food tour of Italy. The three-and-a-half hour class is limited to 12 people and costs $75 per person (including lunch).

Throughout the year, the inn hosts special culinary events that feature local vintners, brew masters, and farmers. Keep an eye on its online calendar, or sign up for its newsletter to stay posted.

Where to Stop

The inn is about 30 minutes from Burlington, home to the **ECHO Aquarium** (**1-877-324-6386** or **802-864-1848,** www.echovermont. org) and plenty of shopping and sightseeing. Head to **Church Street Marketplace** (**802-863-1648,** www.churchstmarketplace.com) for an eclectic mix of homegrown stores, national chains, and restaurants.

Clean up your act with a trip to **Vermont Soaps Organics** (**1-866-762-7482,** www.vermontsoap.com), where saponification (soapmaking) is done the old-fashioned way. Less than 30 minutes away from the inn, stock up on natural soaps, nontoxic cleaners, and certified organic liquid bath and shower gels.

Less than an hour from the inn is the creamy, dreamy home of **Ben & Jerry's Waterbury factory** (1-866-258-6877 or 802-882-1240, www. benjerry.com). Take the factory tour and learn about the company's heartfelt mission and how their ice cream is made. Wind up your tour in the FlavoRoom and sample some of "Vermont's Finest."

Where to Stay

The Inn at Baldwin Creek offers five cozy guest rooms, each tastefully appointed with simple comforts. All rooms feature queen or king beds with luxurious linens and down comforters. A couple rooms have gas-fired wood stoves, and all have private baths—some with clawfoot tubs and one with a whirlpool tub. Room amenities include fluffy bathrobes, personal items, wireless Internet, and air conditioning. Rooms also have a VCR-television with a selection of new and old movies. The main floor offers a comfortable common room with board games and books. The inn also has a heated swimming pool, and guests are also encouraged to explore the gardens and grounds.

Rates start at $85 per person and include a three-course, farm-fresh breakfast cooked daily as well as a bottomless cookie jar and coffee or tea all day. Peak rates are during fall foliage season in mid-September through mid-October. Keep an eye on the website for special getaway packages.

More Good Taste Destinations

Love southern cooking? Follow in the footsteps of America's southern cookin' momma with a Paula Deen tour in **Savannah, Georgia** (1-888-653-6045, www.savannahtours.us). Tours last three and a half to four hours and take you through the historic district and Southside Savannah streets where she got her start. The $61.95 tour price includes lunch at **Uncle Bubba's Oyster House** (Bubba is Paula's brother, 912-897-6101, www.unclebubbas.com), a goodie bag, and a VIP Pass to Paula's **The Lady and Sons Restaurant** (912-233-2600, www. ladyandsons.com) for $61.95 (the VIP Pass gives you priority seating; otherwise, you have to wait in line).

Sample tastes of the windy city with a **Chicago Food Planet** tour (Tickets: 212-209-3370, www.chicagofoodplanet.com). Tastings are on the go as you wind your way through local ethnic eateries and food shops on the three-hour walking tour of Chicago's Near North Neighborhoods. You'll leave with insights into the historical and cultural aspects of the local food scene as well as a dining guide with coupons to enjoy the eateries on your own ($40).

Sip your way through the **Niagara** Peninsula of Ontario's Wine Country region. The **Niagara-on-the-Lake** area alone is home to more than 25 wineries, including unique stops such as **The Ice House Winery** (where the famed Icewine is made). Book a tour through **Niagara Wine Tours International** (**1-800-680-7006,** www.niagaraworldwinetours.com), which offers inclusive stay-and-sip packages with cycling and chauffeured tours. Get more information on the region, including downloadable maps and guides, at the **Wine Council of Ontario (905-684-8070 ext. 221,** www.winesofontario.org).

For gourmet, farm-fresh meals and a pastoral setting, **Blackberry Farm** (**1-800-648-4252** or **865-984-8166,** www.blackberryfarm.com) is an elegant 44-room mountain resort and working farm located 25 miles south of **Knoxville, Tennessee.** Dining at the Blackberry is an epicurean adventure marked by heirloom produce, artisan handmade cheeses, and free-range organic livestock. Cooking schools and wine-tasting events are held throughout the year along with the Enrichment & Adventure Event Series, which explores everything from gardening to canning. The Farmhouse Spa and leisure activities complement the experience.

History Lessons

In This Chapter

* Travel along the path of American history in Boston
* Drink in the historical southern charm of Charleston
* Chart your own course in history in the culturally diverse city of San Francisco
* More historical getaways

History buffs, unite! If history class only whetted your appetite for learning about the stories that shaped the modern world, grab the girls and explore more of the past. In this chapter, we're off to cities where the past and present mingle. Of course, we'll make plenty of cushy stops along the way that feed more than your intellect.

Patriot Tract: Boston, Massachusetts

There's just something about **Boston**—the distinctive accent and fiery pride of its natives; the juxtaposition of a big, modern city blanketed by echoes of its rich historical past; the harbor breezes laced with whiffs of its cultural heritage … whatever it is, the bustling and walkable city of Boston is the perfect spot to take a dip in American history while enjoying the tastes and sites of a New England getaway.

Sights to See

First, get acquainted with the city from the safety of a big duck. **Boston Duck Tours (617-267-3825,** www.bostonducktours.com) tool through Beantown on World War II–style amphibious landing craft (in other words, a "Duck"). Fully narrated by a "ConDucktor," the Duck cruises by historical spots such as the **State House, Bunker Hill, Boston Common, Copley Square, Newbury Street,** and **Quincy Market.** The all-terrain vehicle will splash smack into the Charles River and end your land-water adventure with views of the Boston and Cambridge skylines. Tours last approximately 80 minutes, and tickets are $29.

Next, you'll want to get a closer look at history with a walk on the **Freedom Trail,** a 2.5-mile, red-bricked trail that meanders past 16 major historical sites. The trail takes you to the Boston Common, the "new" State House, Park Street Church, Granary Burying Ground, King's Chapel and Burying Ground, Benjamin Franklin statue and Boston Latin School, Old Corner Book Store, Old South Meeting House, Old State House, site of the Boston Massacre, Faneuil Hall and Quincy Market, Paul Revere's house, the Old North Church, Copp's Hill Burying Ground, *USS Constitution* ("Old Ironsides"), and the Bunker Hill Monument.

Consider taking a guided tour first and then exploring Faneuil Hall, Old Ironsides, or whatever strikes your fancy on your own. Get maps at the **Boston National Historical Park Service (617-242-5642,** www. nps.gov/bost/) or **Freedom Trail Foundation (617-357-8300,** www. thefreedomtrail.org), which offers guided 90-minute tours starting at $12.

You can see more of the city with guided tours by foot, bike, or sea. **Boston by Foot** (617-367-2345, www.bostonbyfoot.org) leads walking trips through the heart of the Freedom Trail, Beacon Hill, Victorian Back Bay, the Waterfront, the North End, Boston Underground, and literary landmarks starting at $12. **Boston Bike Tours** (617-308-5902, www.bostonbiketours.com) offers the Freedom Trail, Harvard, and neighborhood-guided rides starting at $30. **Mass Bay** (617-542-8000, www.massbaylines.com) lines cruises the harbor as live actors bring the history of Boston to life through authentic maritime music, original skits, and storytelling. Harbor tours are $17.50.

Powder Room

Skip the rental car and go mass transit. The Massachusetts Bay Transportation Authority (known as the "T") is a commuter system of rail, subway, bus, and ferry routes to practically every corner of the city. The Massport shuttle bus provides free rides between the T and Logan International Airport terminals. For T schedules, maps, fares, and passes, visit www.mbta.com. Find out more about Massport at www.massport.com.

Art history buffs should make time to wander through the exhibits and gardens of the **Isabella Stewart Gardner Museum** (617-566-1401, www.gardnermuseum.org). Established in 1903 by Isabella Stewart Gardner, an American art collector and philanthropist, the stately building has remained relatively unchanged since her death in 1924—although plans for expansion of the museum are in the works. Admission is $12 per person (with free entrance to anyone named Isabella).

Step into a more recent era of American history with a visit to the **John F. Kennedy Presidential Library and Museum** (1-866-JFK-1960 or **617-514-1600**, www.jfklibrary.org). You'll first watch a short film narrated by the late president followed by freedom to roam the exhibits and galleries. Admission is $10 per person. For a quieter perspective of our 35th U.S. president, visit the home of his birth in Brookline (**617-566-7937**, www.nps.gov/jofi/). Built in 1907, the house is a National Historic Site preserved by the U.S. National Park Service. Admission is $3.

Hungry yet? Get a taste of cultural history with a food tour through **Boston's North End (617-523-6032,** www.micheletopor.com), or dine in an historic home in **Harvard Square.** Weave through the narrow North End streets of one of the oldest Italian communities in America while you enjoy tastes at the bakeries and delis along the way. The three-hour Boston North End Market Tours are $48. Head to the historic **Red House (617-576-0605,** www.theredhouse.com) in Harvard Square, and dine in the charming restored home built in 1802. It's open for lunch and dinner. Save time after your dining experience to explore the many independent bookstores that pepper the neighborhood.

Where to Stop

Make time for a spot of afternoon tea at **Taj Boston (617-598-5255,** www.tajhotels.com/Boston), a tradition since the hotel's opening in 1927. Set in an elegant drawing room with windows overlooking Newbury Street, tea time is marked by fine china, three-tiered silver trays, and a convivial atmosphere—all of which are perfect for clinking your glasses in a toast to your getaway. Choose from fine custom-blended loose-leaf teas that are pre-paired with a menu of delectable sweets, sandwiches, and scones. Apéritifs, sherries, and specialty cocktails are also available to complement your tea experience. Reservations are recommended.

A tad pricey but oh so chic, **Clink restaurant and bar (617-224-4004,** www.clinkrestaurant.com) inside the **Liberty Hotel** offers a piece of history all its own. The hotel was once the site of the Charles Street Jail, and the architecture still echoes its past life. Tucked in the lobby level of the hotel, Clink specializes in tapas-style small plates but also serves gourmet sandwiches for lunch and stepped-up comfort food for dinner as well as revolving wine tasting pours and exotic cocktails. Vestiges of the original jail cell doors remind patrons of the site's history while a dramatic open kitchen and butcher-block tables and bar provide a warm and sociable setting. It's open for breakfast, lunch, dinner, and weekend brunch.

Get your New England lobster fix at **Anthony's Pier 4 (617-482-6262,** www.pier4.com), a landmark family owned and run dining destination since its opening in 1963. Start with traditional New England clam chowder made with native clams or the Boston fish chowder. Get your lobster boiled, broiled, or baked and stuffed, or try the famous broiled Boston scrod fresh from Georges Bank. Reservations are recommended.

Where to Stay

The trick to deciding on your Boston accommodations is pinpointing the area where you want to stay and deciding what type of atmosphere best suits your group.

Located in the Back Bay neighborhood on fashionable Newbury Street, the **Newbury Guest House** takes you back in time with the flavor of an area that has changed little since the 1800s. The rooms are housed in three former single-family Victorian residences built in Queen Anne and Ruskin styles. All rooms have private bathrooms, telephones, TVs, and high-speed wireless Internet. Rooms on the front side of the house overlook bustling Newbury Street while quieter rooms on the back side look out over historic homes across a tree-lined alley. Rates start from $165. *1-800-437-7668 or 617-670-6000. www.newburyguesthouse.com.*

Clarendon Square Inn is tucked on a residential street in a six-story Victorian townhouse built in 1868. Located in Boston's historic South End, Clarendon Square is within walking distance to **Copley Square, Newbury Street,** and **Boston Common.** After an extensive renovation, the inn offers a modern, lively décor that showcases original works from local artists. Cushy amenities such as a rooftop hot tub, plush pillow-top beds, and in-room fireplaces give your stay a homey feel. Rooms start at $155 and include an expanded continental breakfast. *617-536-2229. www.clarendonsquare.com.*

A luxury boutique hotel in Beacon Hill, **Fifteen Beacon** is housed in a turn-of-the-century, 10-story Beaux Arts building. Each of the hotel's 60 guest rooms are individually designed in a modernist style, and each floor contains either a two-room suite or adjoining rooms that can be converted into a suite. Rooms have over-the-top amenities such as bathroom TVs, rainforest showers, and fresh flowers. Of the many unique property details, the building's original cage elevator and its cast-brass lit railing with brass newel post dominate the hotel's lobby and provide guests with a taste of Old Boston. Mahogany walls surround the lobby, and a cozy fireplace radiates a warm welcome. Located on the lobby level are the lounge, the bar, and **Mooo Restaurant.** Rooms start from $395. Check the website for seasonal packages and specials. *1-877-982-3226 or 617-670-1500. www.xvbeacon.com.*

For more information about the Boston area (including maps and special offers), call the **Convention & Visitors Bureau** at **1-888-SEE-BOSTON** or visit www.bostonusa.com.

Chick Wit

As much as I love all my girlfriends, always make sure that you have a little alone time when on trips. There's nothing worse than everybody getting snippy because there's been too much togetherness. I'm not saying go explore a foreign city on your own (bad idea!), but even if it's just an hour to read your book by the pool, you'll really be thankful and you'll prevent fights that seem to start over nothing.

—Lisa, account executive

Southern Belle: Charleston, South Carolina

Southern charm is alive and well in **Charleston**—both in the people who call it home and in the beautifully preserved architecture that lines its streets. From grand plantations and antebellum homes to horse-drawn carriages and magnificent formal gardens, Charleston is a vision of a bygone era that speaks softly of its rich 300-year history. The city has a modern side, too, with chic shops, nationally noted restaurants, and festivals galore that roll out all year long. But it's the "living museum" quality of its lifestyle that has crowned Charleston as a national historic treasure.

Sights to See

Start your journey at the **Charleston Visitor Center** at 375 Meeting Street. From there, follow the **Charleston's Museum Mile** (www.charlestonsmuseummile.org) for the most concentrated wealth of historical and cultural attractions in the city. Of the many sites along the

Museum Mile are the **Confederate Museum, Powder Magazine, Old Exchange & Provost Dungeon, Old Slave Mart Museum, City Hall, Washington Park, Nathaniel Russell House,** 10 stately churches, and more than a dozen other historical homes. You can catch the **DASH Trolley** at any point if your legs give out.

Of the many historical homes to visit, **Drayton Hall (843-769-2600,** www.draytonhall.org) tops the list. A National Trust historic site, Drayton Hall is the oldest preserved plantation house in America open to the public. After seven generations, two great wars, and numerous hurricanes and earthquakes, the main house of this National Historic Landmark, circa 1738, remains in nearly original condition.

Meander among the nearly 40 art galleries of Charleston's historic **French Quarter (843-577-7101,** www.frenchquarterarts.com). Plan your visit to coincide with an Art Walk night, when galleries keep their doors open late. Many serve wine and appetizers and feature special guest artists and exhibits and live music. Art walks are held seasonally; call for details.

Civil War buffs will want to visit **Fort Sumter National Monument (843-883-3123,** www.nps.gov/fomo/). You'll take a narrated 30-minute ferry ride to the Fort, spend an hour exploring, and then head back across the water. The tour onboard **Fort Sumter SpiritLine Cruises (1-800-789-3678** or **843-881-7337,** www.fortsumtertours.com) is $17.

Where to Stop

During your stroll through Museum Mile, stop at **Sticky Fingers Rib House (843-853-7427,** www.stickyfingersonline.com) to refuel. Started by three childhood friends, Sticky Fingers is a Charleston institution that now has hubs scattered across the South. Dig into the hickory-smoked ribs and potato skins at their downtown location on Meeting Street. If a seafood craving strikes, make a detour to nearby **Fish restaurant (843-722-3474,** www.fishrestaurant.net) on King Street where "Naked Fish" and other signature dishes make use of local, sustainable ingredients in a chic and stylish atmosphere.

In the French Quarter, make a date at **Tristan Restaurant (843-534-2155,** www.tristandining.com)—famous for its bold dishes spiked with its signature spicy chocolate barbecue sauce and its contemporary, convivial vibe. It's located on the ground floor of the historic **French Quarter Inn** on the Market Street side. For authentic low-country cuisine in a garden setting, head to **82 Queen** (the name denotes its address, **843-723-7591,** www.82queen.com) for dishes such as she-crab soup, shrimp and grits, aged steaks, and local seafood. Both restaurants serve lunch, dinner, and brunch.

Get yourselves gussied up for a sophisticated evening out at **Circa 1886** (**843-853-7828,** www.circa1886.com). Nestled in the gardens behind the **Wentworth Mansion** in downtown Charleston, Circa 1886 offers a true Charleston fine-dining experience in an elegant and intimate atmosphere. Named for the year the Wentworth Mansion was built, the five-star restaurant boasts an extensive wine list and contemporary cuisine influenced by Charleston's rich history. The menu changes seasonally to take advantage of the freshest local produce and seafood. It's open for dinner by reservation.

Powder Room

Plan your getaway in early March so you can catch the annual **Charleston Food + Wine Festival.** The four-day event celebrates the best chefs with Grand Tasting Tents, Salutes to Charleston Chefs, Dine-Arounds, extravagant parties, a Culinary Village, Gospel Brunch, Wine Seminars, Brewmaster Beer Dinners, and more. For more information, call **843-722-5547** or visit www. charlestonfoodandwine.com.

Where to Stay

Central to the historic district on Marion Square, the **Francis Marion Hotel** offers sweeping views of the harbor and a subtle Charleston charm. Rooms feature upscale amenities such as European bedding with overstuffed duvets and down pillows, wireless high-speed Internet access, and coffee makers. The hotel houses a full-service spa, fitness center, the **Swamp Fox Restaurant & Bar,** a piano bar, café, and gift shop. Rates start as low as $99, and package deals are regularly offered on the website. *1-877-756-2121 or 843-722-0600. www. francismarionhotel.com.*

Just outside Charleston in the charming village of Summerville, the **Woodlands Resort & Inn** is an immaculately restored 1906 classic revival mansion set amid 42 acres of parkland grounds. The resort features 18 luxuriously appointed guest rooms and suites, a country guest cottage, day spa, croquet lawn, red-clay tennis courts, an outdoor swimming pool, and golf privileges at nearby area courses. Rates vary; check the website for special packages. *1-800-774-9999 or 843-308-2106. www.woodlandsinn.com.*

The **Inn at Middleton Place** is located adjacent to **Middleton Place National Historic Landmark**—home to America's oldest landscaped gardens, the **Middleton Place Plantation Stableyards,** and the **House Museum.** The 53-room award-winning inn offers relaxed accommodations with seasonal wood-burning fireplaces, large baths, and views of the **Ashley River.** This rich and diverse natural habitat beckons guests to explore by hiking, kayaking, bicycling, or horseback. Rates start at $179 and include a hot southern-style breakfast, an evening manager's reception, and admission to Middleton Place attractions. Check the website for seasonal offers and packages. *1-800-543-4774 or 843-556-0500. www.theinnatmiddletonplace.com.*

For more historic inns and hotels, call **1-877-946-8772** or visit www. charlestownehotels.com. For B&Bs, visit the **Charleston South Carolina Bed and Breakfast Association** at www.charlestonbb.com or **Charming Inns of Charleston** at www.charminginns.com.

For more information about Charleston (including maps and travel packages), visit www.charlestoncvb.com.

Golden Gait: San Francisco, California

San Francisco offers so many exciting sights to see—and yet so little time! This multifaceted, cross-cultural city can be exhausting for many visitors—from the famed **Fisherman's Wharf** with its rich maritime and cannery history to the bustling **Union Square District** and the iconic **Haight-Ashbury** neighborhood—(defined by its 1960s subculture that still breathes of its eclectic past today). You can't do the entire city in one trip, so take a deep breath and decide on the major areas you want to explore during your getaway. If you've already done the tourist thing, shoot for off-the-beaten path excursions that allow you to see other sides of the city. Hitch a ride on a cable car (still just $5!), take a cultural walking tour, tool through neighborhoods, or enjoy a foggy morning walk through **Golden Gate Park.** History is everywhere in this legendary city. You just have to slow down and you'll see it—one detail at a time.

Sights to See

Like Boston and Charleston, San Francisco has a trail that links its own historically significant spots. A project of the **San Francisco Museum and Historical Society,** the **Barbary Coast Trail (415-454-2355,** www.barbarycoasttrail.org) is a four-mile trail and 20-minute cable car ride that is marked with a series of bronze medallions set in the sidewalks to point the way. The trail connects 20 sites, including the birthplace of the Gold Rush, the oldest Asian temple in North America, a Silver King mansion, the western terminus of the Pony Express, and the largest collection of historic ships in the United States. Guided and audio tours are available, or pick up a map at a local bookstore to explore the trail on your own.

STOP Bad Trip
> While the nickname "Frisco" is making a comeback in some circles, you'll still be pegged as a tourist if you happen to utter it. The controversy of why *not* to use the "F-word" has raged on since the publication of a book called *Don't Call It Frisco* in 1953, and a Laundromat of the same name still exists on Hayes Street. My advice? Just avoid it until it makes its full comeback!

San Francisco has a walking tour for just about everything. Once you've hit the prerequisite sites such as **Alcatraz, Fisherman's Wharf, and Pier 39,** take an off-the-beaten path walking tour. Here's a sampling:

✳ **Foot!** These lively walking tours will show you the funniest routes through San Francisco's quirky history and unique neighborhoods. Foot! tours are part history lesson, part game show, and part comedy show. The tour guides are history buffs by day and seasoned comics, actors, and improvisers by night. Eight different tours are offered. The Go West, Young Woman tour follows the trail of 10 daring divas who changed the course of San Francisco's history. Most tours are about two hours and cost $25, but price varies by number of people. For more information, call **1-800-979-3370** (tickets only) or **415-793-5378**, or visit www.foottours.com.

* **Javawalk.** Javawalk is a caffeine-spiked tour that winds through Union Square, Chinatown, Jackson Square, and North Beach (the city's Little Italy and home of the Beat generation). Led by "Javagirl," the tour covers the city's history from a coffeehouse culture perspective. You'll stop at several North Beach cafés along the way for a quick java jolt. Tours are $25 per person. For more information, call **1-800-979-3370** (tickets only) or **415-673-9255**, or visit www.javawalk.com.

* **All About Chinatown!** Make your way through the colorful maze of Chinatown with a behind-the-scenes tour. You'll learn the history of the fascinating pagodas and buildings, stop at the famed fortune cookie factory, visit an authentic tea house, and get juicy insider details about Chinatown's secret societies. The two-hour tour wraps up with a 10-course dim-sum lunch (total time three hours) for $40 per person ($28 without lunch). For more information, call **415-982-8839**, or visit www.allaboutchinatown.com.

* **Haight-Ashbury Flower Power Walking Tour.** This far-out tour blends hippie history with neighborhood history and architecture. Saunter along the same streets that Janis Joplin, Jimi Hendrix, The Grateful Dead, Jim Morrison, and countless others walked who etched their marks into alternative culture. Tours are about two and a half hours long and cost $20. For more information, call **1-800-979-3370** (tickets only) or **415-863-1621**, or visit www.haightashburytour.com.

* **Victorian Home Walk.** Tour Pacific Heights with its colorful Victorian row houses, famous mansions, and sculpted gardens. Visit the inside of a period Queen Anne Victorian and see famous homes such as the Victorian where the movie *Mrs. Doubtfire* was filmed. Along the way, you'll catch spectacular views of the Golden Gate Bridge and Alcatraz. The two-and-a-half-hour walk is easy,

and the pace is leisurely. The $20 fee (cash only) includes transportation to Victorian neighborhoods from Union Square. For more information, call **415-252-9485** or visit www.victorianwalk.com.

Where to Stop

Suffice it to say, you won't go hungry in San Francisco. An amazing array of culinary delights await in just about every corner of the city.

Union Square is bustling with a bevy of options. Of them, **E&O Trading Company (415-693-0303**, www.eotrading.com) pioneered the Southeast Asian Grill concept in 1997 with its flagship San Francisco location. The three-level rustic space is modeled after an ancient Asian trading warehouse and offers lunch, dinner, and happy hour. Tucked in the **Savoy Hotel** a few blocks from the square, **Millennium (415-345-3900**, www.millenniumrestaurant.com) spins creative and flavorful vegetarian dishes that pair perfectly with its selection of organic wines. Millennium is open for dinner; reservations are recommended.

For seafood fans, an easy choice is the **Crab House on Pier 39 (415-434-2722,** www.crabhouse39.com). Famous for its "Killer Crab"—an entire crab roasted in a secret garlic sauce—and other crab specialties, the restaurant offers spectacular views of the Golden Gate Bridge and Fisherman's Wharf.

For more elegant fare, head to **PlumpJack Café (415-563-4755,** www. plumpjackcafe.com) on Fillmore Street in the **Cow Hollow District.** Food is a visual presentation that delivers with flavors that have earned the restaurant critical acclaim with foodies and locals alike. The wine list is primo, and if you can't decide, order select wines by the glass. Reservations are recommended.

Powder Room

San Francisco offers a great way to sample the flavors of its best restaurants with the annual Dine About Town event. Two times per year for two weeks, more than 100 participating restaurants offer three-course, prix-fixe menus at $21.95 for lunch and $31.95 for dinner. For more information, visit www.onlyinsanfrancisco.com/ dineabouttown.

Where to Stay

If you don't mind the five-block walk to Union Square, **Hotel Carlton** (**1-800-922-7586,** www.jdvhotels.com/carlton) offers great rates and a funky, international ambiance. Each of the guest rooms offers a soft palette of soothing tones punctuated by cheerful colors such as saffron and persimmon and include complimentary wireless Internet access, an in-room laptop safe, a writing desk, telephone, coffee maker, TV, CD player that's MP3 compatible, and other amenities. The onsite Saha Restaurant serves breakfast and dinners that feature Arabic fusion cuisine. Ask about the Girlfriend Getaway experience that includes accommodations in the Sir Edmund Hillary suite, brunch, a visit to Kabuki Springs and Spa (a Japanese-style spa with communal baths), high tea for two, and salsa dancing for $369 each (double occupancy). Rooms start at $89 and include an evening wine reception. Hotel Carlton is part of the San Francisco-based Joie de Vivre group of boutique hotels. For a list of more Joie de Vivre Hotels by location and price range, visit www.jdvhotels.com.

Perched on the edge of the bay at Fisherman's Wharf, **Argonaut Hotel** is in the historic **Haslett Warehouse at The Cannery.** With a history that dates back to 1908 when it was a warehouse, the hotel takes its seaside location seriously with a spirited décor that feels as if you just stepped aboard a luxury cruise ship. Rooms are decorated with white-washed furniture, porthole mirrors, and rich fabrics and are fully stocked with upscale amenities such as bathrobes, coffee makers with complimentary Starbucks coffee, flat-screen TVs, and high-speed Internet. Request a room with a view, and take in amazing sights of the Golden Gate or Alcatraz across the water. The **Blue Mermaid Chowder House,** a lively dining destination adjacent to the Argonaut, serves casual San Francisco fare. Rooms start at $189 and include evening wine. *1-866-415-0704 or 415-563-0800, www.argonauthotel.com.*

The avant-garde **Hotel Diva** (**1-866-427-2861,** www.hoteldiva.com) on Geary Street is in the hub of Union Square. Constructed in 1915, the building originally housed the Somerton Hotel, which was home to many returning World War II soldiers. Now sleek and sexy, the mod guest rooms are styled with cobalt blue carpets, silver accents, and black leather couches and feature flat-screen TVs and iPod alarm clocks.

The Salon Floor rooms boast upgraded goodies such as a complimentary continental breakfast and bottled water, down feather beds and comforters, refrigerators, bathrobes, and iPod docking stations. Guest rooms start at $159; Salon rooms start at $209. The hotel caters to single divas with a Female Frenzy package that comes with accommodations, Booty Parlor Pheromone Body Lotion, a cosmo cocktail four-pack, calling cards, a club list, and compact mirrors, all starting at $139 per person. Hotel Diva is one of seven **Personality Hotels** in San Francisco. Find one that matches your personalities at www.personalityhotels.com.

Savvy Sister

Kimpton Hotels loves women! Argonaut is one of many hotels throughout the United States and Canada that are owned and run by San Francisco-based Kimpton, which offers a Women InTouch program to cater to the travel needs of its female guests. The program includes a comfy and stylish décor, safe environments, caring service, creative travel packages, in-room fitness and spa services, and high-quality amenities. Best of all, the "Forgot It, We've Got It" honor bar provides essentials that you may have left at home, such as eye makeup remover pads, shaving cream, and slippers. Find more information at www.kimptonhotels.com.

For more information about visiting San Francisco (including a free visitors guide), call **415-391-2000** or visit www.onlyinsanfrancisco.com. For a great neighborhood guide including the latest restaurant news, visit the online version of the *San Francisco Chronicle* at www.sfgate.com.

More Historical Destinations

Shoe fanatics should plan a getaway to **Toronto, Ontario.** Home to an amazing array of things to do—from fabulous shopping to lively festivals and a packed theatre schedule—this Canadian city also hides the four-story **Bata Shoe Museum (416-979-7799,** www.batashoemuseum.ca). Located in downtown Toronto, the museum chronicles the history of footwear with a collection of more than 10,000 shoes. Gaze at ancient Chinese bound-foot shoes and Marilyn Monroe's red leather pumps. Admission is $12 per person. For nearby accommodations and attractions, visit www.torontotourism.com.

Discover the Fountain of Youth—or, at least give it a shot—with a trip to **St. Augustine, Florida** (America's oldest continually settled city). See sites such as the Oldest House Museum, the Oldest Wooden School House, the creepy Authentic Old Jail, and the Castillo de San Marcos—a fort constructed in the late 1600s to protect the seaside city from invasion. Learn more about the city's origins at the Ponce de Leon's **Fountain of Youth Archaeological Park,** view it from atop the St. Augustine Lighthouse, or kick back on the beaches of Anastasia State Park. Stay in the heart of the historic walking district in one of the cozy B&Bs (44 Spanish Street is as quaint as they come), or book an oceanfront inn and wake up to the sounds of the Atlantic Ocean waves breaking outside your door. For more information on St. Augustine or to request a visitors guide, call **1-800-653-2489** or visit www.getaway4florida.com.

For an immersion into the past, head to the revolutionary city of **Williamsburg, Virginia.** Colonial Williamsburg's 30-acre historic area is home to restored, reconstructed, and historically furnished buildings where costumed interpreters tell the stories of the men and women of the eighteenth-century city. Make time for a visit to the Spa of Colonial Williamsburg, where they take an historical approach to relaxation and healing. For more information and a visitors guide, call **The Colonial Williamsburg Foundation** (**757-229-1000,** www.history.org).

Part 5

Friends Who Play Together Stay Together: Adventure Trips

The thrills, spills, and adrenaline rush of vacations in the great outdoors is an adventure meant to be shared. In this section, put your physical and mental endurance to the test with water adventures that take you along inspirational shorelines, through bumpy rapids, and on plunges to scenic ocean depths. You'll take time to smell the wildflowers in an expansive wilderness, pedal through trees of immense proportions, scale up a mountainside, and zoom down ski trails. Finally, we slow down the pace with a trot down country roads and dabble in the working ranch and farm lifestyle.

(Photo courtesy of Sophia Field: www.sophiafield.com.)

Navigating the breathtaking Canadian wilderness with Adventures in Good Company.

Water Works

In This Chapter

* Sea kayaking in the islands of northwest Washington State
* Diving and snorkeling along the reefs of the Florida Keys
* Riding the rapids of eastern Tennessee
* More water sport destinations

Call it water therapy. Vacations where the center of activity revolves around placid lakes, turquoise ocean waters, and beguiling rivers have a way of purifying our bodies and cleansing our spirits. In this chapter, we'll paddle our way along cedar-dense shorelines, dive into tepid waters teeming with tropical fish and coral reefs, and hang on for a wild ride through a raging river.

Sea Kayaking: San Juan Islands, Washington

If visions of calm waters and emerald isles dance in your head, pack your bags and head to the **San Juan Islands** in northwest Washington. With more than 400 miles of rocky and sandy waterfront, San Juan County boasts more shoreline than any other area in the nation. Surrounded by three major cities—**Seattle, Vancouver British Columbia,** and **Victoria British Columbia**—the **San Juan Archipelago,** which includes the Gulf Islands of British Columbia, comprises more than 700 islands and reefs. Of the nearly 180 named islands in the San Juans, three of them—Lopez, Orcas, and San Juan—have thriving seaside communities that welcome active, water-loving visitors year round.

Lopez Island is a pastoral island escape ideal for bicycling, kayaking, and kicking back. On the horseshoe-shaped **Orcas Island,** the largest in the county, the slow pace also makes it ideal for calmer water sports and cycling. **San Juan Island** is the most diverse of the three and is home to the historic town of **Friday Harbor.** This quaint, walkable seaport is the center of activity with art galleries, boutiques, bookstores, water-view restaurants, and plenty to do to keep a water enthusiast busy.

Getting to the San Juan Islands can be tricky, but consider it part of the adventure. If you're traveling by car from Washington, you'll catch the **Washington State Ferry** (**1-888-808-7977** or **206-464-6400,** www.wsdot.wa.gov/ferries), the mainland terminal in Anacortes, about 90 miles northwest of Seattle. If you're without a car and prefer to tool around the islands via foot, bike, or moped, you can take the **Airporter Shuttle** (**1-866-235-5247** or **360-380-8800,** www.airporter.com) or **Island Airporter Shuttle** (**360-378-7438,** www.islandairporter.com) buses to the ferry. **Kenmore Air** (**1-866-435-9524** or **360-378-1067,** www.kenmoreair.com) and **San Juan Airlines** (**1-800-874-4434,** www.sanjuanairlines.com) offer daily landplane service flights from the mainland to the islands. Seasonal passenger ferries also run from Seattle, Port Townsend, Bellingham, Victoria British Columbia, and Port Angeles (with a connecting stop in Victoria).

Anchors Away

Sea kayaking is among the most popular of the water sports in this area because wildlife is easily spotted onshore and is not far offshore. Kayak touring and rental outfitters in the area are plenty. You'll find that most don't require previous kayak experience and use stable, double boats that are easy to paddle and maneuver and won't roll.

Here are a few options to get your paddles in the water:

* **Outdoor Odysseys** offers "Women on the Water" sea kayaking and camping tours that take you to islands accessible only by boat. Guided by women, the ladies-only "WOW" trips include cushy pluses such as afternoon wine and Brie, Dutch-oven cuisine prepared with organic produce, and complimentary dry bags. The three-day, all-inclusive trips start at $529 per person. Locally owned and operated, Outdoor Odysseys has been guiding kayak trips in the area for more than 20 years and also offers shorter and longer duration coed tours. For more information, call **1-800-647-4621** or **206-361-0717,** or visit www.outdoorodysseys.com.

* **Sea Quest Expeditions** offers orca whale-watching kayak trips that are led by guides with biology or environmental science backgrounds. These trips are designed to take you into the heart of a whale habitat while showcasing the natural beauty of the islands. All-inclusive two-, three-, and five-day women-only expeditions are $339, $499, and $749, respectively. Shorter and longer coed trips are also available. For more information, call **1-888-589-4253** or **360-378-5767,** or visit www.sea-quest-kayak.com.

* **Adventure Associates of Washington** has women-only sea kayaking expeditions that range from three to six days, starting at $495. Custom and multi-sport expeditions are also available. For more information, call **206-932-8352** or visit www. adventureassociates.net.

* **Osprey Tours** and **Shearwater Sea Kayak Tours** both run operations from Orca Island. Get your feet wet with Osprey's one-hour kayak trip to see the adorable Harbor Seals for $50. Day trips to the secluded Sucia Island with Shearwater are $125. Both offer other tour options. For more information about Osprey, call

1-877-376-3677 or **360-376-3677,** or visit www.ospreytours.
com. For more information about Shearwater, call **360-376-4699**
or visit www.shearwaterkayaks.com.

Where to Stop

San Juan Island is home to some 40 charming restaurants and cafés.
Head to historic Friday Harbor for a handful of great options. **Mi
Piace Coffee House Restaurant** (360-378-6477, www.mipiacecoffee.
com) offers fresh-roasted coffee, pastries, soups, and paninis in a
warm atmosphere. **Steps Wine Bar & Café** (360-370-5959, www.
stepswinebarandcafe.com)
rounds out its offerings with succulent seafood dishes, tantalizing
desserts, an extensive wine list,
and a contemporary vibe. The
Backdoor Kitchen (360-378-
9540, www.backdoorkitchen.
com) has an international flair
and a garden setting, while
Coho Restaurant (360-378-
6330, www.cohorestaurant.
com) is known for its culturally
diverse cuisine that shows off
local fresh ingredients.

Savvy Sister

Would a whale be so rude
as to bump your kayak and
scare you half silly? Never!
Or so say the folks at Sea
Quest Expeditions. Whales are
extremely aware of their environment and do not collide with
boats. So, quit your worrying and
just have fun!

Besides outdoor water adventures and exploring the towns and hamlets,
art lovers can usually catch an art show or special exhibit at any number
of the galleries found on the islands. Visit the **San Juan Islands Artist
Community** website (www.sanjuanartistcommunity.com) for a list of
events, workshops, and current gallery exhibits.

Where to Stay

Keep in mind that high season is generally from May through
September, so rates will increase at most hotels and inns—and rooms
will fill up during summer holidays and weekends.

A block and a half from the Washington State Ferry terminal and Friday Harbor Marina, **Friday Harbor House** is perched atop a bluff that looks out over the harbor. Each of the 23 modern-style guest rooms and suites have fireplaces, sitting areas, oversize jetted bathtubs, and upscale amenities. The onsite **Harbor View Restaurant** features locally caught seafood and local produce. Rates start at $150. Keep an eye on the website for seasonal packages. *360-378-8455. www. fridayharborhouse.com.*

The beachy, modern vibe of **Elements Hotel & Spa** makes it a comfortable spot to crash in Friday Harbor. Stay with the theme by booking a Sea Place room, which has two queen beds, a full kitchen, and an intimate dining area. None of the rooms are huge, but all offer access to a heated indoor pool, Jacuzzi, sauna, and fitness studio. Guests have complimentary use of beach cruiser bikes, wireless Internet service, and can order room service from the nearby Backdoor Kitchen. For a more Zen-like experience marked by an eco-intelligent décor, ask about its sister property, the nearby **Bird Rock Hotel** (1-800-352-2632 or 360-378-5848, www.birdrockhotel.com). *1-800-793-4756 or 360-378-4000. visit www.hotelelements.com.*

If you prefer a more out-of-the-way landing spot, Orca Island offers several choices from resorts to boutique inns. With three buildings and rooms at various price ranges, **The Outlook Inn** offers something for everyone. The elegant Bay View Suites have gas fireplaces, Jacuzzi bathtubs, private balconies, and king beds and start at $155. The smaller East Building rooms start at $74, and rooms in the main building share a bath and start at $54. *360-376-2200. www.outlookinn.com.*

For more information on the area, including visitors guides and maps, call **1-888-468-3701** or visit www.guidetosanjuans.com.

Snorkel and Dive: The Florida Keys

Crank up the Jimmy Buffett tunes, grab your flip-flops, and plan yourselves a tropical outdoor adventure in the **Florida Keys.** A chain of islands that begins just south of Miami, the Florida Keys are connected by more than 40 bridges over the Atlantic Ocean and Gulf of

Mexico. For diving and snorkeling enthusiasts, the shallow water flats, mangrove islets, coral reefs, and shipwrecks found off the waters are a paradise alive with brilliant undersea creatures. The entire coastal area of the Keys has been designated as a National Marine Sanctuary. The laid-back lifestyle, subtropical climate, and lively characters who call the islands home set the scene for a fun and memorable outdoor getaway.

Dive In

The hot spot in the upper keys for taking the plunge is **Key Largo.** With its shallow reefs and deep wrecks, you could spend your entire trip just exploring the waters off the upper key. Among its most famous dive sites are the **Key Largo Dry Rocks,** where the 9-foot-tall, 4,000-pound Christ of the Deep statue sits submerged in 25 feet of water.

Key Largo is also home to **John Pennekamp Coral Reef State Park (305-451-6300,** www.pennekamppark.com). Pennekamp is open to camping, fishing, picnicking, and swimming in designated areas. The park offers snorkeling tours ($29), scuba tours ($50), glass-bottom boat rides ($22), canoe and kayak rentals, and boat rentals. The vehicle entrance fee varies by the number of people in your party.

Ｑ *Savvy Sister* _____

The acronym, "self-contained underwater breathing apparatus" indicates that scuba diving is a serious sport and requires training and certification. If you decide to take dive classes during your trip, look for instructors certified by a major diving association. The most recognized scuba associations are the National Association of Underwater Instructors (NAUI), the Professional Association of Diving Instructors (PADI), Scuba Schools International (SSI), and Professional Diving Instructors Corporation (PDIC).

Understandably, most first-timers to the Florida Keys make a beeline to Pennekamp Park for their first plunge. But plenty of other Key Largo dive shops offer trips into the protected reefs. The rates might be higher, but you'll usually get more personal attention and avoid the hustle and bustle of park central. Note that if you're not the least bit interested in getting wet, most outfitters will allow "bubble watchers" along for the ride for a discounted fee.

Here are a few more places to take the plunge in Key Largo:

* **Horizon Divers** offers scuba and snorkel trips, instruction, equipment rentals, and sales. Diving trips start at $75; snorkeling starts at $45. Rates are per person. Private guides and night dives are available. For more information, call **1-800-984-DIVE** or **305-453-3535**, or visit www.horizondivers.com.

* **Scuba-Do Diving Charters** has been around for nearly 20 years and offers reef and wreck diving, instruction, snorkeling, and private charters. Dive charters start at $80; snorkeling starts at $55. The full-day scuba refresher course includes an afternoon charter trip for $180. Rates are per person. For more information, call **1-800-516-0110** or **305-451-3446**, or visit www.scuba-do.com.

* Backed by 30 years in the biz, **Quiescence Diving Services** offers snorkeling, diving, instruction, tank inspection, equipment rentals, and sales. Diving trips with tanks and weights included are $75; snorkeling is $45. Rates are per person. Twilight and night dives are available. For more information, call **305-451-2440** or visit www. keylargodiving.com.

Powder Room

Save a buck by asking about lodging packages if you prebook your charter excursion. Many dive shops have relationships with local hotels and can get you a deal when you book accommodations through them.

As you make your way down to the Conch Republic (Key West, that is), you'll find ample places to dive in along the way. Here are some "key" stops:

* **Islamorada.** Head to the Holiday Isle Dive Shop, a diving destination since 1972. Depending on which you choose, you'll explore areas such as the colorful Hens & Chickens patch reef, Pleasure Reef, Secret Garden, and Davis Ledge (where you can rub a Buddha belly for good luck). Afterward, you can grab a famous rum runner at the **Tiki Bar** (rumored to be the birthplace of the frozen libation) or a bite at **Rumrunners Island Bar.** Scuba trips are $50 without equipment, and snorkel trips are $30. For more information, call **1-800-327-7070 ext. 644** or **305-664-3483**, or visit www.diveholidayisle.com.

 * **Marathon. Tilden's Scuba Center** has two dive shops at each end of Marathon, so if you blow by the first one, stop at the second. Tilden's offers plenty of underwater adventures with nearly 30 reefs off the waters to explore (along with a few shipwrecks). Scuba trips start at $60 with no equipment while snorkel trips start at $35. If you prefer to stay dry, the Champagne Sunset Cruise is $45. For more information, call **1-888-728-2235** or visit www.tildensscubacenter.com.

 * **Lower Keys. Looe Key Reef Resort & Dive Center** in **Ramrod Key** offers full-day reef trips for every level, including diving and snorkeling. Divers are $80 (includes tanks and weights), and snorkelers are $40. Wreck trips and custom charters are also available. After your dive, kick back at the **Looe Key Tiki Bar** for drinks and pub grub. For more information, call **1-800-942-5397** or **305-872-2215,** or visit www.diveflakeys.com.

 * **Key West.** The most historic, lively, and southernmost point of the Florida Keys, Key West also offers a bounty of undersea treasures. **Dive Key West** is backed by more than 35 years in the biz and besides snorkel and dive trips also offers scuba instruction and certification. Dive trips are $69 with no gear, and snorkel tips are $49. For more information, call **1-800-426-0707** or **305-296-3823,** or visit www.divekeywest.com.

 Powder Room

 If you're already a certified diver, don't forget to pack your certification card and log book! Consequences vary by outfitter, but you'll likely end up having to take a refresher course.

Where to Stop

It's not so much about *where* to eat in the Florida Keys but *what* to eat: conch fritters, conch salad, conch soup, Florida lobster tails in season, peel-and-eat shrimp, and key lime pie. Get a head start in Key Largo at the **Conch House (305-453-4844,** www.keylargocoffeehouse.com), the **Fish House (305-451-4665,** www.fishhouse.com), and **Snapper's (305-852-5956,** www.snapperskeylargo.com). Go for the Caribbean lobster and conch ceviche or cracked conch at the Conch House. At

Snapper's, watch the sunset from the waterfront while you nosh on raw bar items or peel-and-eat shrimp. At the Fish House, start with conch fritters, the fresh catch of the day, and end with a slice of award-winning key lime pie.

The Florida Keys offer a multitude of activities, but I'm pretty sure it's a sin to leave Key West without a visit to the **Hemingway Home & Museum (305-294-1136,** www.hemingwayhome.com) and **Sloppy Joe's (305-294-8759,** www.sloppyjoes.com). The home tour is just $12 and leads you through the 1850s house that is still furnished with items the Hemingway family used after they purchased it in 1931. Take your allergy medicine if you're allergic to cats, however, because the 60 residents now are of the feline persuasion—most of which have six toes (ask your tour guide for details). Afterward, head to the famous Sloppy Joe's on Duval Street and raise a glass to former patron Ernest Hemingway.

Where to Stay

The Florida Keys have no shortage in lodging choices. From sprawling resorts to beach-style motels, you'll find it all. In Key Largo, you can stay at the super cushy **Marriott Key Largo Bay Beach Resort (305-453-0000,** www.marriottkeylargo.com) with its own dive crew, a full service spa, restaurants, and poolside bars. Rates are from $169. Or head farther south to the **Island Bay Resort (1-800-654-KEYS** or **305-852-4087,** www.islandbayresort.com) in Tavernier, centrally located between Key Largo and Islamorada. Expect brightly colored bedspreads with starfish and palm trees and unique Florida character to each of the 10 cottages. The Conch Key and Sunset Cottages sleep three, or request the Coral Reef and Key Largo Cottages, which adjoin to sleep four. All rooms have fully equipped kitchenettes, private wood decks, and barbecue grills. The best part is a west-facing private beach and dock with killer sunsets. Room rates start at $159.

For what feels like your own island paradise, **Hawk's Cay Resort** is a water lover's wonderland. Located on Duck Key, south of Islamorada and north of Marathon, Hawk's Cay is perched on its own 60-acre island. Amenities include an outdoor heated pool, an adults-only pool, Jacuzzi, tennis courts, full-service spa, and four restaurants. Guest rooms offer an island-style décor with private balconies—many overlooking the ocean. The resort offers a host of recreational outlets, from snorkeling and sailing to water skiing and dolphin interaction at the Dolphin Connection center. Rates start at $220. *1-888-443-6393 or 305-743-7000. www.hawkscay.com.*

Powder Room

Take a dip with the dolphins at the **Dolphin Connection** center at Hawk's Cay, which is open to nonresort guests and offers several programs for interacting directly with the chummy mammals. The Dockside Dolphins experience is $50 for resort guests and $60 for nonresort guests and allows you to shake fins with the dolphins from the training docks. The Dolphin Discovery program gets you up close and personal with them in the water and is $135 for guests, $150 for nonresort guests. For more information, call **1-888-814-9154** or visit www.dolphinconnection.com.

In Key West, live like a native and book one of the many adorable B&Bs tucked along the streets. One such charming spot is **Courtney's Place Key West Historic Cottages & Inns (1-800-869-4639** or **305-294-3480,** www.courtneysplacekeywest.com). The eight guest cottages, three efficiencies, and six private guest rooms are central to Old Key West and are nestled among tropical gardens and a petite pool. The two-bedroom Bahamian Cottage is ideal for a group of four and has a kitchen, porch, living area, and feminine (but not frou-frou) décor. Rates start at $109 and include a continental breakfast. If the cottages are full, ask about the sister property, the **Seaport Inn (1-800-869-4639** or **305-294-3480,** www.seaportinnkeywest.com).

For more information on the area (including free maps, brochures, and special offers), call **1-800-FLA-KEYS** or visit www.fla-keys.com.

Whitewater Rafting: Pigeon River, Tennessee

Whitewater rafting is quite possibly the most thrilling water ride you could take outside a theme park. And taking a ride on the **Pigeon River** in the **Great Smoky Mountains** is a scenic spot to get your feet wet. Surrounded by national park forest, the Pigeon has carved its rocky riverbed through some of the most dramatic country in eastern Tennessee.

The lower section of the river is the place for beginners. Marked by Class I and II rapids with one Class III area, the six miles of the lower section equates more to a float trip and is the best ride to get started while still experiencing the thrill of riding the rapids. Take a day off to explore, and then hit the Upper Pigeon—where you'll be immediately confronted with fast-moving water and giant waves. The upper area, or Big Pigeon River, boasts 12 Class III and 3 Class IV rapids.

⚲ *Savvy Sister*

The International Scale of River Difficulty classifies a stretch of river according to difficulty. Here's how it breaks down: Class I is easy (you're bored), Class II is medium (you're having fun now), Class III is difficult (you're giddy), Class IV is very difficult (you're hanging on for dear life), Class V is extremely difficult (you're screaming uncontrollably), and Class VI is unrunnable (turn around and go home). For a more complete definition of each class, visit www.americanwhitewater.org. If you want to try your hand at the sport in a more predictable environment, visit the **U.S. National Whitewater Center** in **Charlotte, North Carolina,** home of the world's largest man-made course. For more information, call **704-391-3900** or visit www.usnwc.org.

River Trippin'

The Pigeon River is surrounded by a slew of rafting outfitters. Pigeon rafts load in **Hartford, Tennessee.** Here are a few tips to get your feet wet:

* **Rafting in the Smokies** offers two set trips. Lower Pigeon Float trips are 2 hours and start at $35. The Big Pigeon Upper trips are one-and-a-half hours and start at $39. For more information, call **1-800-PRO-RAFT** or **865-436-5008,** or visit www.raftinginthesmokies.com.

* **Wildwater Rafting** offers Lower Pigeon guided trips starting at $35 and Upper Pigeon trips starting at $39. Trips times are about two hours. Rafting excursions on the Nantahala River (about an hour from the Pigeon base) are also offered. For more information, call **1-800-451-9972** or visit www.wildwaterrafting.com.

* When you're ready to take on bigger rapids, take a trip up to the Nolichucky River in Erwin, Tennessee (less than two hours from Hartford). The Nolichucky River Whitewater Rafting trip with **Mountain Adventure Guides** is a full day on the rapids and includes lunch for $71 per person. Excursions are also offered on Nantahala and French Broad Rivers—each a little more than an hour from the Pigeon River area. For more information, call **1-866-813-5210** or **423-743-7111,** or visit www.mtnadventureguides.com.

* If tubing is more your thing, **Smoky Mountain River Rats** offers tubing and kayak excursions out of Townsend (about an hour from Pigeon base). The tubing float adventure starts at $13 per person and lasts about an hour. Rafting and tubing combo packages are available. For more information, call **865-448-8888** or visit www. smokymtnriverrat.com.

(STOP) *Bad Trip*

Depending on when you go, the river waters can be chilly—and you'll get wet. To avoid shivering your way down the rapids, dress properly in cooler weather. The layer closest to your body should be a snug-fitting, wicking fabric. (No cotton undies, ladies—trust me!) Wet suits may be suggested (and provided) by your outfitter. Wear them! No, they don't make you look fat—and they'll keep your core toasty.

Where to Play

You could head to **Dollywood** (**1-800-365-5996,** www.dollywood.com) in **Pigeon Forge** if that's your thing. The theme park has rides, shows, shopping, and restaurants and is home to the **Southern Gospel Music Hall of Fame & Museum.** (The two million people who visit annually can't be wrong.) Tickets start at $50 depending on the season. Or you can opt for a quieter stroll through **The Old Mill Square** (**865-428-0771,** www.oldmillsquare.com). Not far from Dollywood, the Old Mill is listed on the National Register of Historic Places and is a complex of restaurants, pottery, craft shops, and old-fashioned candy and food stores.

As for places to refuel, be prepared to stray from your diet for a date with down-home, country cooking. A family owned restaurant since 1960, the **Pancake Pantry (865-436-4724,** www.pancakepantry.com) is a Gatlinburg hot spot for breakfast and lunch. The restaurant serves nearly 25 varieties of pancakes—from old-fashioned buttermilk to sweet potato pancakes—as well as gourmet sandwiches and boxed lunches to go. Doors open at 7 A.M., so get there early and beat the crowd.

After a day of thrill-riding through the rapids, nothing beats an ice-cold beer—and with locations in Pigeon Forge and Gatlinburg, **Smoky Mountain Brewery** (Pigeon Forge: **865-868-1400,** Gatlinburg: **865-436-4200;** www.smoky-mtn-brewery) hits the spot. To accompany its handcrafted microbrews, the restaurant serves wings, burgers, steak, pasta dishes, specialty pizzas, and hearty sandwiches.

Where to Stay

Pigeon Forge and Gatlinburg both offer standard chain hotels at great rates. For an affordable option in Gatlinburg, however, stay at the riverfront **Rocky Waters Motor Inn (1-800-824-1111** or **865-436-7861,** www.rockywatersmotorinn.com). You'll have a choice of standard guest rooms, suites with Jacuzzis, or rustic cabins. Rooms have refrigerators, microwaves, coffee makers, and TVs; most also have fireplaces and private balconies overlooking the Pigeon River. Rates start at $69 and include a continental breakfast. Check the website for seasonal deals.

For a more cushy experience, stay at the **Eight Gables Inn (1-800-279-5716,** www.eightgables.com) in Gatlinburg. The cozy country inn houses 19 rooms and suites, each with private baths, TVs, feathertop beds, plush bathrobes, and personal amenities; several also have fireplaces and whirlpool tubs. You can't ask for better views, and the spacious inn is surrounded by gardens, gazebos, and outdoor sitting areas. Rates start at $140 and include a full breakfast, afternoon tea, and evening desserts.

Chick Wit

Don't forget to tip the crew—especially if they take good care of you! That's how they primarily get paid.

—Jan, publishing executive

For more lodging options and area attractions, visit www.escapetothesmokies.com.

More Water Sport Adventures

If the thrill of riding an ocean wave is calling you, try your hand at surfing on the sunny shores of **Santa Monica, California. Learn to Surf LA (310-663-2479,** www.learntosurfla.com) offers progressive lessons for every level in private or group classes. Group lessons start at $75; private lessons start at $120. Stay at the stately **Shutters on the Beach (310-458-0030,** www.shuttersonthebeach.com) in Santa Monica, and treat yourselves to a Beach Buff body treatment (90 minutes for $230) at the hotel's exclusive **One Spa.**

Take in the natural beauty of **Alaska** by tooling along her lakes and rivers in a canoe. **Wilkinson Expeditions (1-888-783-4332,** www.alaskatrips.com) boasts a custom camping experience for canoeing expeditions that includes all meals, ground transportation, and equipment. Prices start at $750 per person for three days and two nights. **Alaska Outdoors (1-800-320-2494** or **907-357-4020,** www.travelalaskaoutdoors.com) has multisport, seven-day camping adventures where canoeing, hiking, a wilderness bus tour, meals, and equipment are included for $1,025.

You'll never quite appreciate the immense beauty of the **Grand Canyon** in **Arizona** until you're floating along the **Colorado River** and gazing up at its majestic walls. Backed by nearly 40 years of rafting the waters of the Grand Canyon, **Arizona River Runners (1-800-477-7238,** www.raftarizona.com) offers guided rafting trips for every level—from three-day to two-week adventures. The Three-Day Escape all-inclusive package starts at $985 per person and includes a helicopter ride to the floor of the Grand Canyon.

Nature Girls

In This Chapter

* Hiking hut to hut through the Canadian wilderness
* Biking through the California redwoods
* Scaling the craggy mountains of West Virginia
* Skiing down the slopes of southwestern Colorado
* More natural adventures

Calling all nature lovers and outdoor enthusiasts! In this chapter, we'll see the world from a perspective uncluttered by city trappings. We'll trod down hills, scramble up rocks, and feel the exhilarating rush of crisp air as we pedal through towering tree-lined paths and ski down mountain trails. All that these getaways require is a shared admiration for the beauty of nature and maybe an ounce of courage. Don't forget that giant tube of sunscreen, and off you go!

Hike: Canadian Wilderness

No cars, no kids, and no responsibilities. Just you, your comrades, and a friendly guide trekking across a landscape framed by snow-dusted mountain vistas, placid lakes, wildflowers, and a night sky ablaze with brilliant stars. Sound good? Founded in 1999 by outdoor enthusiast Marian Marbury, **Adventures in Good Company (1-877-439-4042,** www.adventuresingoodcompany.com) has created outdoor adventures just for women. One of many trips offered throughout the year, Hiking Hut to Hut in British Columbia is a rare opportunity to experience the stunning Canadian wilderness without having to haul a huge camping pack. All you have to do is get yourselves to Seattle, Washington, and the rest is a cake walk through the woods—albeit a vigorous one!

> ### Chick Wit
> Try to plan your outdoor adventure trips around your monthly cycle. It's just one less thing to bother with when you're enjoying the great outdoors.
> —Karen, physical therapist

Walk on the Wild Side

The five-day adventure will take you through **Wells Gray Park.** Considered one of the best-kept secrets in **Canada,** the stunning wilderness is a one and a half–million-acre wonderland of mountain peaks, unspoiled lakes, and lush meadows with an infinite variety of mountain wildflowers. In fact, the park is so remote that you're unlikely to see other people throughout the entire trip. But rather than roughing it on your own, you'll have an experienced guide to keep you on target. At the end of each day, you'll have a comfy place to crash—and meals are already planned ahead.

You'll start the adventure in Seattle, where you'll need to get yourselves to the designated hotel in Clearwater, British Columbia. Once there, the group of 10 women (maximum) will gather for introductions and a welcome dinner. Bright and early the next morning, you'll set off for the trailhead.

Each day will vary, but typically you'll hit the trail by 9 A.M. and hike anywhere from three to eight hours per day with stops along the way for lunch and scenic snapshots. You'll travel through mature forests and lush meadows, down valleys and high above rushing waterfalls, along wildlife trails, and to the banks of numerous lakes. Nights will be spent in cozy, heated huts. After five days out on the trail, you'll head back to the motel, clean up, and celebrate the trip over a farewell dinner.

The trip is rated M+, meaning that it's best suited for gals in good physical condition who regularly work out three to four times per week. Backpacking experience is a plus. Good hiking shoes are also a must. Besides hiking for a good part of each day, you'll need to carry a light pack (15 to 20 pounds) for your clothes, personal items, and sleeping sack. Three months before the trip, you'll get a detailed list of everything you'll need to pack.

Powder Room

Bandannas are a nature girl's best friend, according to the folks at Adventures in Good Company. You can use them for bad hair days, as sweatbands, as halter tops, as towels, and even as emergency coffee filters. You'll find more practical tips on the Adventures in Good Company website at www.adventuresingoodcompany. com. For more hiking advice on everything from trekking poles to hygiene, visit www.lowergear.com.

The all-inclusive price of $1,350 includes guide services, two nights motel lodging, four nights in the huts, all meals from dinner Monday through Sunday breakfast, and round-trip transportation from Clearwater to the trailhead. Airfare and transportation to Clearwater is not included, but the staff will organize transport on a cost-share basis from Seattle.

The food is mainly vegetarian, but the staff makes sure that meat is available at some meals for those who prefer it. Meals are hearty, healthy, and so tasty that past participants have begged for the recipes—most of which are now posted on the website. You'll find African Ground Nut Soup, Alpine Pesto Spaghetti, Wild Forest Mushroom Couscous, and Powerballs (to name a few). With advance notice, they can accommodate most dietary restrictions or allergies.

Where You'll Stay

Although certainly rustic, the huts are comfortable, heated, and equipped with the basics. The first hut you'll stay in is the Trophy Mountain Chalet, which has a large living area downstairs and one large room upstairs with divided sleeping compartments. The second one is the Discovery Cabin, where you'll find a spacious open loft instead of a second floor. Neither cabin has running water and instead has outhouses or a composting toilet and a small room with a wash basin for washing up at the end of the day (not to mention numerous opportunities to go jump in a lake). The huts are stocked with games, books, and other diversions as well as slippers for group use.

Bike: Redwood Country, California

Why pedal your way through the **Redwood country** of California? Well, in case you haven't heard, redwoods are big—in fact, the stately sequoias are the tallest and among the most massive tree species on Earth. You can cover a lot more territory by bike than on foot, and you won't have to strain to see the sights from a car window. Plus, after an invigorating bike ride, you'll have your choice of quaint spots to land in the evenings. From the picturesque village of **Ferndale** up to the seaside towns of Trinidad and Crescent City, the northern coast of California merges cozy creature comforts with awe-inspiring natural beauty.

If you're an equipment freak and have to ride your own bike, a road trip up the northern California coastline is well worth the sights (depending on your starting point). If you decide to rent a bike, you'll find several places to rent them. **Bay City Bike (415-346-2453,** www.baycitybike. com) in **San Francisco** rents bikes starting at $27 a day. Or get one at the **Life Cycle Bike Shop (707-822-7755)** in the green-friendly college town of **Arcata** (rumored to have more Toyota Prius hybrids per capita than any town in the United States), where they rent bikes for $25 a day. Life Cycle is also a great place to stop if you have any bike needs. The family-run business has been around for more than 30 years.

Pedal to Paradise

Your first stop should be at one of the five National Park Service visitor centers to pick up maps and chat with park staff about trail and road conditions. All have restrooms, gift shops, and picnic areas and are generally open spring through fall, 9 A.M. to 5 P.M. Listed from the northernmost to southernmost, the centers are as follows:

* **Hiouchi Information Center:** located on U.S. Highway 199 in Hiouchi; **707-458-3294**

* **Jedediah Smith Visitor Center:** located on U.S. Highway 101 in Hiouchi; **707-458-3496**

* **Crescent City Information Center:** located on 1111 Second Street in Crescent City; **707-465-7306**

* **Prairie Creek Visitor Center:** located just off U.S. Highway 101 along Newton B. Drury Scenic Parkway in Orick; **707-465-7354**

* **Kuchel Visitor Center:** located on U.S. Highway 101 in Orick; **707-465-7765**

(STOP) *Bad Trip*

Remember the old saying, "Leaves of three, let them be"? Poison oak is found in various forms throughout the redwood parks. Look for the three distinctive smooth, shiny leaflets in bright green or red. Contact with leaves can leave you scratching uncontrollably, so wash thoroughly if you brush up against it. Stay on trails, and tuck your pants legs into your socks to avoid ticks from creeping up your britches. Eek!

The park is famous for its unpaved scenic roads—most of which do not allow trailers and motor homes and are great for tooling along on a bike. Take frequent breaks to give your neck a break from peering up so much. Try one of these routes:

* **Howland Hill Road.** In the heart of the redwoods, this six-mile gravel road in **Jedediah Smith Redwoods State Park** is a narrow, winding corridor shadowed by ancient redwoods. Located at the

northern end of the park, the road is accessible from Highway 101 south of Crescent City by turning onto Elk Valley Road or from Highway 199, two miles east of the Hiouchi Information Center.

* **Davison Road.** This narrow eight-mile road passes through a young redwood forest to the sandy shores of **Gold Bluffs Beach.** Keep your eyes peeled for elk! Located on Highway 101 south from Crescent City 30 miles or north 2 miles from Orick. A state park day-use fee is required.

* **Cal-Barrel Road.** Pedal along this three-mile road through old-growth forest in **Prairie Creek Redwoods State Park.** Also a narrow, winding road, the slow going will give you plenty of time to take in the colossal redwoods that rise like pillars in the sky. The turnoff is located north of the Prairie Creek Visitor Center on Newton B. Drury Scenic Parkway.

If you want to take off on a trail, here are a few of the back-country routes that the National Park Service recommends specifically for biking. (Mileage noted is one-way.)

* **Ossagon Trail Loop.** A 19-mile loop (when combined with the Coastal Trail Gold Beach section), this trail offers steep terrain that rewards you with a spruce forest and views of the ocean. It's accessed via Newton B. Drury Scenic Parkway at milepost 132.9.

* **Coastal Trail, Gold Bluffs Beach section.** This easy three-mile trail offers great ocean views and the occasional elk sighting. It's accessed via Ossagon Trail or Davison Road.

* **Coastal Trail, Last Chance section.** A six-mile route with some steep sections, this trail leads through the redwoods with coastal views along the way. It's accessed at the end of Enderts Beach Road or milepost 15.6 on Highway 101.

* **Davison Trail.** Start at Elk Meadow Day Use Area or at the south end of Elk Prairie campground for an easy two-mile ride. Combine with Streelow Creek Trail and Davison Road for a seven-mile loop. Carry on to Lost Man Creek trailhead for another couple miles. This route varies from easy to moderate with a few steep grades and will take you through old-growth and second-growth forests.

Download a bike route map including mileage and difficulty ratings at www.nps.gov/redw. Click **Plan Your Visit** to access the current visitor's guide, and click **Brochures** to get a bike route map. Call the park's main redwood office at **707-464-6101** for more information.

Where to Stop

Leave your bikes back at the hotel for a day or two of exploration. Take a hike through the **Lady Bird Johnson Grove,** or hit a few notorious tourist stops.

It seems almost sacrilegious to increase your carbon footprint just to drive through a tree, but it gives you a real appreciation for their massive size. So, take the hybrid. The three sites left (one fell in 1969 under heavy snow) are the **Klamath Tour-Thru Tree** in **Klamath** off the Terwer Valley exit, the **Shrine Drive-Thru Tree** in **Myers Flat,** and the **Chandelier Tree** in **Drive-Thru Tree Park** in **Leggett.**

The **Trees of Mystery** center (**1-800-638-3389** or **707-482-2251,** www.treesofmystery.net) in Klamath (south of Crescent City) is a roadside tourist attraction worth a camera-snapping stop. You can take a 10-minute ride on the SkyTrail gondola through the tree tops, marvel at the sky-high statues of Paul Bunyan and Babe the Blue Ox, and take a walk by trees that have strange twists and formations. Adults are $13.50, which includes the SkyTrail ride and trail access.

Savvy Sister

Speaking of carbon footprints, major car rental companies are now doing their part to help us clean up our acts. Enterprise, for example, now offers a fleet of hybrids and ethanol flex-fuel vehicles as well as an optional Carbon Offset Program where you can contribute a little more than a buck per rental to a charitable foundation that works to offset carbon emissions. Find out more at www.keystogreen.com.

Where to Stay

Ferndale and Eureka both offer accommodations that take you back in time to the Victorian era. In Ferndale, stay in the heart of downtown at **Victorian Inn** (1-888-589-1808, www.victorianvillageinn.com), an historic space that lives up to its name with an elegant Victorian décor and vintage accents. Rates start at $125 and include a morning meal. In Eureka, stay at the stately **Carter House Inns** (1-800-404-1390 or 707-444-8062, www.carterhouse.com) and wander the flower and herb gardens after an elegant meal at the inn's award-winning Restaurant 301. The property offers a choice of room types spread out among the Hotel Carter, Carter House, Carter Cottage, and Bell Cottage. Rooms start at $155; watch the website for special packages.

Trinidad offers a handful of charming inns that take advantage of the breathtaking coastal views. Among them, the **Trinidad Bay Bed & Breakfast** (707-677-0840, www.trinidadbaybnb.com) is a Cape Cod–style inn that overlooks the bay and **Memorial Lighthouse.** The inn has four comfy guest rooms, each with a king-size bed, luxurious linens, private baths, and spectacular ocean and garden views. Stick with the theme by booking the Redwoods room, which affords fantastic views of Trinidad Bay and sunsets to the west. The room has a king bed, a large bathroom with shower, a reading chair, and a table for two next to the Cape Cod–style dormer window. Rates start at $200 and include a three-course breakfast.

Another Trinidad destination is the **Turtle Rocks Ocean Front Inn** (707-677-3707, www.turtlerocksinn.com). Situated on three seaside acres, this B&B features rooms with private, glassed-in decks that overlook the ocean. Catch sea lions sunning on the rocks while you take in the cool breezes. Rooms start at $165 and include a full gourmet breakfast.

For more bed-and-breakfast inns, visit www.northernredwoods.com. Get Arcata lodging information at www.arcatastay.com (check out the **Rose Court Cottage**—so very cute!) and additional Trinidad information at www.trinidadcalif.com. If you plan to head north to Crescent City, find hotel listings and vacation rentals at www.northerncalifornia.net.

For more on the California Redwood Coast (including package deals and a visitor's guide), call the **Humboldt County Convention & Visitors Bureau** at **1-800-346-3482** or visit www.redwoods.info.

Climb: Seneca Rocks, West Virginia

Ready to rock? Reach new heights and tighten the bonds of your friendships with a rock-climbing excursion. Scaling a mountain face isn't as scary as you might think—especially once you know what you're doing. Little Miss Girly-Girl whose palms sweat when driving on overpasses (that would be me) has even done it. And a popular and immensely scenic area to learn the art of rock climbing is **Seneca Rocks, West Virginia.**

Less than a three-hour drive from Charleston, West Virginia, and four hours from Washington, D.C., Seneca Rocks is home to a massive crag of the same name that rises above the **Spruce Knob-Seneca Rocks National Recreation Area** in the eastern panhandle of the state. A playground for rock climbers and nature lovers, Seneca Rocks is particularly good for rock climbing because of the varying degrees of routes and the geology of the rock itself.

Learn the Ropes

This tiny town is home to a couple top-notch climbing schools. The one where I broke in my climbing shoes was **Seneca Rocks Mountain Guides and School of Rockcraft (304-567-2115,** www.senecarocks. com). The school boasts a three-to-one student-to-instructor ratio and offers beginning to advanced instruction.

The Basic Rockcraft program is two or three days. The first day, you'll hike out to the rocks for instruction on the fundamentals of traditional multi-pitch technical climbing. After learning to tie the necessary knots, handling the rope, constructing natural anchors, belaying, and rappelling, you'll take your first climb toward the Seneca Rocks summit. The two-day course is $295; three days are $375. The fee includes guide services, climbing shoes and equipment, and use of the indoor rock wall. Ladies-only rock-climbing clinics are held at various times throughout the year for the same rates and are led by a female guide.

The other place in town is the **Seneca Rocks Climbing School (1-800-548-0108** or **304-567-2600,** www.seneca-rocks.com). Prices are exactly the same for the two or three days of the Comprehensive Basic course, and a women's-only course is also available.

The major difference in the two schools may be that Seneca Rocks Mountain Guides has a killer coffee shop called **Ground Up,** while Seneca Rocks Climbing School houses the **Gendarme Climbing Shop** (where you can pick up climbing and backpacking gear). Both require that you bring along your own water and lunch for the day. They differ somewhat in their approaches toward climbing techniques, but both are staffed by enthusiastic, skilled guides who love what they're doing.

Savvy Sister

The Yosemite Decimal System is a numerical rating system used in mountaineering to classify the difficulty of hikes and climbs. Rock climbing is rated as Class 5, and routes are rated as 5.0, 5.1, 5.2, and so on (according to difficulty). Here's a witty (although accurate) way of defining Classes 1 through 4 courtesy of www. climber.org: Class 1: you fall, you're stupid; Class 2: you fall, you break your arm; Class 3: you fall, you break your leg; Class 4: you fall, you are almost dead (you can't breathe or move your arms, legs, and head); and Class 5: you fall, you are dead. Learn the ropes with *The Complete Idiot's Guide to Rock Climbing* by Stefani Jackentha (Alpha Books, 1999).

Where to Stop

If your thrill-o-meter isn't quite too full, head to the **Nelson Rocks Preserve (304-567-3169,** www.nelsonrocks.org) in nearby **Judy Gap,** home to one of the few via ferrata systems in North America. Italian for "iron way," a via ferrata is a long climbing route with permanently fixed bolts, cables, and rungs. You won't need climbing experience to tackle it—just nerves of steel as the ascent takes you up some 1,000 feet and over a bridge straight from an *Indiana Jones* movie. You'll stay anchored to the cable via a harness and a Y-shaped lanyard with cara-biners (a D-shaped ring with a spring catch on one side) at the two ends. Every six or eight feet, you'll clip into the other side of the anchor point, one carabiner at a time, so that you always stay clipped into the cable. Seems easy enough—but as the website warns, it could be one of the most intense adventure experiences you'll ever have.

Keep your shoes firmly on the ground with a hike to the observation tower that sits atop Spruce Knob, West Virginia's highest peak. The gentle Whispering Spruce Trail is just a half-mile walk from the parking area and leads to the stone lookout tower. About a mile and a half from there is a picnic area with tables, grills, and rustic restroom facilities.

When the time comes to refuel, you'll find a handful of family-owned places for down-home cooking and friendly service. Frequented by the local climbing community, **Harper's Front Porch Restaurant (304-567-2555)** is located over **Harper's Old Country Store** at the junction in Seneca Rocks and affords spectacular views of the landscape. For sandwiches on your climbing days, stop by the **Macksville Mart (304-567-3100)**, a small grocery and gas station adored by locals. Both **Yokum's (1-800-772-8342** or **304-567-2351,** www.yokum.com) and **Valley View (304-567-2496)** are touted for their breakfasts and also serve lunch and dinner.

Where to Stay

Dust off your camping gear and crash at one of the local campgrounds—both within walking distance from the schools. Run by the U.S. Forest Service, **Seneca Shadows Campground (1-877-444-6777** or **304-567-3082,** www.recreation.gov) has hot showers, electric hookups, and group campsites. The **Princess Snowbird Campground** is on the grounds of **Yokum's Vacationland (1-800-772-8342** or **304-567-2351,** www. yokum.com/lodging.htm), where you'll also find a motel and rustic cabins.

For a bit more privacy and lots more amenities, book a cabin at **Harman's North Fork Cottages (1-800-436-6254** or **304-257-2220,** www.wvlogcabins.com), about 12 miles from Seneca Rocks near the Smoke Hole Caverns. All cabins have kitchens and decks, and most have outdoor hot tubs. Rates are $99 and up. Cabins range in size and can sleep between two and eight adults.

Ski: Telluride, Colorado

Located in southwest Colorado's San Juan Mountains, **Telluride** sits at 8,750 feet above sea level and is a beloved skiing destination for its Old West, small-town charm. A National Historic Landmark District,

Telluride is a walkable, quaint town with Victorian homes and storefronts (not a single chain restaurant or shop) and friendly locals with equally friendly masters (dogs make up a modest town majority).

At an altitude of 9,500 feet, the town of **Mountain Village** is home to the ski resort headquarters as well as restaurants, lodging, and shops. Telluride and Mountain Village are connected by a free Gondola transportation system—the only one of its kind in North America. With the free Galloping Goose bus system (running on nontoxic, biodegradable, vegetable oil-based diesel fuel), you'll have little need to use a car in Telluride or Mountain Village.

Down the Ski Bunny Trail

With more than 90 ski runs, the **Telluride Ski Resort (1-800-778-8581,** www.tellurideskiresort.com) experience offers terrain for every skier's level—from long, wide, groomed trails that wind past celebrity homes to challenging mogul runs in remote areas. Even beginners can ride to the highest peaks and enjoy terrain and views typically accessible only by experts. Besides the gondola, the resort has a generous system of ski lift chairs—including two high-speed gondolas and seven high-speed quads. The ski season typically runs from Thanksgiving week through early April. Because lift tickets can cost a pretty penny, save some green by buying tickets online in advance and save up to 15 percent off the ticket window rate.

Powder Room

As a novice skier who has retained my novice status after almost a decade of skiing, my best advice for newbies is to sign up for a class. Do not attempt to take directions from your friends, or I guarantee you some face-plant time. With a class, you'll stay on terrain suited for your level while you pick up all the basics (and usually a friend or two).

Another reason to love Telluride is that since 1981, the **Telluride Ski and Snowboard School** has held Women's Weeks throughout the year, where women-only clinics are led by female ski instructors. You'll be matched with women within your same ski level for expert instruction that includes a video analysis of your ski technique and use of the timed race course. The three or five-day clinics include après-ski events, a celebration dinner, and various other pluses such as shopping excursions, wine and chocolate tastings, and spa treatments. Inquire about Women's Week through the ski resort.

Where to Stop

Telluride and Mountain Village offer boutique shopping, exquisite galleries, restaurants for every taste, and a hopping nightlife. On a recent trip there—overcome by a cupcake craving—my sister-in-law and I happened upon **Baked (970-728-4705,** www.bakedintel.com) in Telluride in our sugar-starved search. Baked is an off-the-beaten-path bakery and deli with fresh pastries, sandwiches made with homemade breads, and hearty soups. There weren't any cupcakes (that day, anyway!), but they had the best sprinkled cake donuts that I've downed in a long time. We also stumbled upon **The Sweet Life (970-728-8789,** www.thesweetlifeinc.com), the cutest little candy and gift shop with a '50s-style diner that serves burgers, root beer floats, and homemade ice cream. We never found our cupcakes, but the sugar rush kept us going for hours.

Speaking of my sister-in-law, we are two kernels on a corn cob when it comes to traveling and agreed it would be in our best interests to feign a ski injury to spend the day at a spa (she actually was injured). The **Golden Door Spa (1-800-772-5482,** www.goldendoor.com) at the **Peaks Resort** fit the bill with a bubbling mineral-infused whirlpool, a eucalyptus steam room, gorgeous mountain views, and pampering spa and salon services. Another enticing retreat in town is **Atmosphere Spa (970-728-0630,** www.telluridespa.com). Located just inside the **Camel's Garden Hotel** near the base of the Gondola, the day retreat offers a cozy atmosphere and a full menu of body and skincare treatments.

For ski days, you'll likely refuel on the slopes. When dinner rolls around, you'll have a ton of choices. **Brown Dog Pizza (970-728-8046,** www.browndogpizza.com) and **Smuggler's Brew Pub & Grille (970-728-0919,** www.smugglersbrew.com) are solid spots for casual, budget-friendly fare. **Honga's Lotus Petal Restaurant (970-728-5134,** www.hongaslotuspetal.com) is a local favorite for its lively Asian dishes and loose-leaf teas. **Cosmopolitan Restaurant & Tasting Cellar (970-728-1292,** www.cosmotelluride.com) offers succulent entrées such as grilled Colorado lamb rack served with spinach–goat cheese potatoes and vegetable cannelloni made with fresh herb pasta. Dine at 10,000 feet inside **Allred's (970-728-7474,** www.allredsrestaurant.com), just off the top of the gondola in Mountain Village. End your evenings at **The Bubble Lounge (970-728-9653,** www.telluridebubblelounge. com), where you'll get a natural high from the O$_2$ Bar while sipping on a specialty martini.

Where to Stay

As with most ski areas, your best bet is to find a privately owned condo or townhouse that comes with all the amenities of home, such as kitchens, private baths, and separate bedrooms. Many properties in Telluride and Mountain Village are ski-in, ski-out and offer packages that include discounted lift tickets or rental equipment. Start your search at one of the following property management companies: **Accommodations in Telluride, 1-866-754-8772,** www.vacationtelluride.com; **Telluride Rentals, 1-800-970-7541,** www.telluride-rentals.com; or **ResortQuest, 1-877-826-8043,** www.resortquesttelluride.com.

You can also stay in the heart of it all at ski-in, ski-out accommodations at Mountain Village. For a list of **Mountain Village properties,** call **1-800-778-8581** or visit www.tellurideskiresort.com.

For more information about Telluride or to request a visitor's guide, call **1-888-605-2578** or visit www.visittelluride.com.

More Nature Adventures

If you like all-inclusive, preplanned adventures, **Backroads (1-800-462-2848** or **510-527-1555,** www.backroads.com) offers outdoor trips worldwide with accommodations that vary from rustic camping to luxurious inns. The guided trips have earned the nickname "snack roads" for their stellar meals, and you can find a trip for just about every fitness level. Established in 1979 for small-group walking tours, **Country Walkers (1-800-464-9255,** www.countrywalkers.com) offers a handful of adventure trips just for women. From trailing the fall foliage in Vermont to following rural footpaths in Ireland, all Country Walkers Women's Adventures offer superb cuisine, knowledgeable tour guides, and authentic accommodations.

With a little more than 400 residents, no traffic lights, and one restaurant, there's not much to do in the tiny town of **Hulett, Wyoming**— except crash for the night after scaling a giant rock. The nearby **Devil's Tower** is America's first national monument and rises 1,267 feet above the Belle Fourche River. **Devil's Tower Climbing School (1-888-314-5267** or **307-467-5267,** www.devilstowerclimbing.com) offers instruction and guided climbs. And as for that one restaurant, the **Ponderosa Café & Bar (307-467-5335,** www.theponderosacafe.com)—rumor has it that it's darn good! Find lodging in Hulett and Devil's Tower at www.wyomingtourism.org.

Whistler Blackcomb Ski Resort (1-866-218-9690, www.whistlerblackcomb.com) in **British Columbia, Canada,** takes care of the ladies with "no-men-allowed" clinics throughout the season. The Roxy Snowboard and Ski Camps provide women the ability to master skiing and snowboarding, along with fun events for unwinding. You can even take part in women's gear buy-nights at some of the best ski and snowboard shops in town, offering deals and tips on the latest equipment designed just for women as well as refreshments and wine. Whistler is also a great ski town with its extensive shopping, a wide variety of excellent food, and a happening nightlife.

Real Cowgirls Don't Wear Stilettos

In This Chapter

* ✳ Looking the part

* ✳ Ride and relax at Alisal Guest Ranch in California

* ✳ Kick up the dust at Ranchos de los Caballeros in Arizona

* ✳ Work for your keep at Double E Guest Ranch in New Mexico

* ✳ More ranch destinations

Okay, gals … it's time to pull on your cowgirl boots and trade in your city slicker comforts for the thrill of the open range.

Dedicated to getaways beyond the conveniences of urban life, this chapter takes you down dusty trails, through pastoral fields of grazing animals, and back to a simpler time. And don't worry—while your manicured hands might get dirty, I've wrangled up places where you and your crew will have a soft place to land at the end of a hard day's play.

Saddle Wear

Let's be honest. Straddling a giant moving barrel is not an activity that most of us modern gals do on a daily basis—and horseback riding can unleash aches and pains in the strangest places. A few key items can *help* alleviate some of that discomfort. Leave the designer jeans at home and opt for relaxed riding jeans—preferably Wranglers or a style that doesn't have a double inseam to avoid the dreaded chaffing. Sunglasses are good, but if you plan to do more than trot, a cowboy or wide-brimmed hat with a secure chin strap is better. Depending on what level rider you are, riding boots are also an option because they fit snugly in the stirrups. A supportive or exercise bra is a must, and if you plan to ride more than a few days in a row, bring along padded bicycle shorts. No one likes a sore saddle.

> **Powder Room**
>
> For a crash course on gear and riding technique, pick up *The Complete Idiot's Guide to Horseback Riding* by Jessica Jahiel (Alpha Books, 2000).

Country Roads: The Alisal Guest Ranch and Resort

1054 Alisal Road, Solvang, CA 93463. 1-888-425-4725 or 805-688-6411. www.alisal.com.

Located 40 miles north of the seaside town of **Santa Barbara, Alisal Guest Ranch** serves up charming, ranch-style accommodations with a heaping side of cowboy hospitality. Alisal, which translates to "grove of Sycamores" in the Chumash language of the Native Americans of that area, is shaded by sycamores and century-old oak trees. The working cattle ranch has a history that dates back to the mid-1800s, when conquistador Raimundo Carrillo received the land as payment for his services to the Mexican government. Fast-forward a few hundred years, and the independently owned property has been home to legendary trotters, Kentucky Derby standouts, and a growing roost of vacationers.

The 10,000-acre property is dotted with 73 cottages available in one-room studios and one-bedroom suites. The California ranch design of the rooms is punctuated by cowboy artwork, wood-burning fireplaces with complimentary firewood, high-beamed ceilings, rustic-style beds, and picture windows. Most rooms have semiprivate patios, and all have mini kitchenettes—but for the sake of peace and quiet, you won't find televisions or phones (which are available in common areas throughout the property).

Room rates start at $475 and include lavish breakfasts and dinners at the Alisal Ranch Room. The larger one-bedroom suites sleep four to six depending on the room and start at $550.

STOP *Bad Trip*

While city slickers are welcomed like old hats at working ranches, their wireless trappings are not as widely embraced. Use of cell phones and other gadgets in any public area is a no-no. As a courtesy to your hosts and those in your party, stash your phone in your room and use it in private at the beginning or end of your day when necessary.

Activities on tap include riding and roping, nature walks, tennis, golf, scenic trail rides, and poolside lounging. Guided fishing trips and sail-boats are up for the taking at the resort's private spring-fed lake. In May 2008, the ranch unveiled a spanking new fitness center and spa with cardio and weight training equipment, a yoga and pilates studio, and six spa treatment rooms. In the summer months, top off your day with live country music in the **Oak Room** bar or head out to the historic **Maverick Saloon** in nearby **Santa Ynez** for live country western and classic rock tunes.

Cowgirl Bootcamp

One of its most requested packages, Cowgirl Bootcamp is a women-only adventure held on predetermined dates throughout the year. After basic riding instruction, wranglers-in-training hit the trails on horseback with resident cowgirls Lori Bart and Katie Carter. More adventurous riders can try their hands at barrel racing and lasso lessons in the authentic Western rodeo arena or saddle up for an invigorating morning ride that ends with a flapjack breakfast at an historic adobe.

Don't let the term "bootcamp" rattle you. Bootcamp comes padded with cushy touches to soothe your inner diva. Cowgirls will ease into their adventure with a welcoming gift basket packed with Western Remedies beauty balms, edibles, wine, an official Cowgirl Bootcamp tee, and other surprises.

The all-inclusive package includes studio accommodations for four days and three nights, evening cocktail receptions, three meals per day including wine with dinner, a private winemaker's presentation, a gourmet lakeside picnic lunch, daily horseback rides, line dancing, fly-fishing lessons, and nightly hoedowns. Rates include taxes and service charges and start at $2,450 for double occupancy. By booking a minimum of 10 guest rooms, you can arrange for a private bootcamp outside regularly planned times.

Outside the Ranch

For a taste of something completely different, take a day trip into town. Founded in the early 1900s by Danish immigrants, **Solvang** has been dubbed "more Danish than Denmark" because of its Scandinavian architecture, traditional bakeries, and Danish import stores. Grab a strudel and coffee at **Olsen's Danish Village Bakery (1-800-621-8238,** www.olsensdanishbakery.com), or stop into the **Solvang Restaurant (1-800-654-0541,** www.solvangrestaurant.com) for a plate of aebleskiver—a traditional Danish delicacy best described as tennis ball–shaped pancakes dusted in powdered sugar and served with raspberry jam. The windmill-laden town is home to more than 150 shops, including the **Solvang Shoe Store (1-888-384-2564,** www.solvangshoe. com)—a specialty clog shoe haven. If you've never had your picture taken with a giant red clog, here's your chance. For more information about Solvang, contact the Solvang Visitors Bureau at **1-800-468-6765** or visit www.solvangusa.com.

Trail Blazin': Ranchos de los Caballeros

1551 South Vulture Mine Road, Wickenburg, AZ 85390. **1-800-684-5030** *or* **928-684-5484**. *www.sunc.com.*

Although the manly name of this way-out West destination may lead you to think otherwise, the cowgirl spirit is very much alive and well at **Ranchos de los Caballeros.** A little more than an hour's drive from sprawling **Phoenix,** the ranch is perched on 20,000 acres of Sonoran desert, where giant agave and towering saguaro cacti wave a friendly "how do you do" at passersby. The resort was given its name when it opened in 1948 as a nod to the Spanish caballeros (or "gentlemen on horseback") who explored the dusty Southwest and cultivated the traditions that shaped this area. The property has been family owned and operated since its opening, and visitors are likely to catch a glimpse of owner and lifelong ranch resident Dallas "Rusty" Gant Jr.—also former mayor of his hometown of Wickenburg.

Handcrafted oak furniture, Mexican tile work, local cowboy artwork, Native American throws, and the warm hues of the Southwest blanket the main lodge and resort accommodations with a rustic yet upscale vibe. The 79 ranch-style rooms and suites snake through the property in individual or adjoining casitas and are equipped with modern frills such as televisions, phones, and mini kitchenettes. The resort offers five room types, from the economical Ranch Rooms with one king or a double and twin bed to the Maricopa Suites with a private king bedroom with a queen-size murphy bed and fireplace in the living space. The midsize Sunset Rooms offer the best desert views; some have gas kiva fireplaces and all have window seats, large patios, and can be converted into two- or three-room suites.

Luxury amenities such as a pristine 18-hole golf course, tennis courts, and a heated pool meet wild west activities such as trap and skeet shooting, horseback riding, and team penning for an eclectic experience. Set in a restored 1940s ranch house, the Spa at Los Caballeros boasts spacious spa suites draped in natural sunlight, a full menu of skin and body treatments, and a cowboy-Zen vibe punctuated by authentic period furniture.

Room rates vary with availability but generally start at $400 for double occupancy and include 3 square meals daily and full use of ranch facilities. Rates increase slightly during high season (the weekend before Christmas through mid-April), so you get more for your buck in October, November, and mid-April through mid-May. The resort closes down during the sizzling summer months in mid-May and opens for business in early October.

Giddy-Up Gals Getaway

There's a saying in Arizona: "You only hug a cactus once." This little gem is among the many bits of desert wisdom you might pick up during the Giddy-Up Gals Getaway. A weekend dedicated to dipping a novice cowboy boot into the ranch lifestyle, this short but sweet getaway is a laid-back adventure laced with fun and relaxation.

Limited to approximately 18 women, the Giddy-Up Gals Getaway includes a basic education in horse and tack, riding instruction, and an afternoon of coached penning where cowgirls team up to herd steer into a framed pen.

The all-inclusive package starts at $598 per person during the off season ($818 during high season) and includes three days and two nights accommodations, three gourmets meals per day, unlimited trail rides, a hang-on-to-your-hats hayride to a starlit cookout complete with a balladeer and bonfire, and plenty of free time for walks through the spa labyrinth or nature hikes with the resident naturalist. Alcohol is not included, but the homegrown prickly pear margaritas at the saloon are worth the splurge. Package dates are preset, but call the ranch for more details on planning a private getaway.

Outside the Ranch

Historic downtown **Wickenburg** is a worthy detour, especially if you've got a hankering for authentic Western wear. Take a historical walking tour of the dusty Old West town, or wander through the galleries, shops, or the **Desert Caballeros Western Museum (928-684-2272, www.westernmuseum.org)**. For souvenirs, stop by the **Old Livery**

Mercantile (**928-684-3298,** www.oldlivery.com) where you'll find miles of Arizona trinkets and handicrafts. For cowgirl wear and accessories, shoot into **Buckshot Babe's (928-684-0750,** www.buckshotbabes.com) or **Cowgirl Salvage (928-684-6112,** www.cowgirlsalvage.com). Pull up a stool at the town's oldest bar, **Rancho Bar 7 Restaurant (928-684-2492),** where the bar itself is the original cherry wood structure built in 1937 and home to bartender Uncle Wes, who at age 87 has worked at the bar five days a week since 1942. The town is spilling over with Old West folklore, so be sure to strike up a conversation with a local. They might look tough (it's the seething Arizona sun) but are quick to offer friendly advice and town tidbits. For more information on Wickenburg, contact Wickenburg Travel Guide (**928-684-5479,** www.outwickenburgway. com).

Ranch Hand: Double E Guest Ranch

67 Double East Ranch Road, Gila, NM 88038. **1-866-242-3500.** *www. doubleeranch.com.*

Dude, where's the pool? The flat-screen TV? The hot tub? Y'all pulled your pony up to the wrong dude ranch if that's what you're after. **Double E Guest Ranch** proprietors Debbie and Alan Eggleston take the business of ranching and wrangling seriously, and a trip to their working cattle ranch is as close as it gets to an authentic cowgirl experience.

Tucked in the southwest corner of New Mexico in the tiny town of **Gila** (pronounced *HEE-la*), Double E is between a three-and-a-half and five-hour drive from **Phoenix, Tucson, Albuquerque,** and **El Paso.** (If you plan to fly, check flights and rental car rates at nearby Silver City Airport.) Rugged, remote, and layered in legends of the Old West, the **Gila National Forest** frames the ranch with mountain vistas punctuated by brilliant blue skies. And at an altitude of 5,000 feet, temperatures are moderate (even in the summer), and the ranch is open to guests year round.

The ranch can accommodate up to 14 guests at a time. Sleeping quarters range from seven single-room guest cabins with private decks and full baths to an 1,800-square-foot log home that houses up to five and has a washer and dryer. Rooms include mini refrigerators, coffee makers, and microwaves. The rustic décor is undeniably cowboy Western, and the owners are quick to note that the rustic décor was no accident. They don't mind a little dirt, so if you don't kick your boots off at the door, no one's going to get hurt.

Hearty, home-cooked meals are served family style at ranch "headquarters," where guests and staff eat three square meals daily together unless lunch is packed and enjoyed trailside. Alcohol is bring your own. And don't go skipping dinner. Not only will you need the sustenance come morning, but plans for the next day's activities are up for discussion over the cook's fresh-made signature dishes such as beef brisket, green chili enchilada burritos, and banana cream pie. While the Egglestons run a tight ship and keep their rates low by counting on guests to help with ranch chores, the days are flexible and the pace is unhurried.

Rates start at $215 per person and include breakfast, lunch, and dinner along with the use of horses and basic riding instruction.

Cowgirl Camp

If I haven't scared you off yet, than you and the gals are ready for immersion in a true giddy-up experience. Cowgirl Camp Level I for beginners and Level II for more experienced riders are five-day, women-only programs held up to two times per month at preplanned weeks throughout of the year. The ranch is open year round and can usually accommodate groups outside the planned weeks with advanced notice.

Level I campers will ease into their experience with a full day dedicated to horsemanship and trail riding. For the next three days, novices will learn the basics of team penning, barrel racing, roping, and roundups. Depending how sore your saddle is, the final day is a choice between hunkering down in a hammock or a trail ride to Native American ruins or through the Gila wilderness.

Level II campers will experience a similar itinerary but will also learn single-steer reining, practice cattle driving in the open range, and dabble in mounted shooting with Cowboy Mounted Shooting Top Ten World Champion and ranch owner Alan Eggleston.

Cowgirl Camp Level I starts at $1,125 and Level II at $1,250 and includes six days, five nights cabin accommodations, three meals daily, and shuttle pickup and drop off in Silver City.

Outside the Ranch

Gila is little more than a one-pony town, but within a few hours drive of nearby **Silver City,** you can get to the **Gila Cliff Dwellings National Monument.** The winding drive lands you within a short walk to the ancient dwellings of the Mogollon (pronounced *mow-gee-on*) people who inhabited the area in the late 1200s.

For more information, contact the **National Park Service** at 575-536-9461 or visit www.nps.gov/gicl.

Powder Room

When you travel with a group, splitting meal checks can be a splitting headache. If the gals agree that the majority of your meals will be eaten at onsite dining facilities, look for properties that offer an American plan—which means your room rate includes three meals a day. A modified American plan means your quoted rate includes two meals per day.

More Ranch and Rural Destinations

For more ranching fun, hit up the **Bar W Guest Ranch** in **Whitefish.** The Cowgirl Up package at the family-run and owned guest ranch includes six nights lodging, meals, a private vintner's presentation, team penning, an evening cocktail reception, step and square dancing lessons, optional activities such as roping and barrel racing, and two hours of pampering (including its signature honey and hot cream rock foot massage). Packages start at $1,385 for double occupancy. *2875 Highway 93 West, Whitefish, MT 59937.* **406-863-9099** *or* **1-866-828-2900.** *www.thebarw.com.*

An idyllic country setting an hour west of **Houston,** the **Blisswood Bed & Breakfast** offers charming cottages and cabins for reasonable rates. Options range from the cozy Writer's Cabin, which sleeps three and starts at $159 per night, to the three-bedroom Ranch House Studio, which sleeps up to eight and starts at $189. Rent the entire Dog Trot House for $299, which sleeps up to six and has its own indoor Jacuzzi tub and outdoor pool. Cowgirl Camp and Girlfriend Getaway packages are available with horseback riding and massage or facial services, starting at $229 per person plus the cost of lodging. *13300 Lehmann Legacy Lane, Cat Spring, TX 78933.* ***713-301-3235.*** *www. blisswood.net.*

Check out Cibolo Creek Ranch in Marfa, Texas. If Marfa sounds faintly familiar, it's likely because the town was the backdrop for two of 2008's most decorated movies: *No Country for Old Men* and *There Will Be Blood.* It was also the site of the 1956 film *Giant* with Elizabeth Taylor, Rock Hudson, and James Dean. Steeped in its own history, the ranch's rooms and suites are tucked in three historic forts, each individually appointed with Mexican antiques, hand-stitched quilts, and most with adobe fireplaces. Rooms start at $475 double occupancy for two, including three meals daily. Activities abound, from horseback riding and hiking to soaking in the outdoor hot tub. *HCR 67, Box 44, Marfa, TX 79843.* ***432-229-3737*** *or* ***1-866-496-9460.*** *www.cibolocreekranch.com.*

The Montana Cowgirl package at **Triple Creek Ranch,** which is offered exclusively in the summer months, includes 4 nights double occupancy in a luxury cabin (standalone cabins with private decks and most with wood-burning fireplaces and outdoor hot tubs), use of a golf cart to explore the property, all meals and snacks, ranch activities, a cattle drive adventure, and two custom-made Triple Creek Ranch keepsake cowgirl hats for $4,220 for two people. *5551 West Fork Road, Darby, MT 59829.* ***406-821-4600*** *or* ***1-800-654-2943.*** *www.triplecreekranch. com.*

Find more guest ranches at duderanch.org and farm destinations in Pennsylvania at pafarmstay.com or in Maine at www.mainefarmvacation. com.

Part 6

The Road Less Traveled: Quirky, Wacky, and Wild Excursions

If you've said to yourself on more than one occasion, "I've always wanted to do that," well … here's your chance. Volunteer vacations not only take you to places off the tourist map but also fill your heart with a renewed sense of accomplishment. Next, we take off in search of ghosts, dabble in the spiritual world, and walk through a vortex. We take a trip to annual festivals and fulfill unrequited fantasies. Finally, we wrap up our whirlwind girlfriend getaways tour with the only way possible—by tripping to Las Vegas for anything-goes excursions.

(Photo courtesy of Troy Snow, Best Friends Animal Society.)

Dogtown resident Mr. Bones entertains volunteers at Best Friends Animal Society in Kanab, Utah.

Volunteer Vacations

In This Chapter

* ✳ Work together to improve hiking trails at national parks

* ✳ Help out at the nation's largest animal sanctuary

* ✳ Rebuild and socialize communities in rural U.S. locations

* ✳ Assist with wildlife and environmental studies with a team
  of scientists

* ✳ Other volunteer vacations

What, you may ask, work during a vacation? Seriously? Although
it might sound counter-intuitive to combine the concept of
hard labor with a fun getaway, volunteer vacations can be quite
rewarding—especially if you buddy up with your closest friends
and share the adventure. Come on … what better way to knock
that little twinge of guilt to the curb that comes from leaving
your cares behind when you know you're doing something for
the greater good?

And not all vacations require hard labor, by the way. Many take you beyond the barriers of where tourists roam and into the most breath-taking locations in the country. Most are extremely affordable, and the registration fees (your accountant will be glad to know) are tax deduct-ible in most cases.

American Hiking Society

Your mission, should you chose to accept it, is constructing or rebuild-ing footpaths, cabins, and shelters in and around America's most scenic hiking trails. Founded in 1976, **American Hiking Society (301-565-6704,** www.americanhiking.org) is a national, recreation-based non-profit organization dedicated to promoting and protecting America's hiking trails, the surrounding natural areas, and the hiking experience itself.

American Hiking Society's Volunteer Vacations offer you and the girls an economical, fulfilling way to explore some of the most scenic hills and valleys of the country while doing your part to improve the hik-ing experience. Sure, you'll get your hands dirty—but after a week out on the trails, not only will your lungs be pumped with fresh outdoor air but your head will also fall peacefully onto your sleeping bag each night, knowing you have made a difference. Heck, you may even lose a pound or two. Many American Hiking Society volunteers are so inspired by the sense of accomplishment they get from these trips that they return year after year.

The Volunteer Program

American Hiking makes its volunteer programs easy to love, because with a few exceptions, the flat fee is all inclusive. You just get yourselves to the rendezvous location with the proper gear, and everything else is done for you.

The registration fee for each trip is $275 per person ($245 for American Hiking members). The tax-deductible fee includes meals (except when you opt to eat out in a nearby town), park entrance fees, campground fees and back-country permit fees, a crew member T-shirt, and a year's membership to American Hiking for new participants. Tools, camp cooking gear, and first-aid equipment are provided by the host, but you'll be responsible for your own gear and personal items such as sunscreen and bug repellent. You will be provided with a list of required and recommended items once you register.

Powder Room

Membership has its perks. The $30 membership fee is wrapped up with the initial cost of your trip and includes a quarterly *American Hiker* magazine, a subscription to *Backpacker Magazine,* members-only discounts on books and gear at partnering retailers, and the satisfaction of knowing that you're supporting hikers and protecting and maintaining trails as well as the lands and waters around them. Join at www.americanhiking.org.

Crews are made up of 6 to 20 volunteers accompanied by a crew leader. Most trips require backpacking or day hiking, and accommodations vary from primitive campsites to bunkhouses or cabins.

A typical day starts with a hearty breakfast. You'll hit the trail generally by 8 A.M., work six to seven hours, and return to camp in time to enjoy a long, lazy afternoon. All participants are expected to lend a hand with camp chores such as cooking, washing dishes, collecting firewood, and maintaining tools. Evenings are spent with plenty of free time to relax, and most trips are padded with time off to explore the local area.

As far as fitness level goes, no particular outdoor experience is necessary—and each trip offers a wide variety of tasks with something for everyone to do. But nearly all of the projects require participants to be in decent physical condition. If you have any questions about your fitness level, make an appointment with your physician. Trips are rated easy to moderate, moderate to difficult, and strenuous to very strenuous. Consult the American Hiking Society website (www.americanhiking.org) for a complete description of each ranking.

Where You'll Go

Once you've decided on the ideal trip rating for your group, the next decision is which way to point that shiny new compass of yours. The

Volunteer Vacations schedule boasts an average of 75 projects in 30 states, from Alaska to West Virginia, in nearly every month of the year.

For a trip ranked easy to moderate, the **Longhorn Cavern State Park** location will take you deep inside one of the few river-formed caverns in **Texas.** Your team of 20 volunteers will work inside the cavern to repair or replace trails damaged by flooding and outside the cavern on the tree-shrouded 1.5-mile Backbone Ridge hiking trail. The trip concludes with a cavern tour and a two-hour Vanishing Texas scenic cruise along the rugged Colorado River Canyon.

Classified as moderate, the **U.S. Virgin Islands National Park** trip offers breathtaking terrain—and, except for a tropical rain shower or two, picture-perfect weather. Sites are located on the exotic island of **St. John** in the **U.S. Virgin Islands.** Camp out on a white sandy beach with star-filled skies to lull you to sleep. This trip has a maximum of 15 people, and the work focuses primarily on restoring the trails used for nature and historical ruins tours with extensive erosion damage. Volunteers will construct drainage structures or clear the exotic vegetation that tends to take over the ruins.

If you decide on a more strenuous adventure, the **Golden Gate National Recreation Area** stretches 70 miles north and south of the **Golden Gate Bridge,** creating an 80,400-acre greenbelt along the Pacific Ocean. From Tomales Bay in the north to the San Mateo watershed in the south, the parks include ancient redwoods, historic landmarks, miles of trails, rocky shorelines, rare and endangered species, lush coastal wilderness, and breathtaking vistas. A small group of eight takes on trail maintenance, repair, and enhancement along the coastal trails. The trip includes a behind-the-scenes tour of Alcatraz Island.

(STOP) *Bad Trip*

Know your limits. Before you sign yourselves up for a week of primitive living, be sure you're comfortable with the work environment. If you've got a touch of claustrophobia, for example, working in a cavern might not be the best option. If you're afraid of bugs, snakes, and creepy crawlers, you might want to opt for a spa vacation instead (see Chapter 8).

Best Friends Animal Sanctuary

5001 Angel Canyon Road, Kanab, UT 84741. **435-644-2001.** *www. bestfriends.org.*

Unconditional love, anyone? You and your animal-lovin' pals can cuddle up with some very deserving creatures at the **Best Friends Animal Sancutary** for an unbelievably rewarding getaway. A temporary home for some and a permanent home for others, Best Friends operates the country's largest sanctuary for homeless pets. An average of 2,000 abused and abandoned animals—including dogs, cats, birds, rabbits, goats, horses, and pot-bellied pigs—find the special care, unconditional love, and safe environment they need.

Formed in 1970, the organization has blossomed from a simple philosophy: kindness to animals helps build a better world for all of us. They work with shelters and rescue groups to advance initiatives that decrease the number of homeless pets, including adoption, spay/neuter programs, and humane education. And vital to keeping the birds chirping, the dogs barking, and the cats purring are the nearly 5,000 volunteers who lend a hand each year.

Surrounded by the painted canyons of southern Utah, the sanctuary is located on a 33,000-acre ranch at **Angel Canyon,** just outside the western town of **Kanab.** The canyon is at the heart of the famous Golden Circle of national parks, about 30 miles from **Zion National Park** and within a two-hour drive to the **Grand Canyon, Bryce Canyon,** and **Lake Powell.** Angel Canyon has long been a mecca for people who have a soft spot for animals and nature and is famous for playing the backdrop in dozens of movie and TV westerns going back to the 1950s, including *The Lone Ranger* and *The Outlaw Josey Wales.*

The Volunteer Program

Volunteer opportunities at Best Friends are flexible based on what you and the girls are looking to do. Your first step is contacting the Best Friends Volunteer Office and organizing your stay through them. How long you stay depends entirely on what you decide. You can volunteer for a week or for a few days and combine your visit with an exploration of nearby national parks.

Powder Room _____

Besides serving as a stopover for national park tourists, Kanab, Utah, is also the commercial seat for the surrounding ranches and farms. A day trip to Kanab is worth the trek to take in spirited hot spots such as **Nedra's Too** restaurant, the **Rocking V Cafe** (part restaurant, part art gallery), and the **Crescent Moon Theater** for live cowboy poetry readings. For more information, contact the **Kanab City Office** at 435-644-2534 or visit www.visitkanab.info.

The sanctuary offers seven main areas where you can lend a hand: Dogtown, Kittyville, Parrot Garden (indoor birds), Piggy Paradise (pot-bellied pigs), Wild Friends (outdoor birds), Horse Haven (also home to sheep, goats, and burros), and the Bunny House. Two volunteer sessions are held each day (mornings and afternoons). Volunteer opportunities within the animal areas can vary from helping with daily chores (cleaning, sweeping, scooping, and emptying litter pans), feeding the animals, cleaning their living areas, grooming them, taking them for walks, and socializing with them. Personal attention to these critters, no matter how small, is a huge part of the sanctuary's mission.

You can also opt to help out in the landscaping department, greenhouses, maintenance department, or the Angel's Rest pet cemetery. Depending on the time of year and changing needs, you can also volunteer to help with projects such as building, fence repair, and other various tasks.

What to Bring

Besides the prerequisite sunblock, shades, hats, and other necessities, be sure to bring an old pair of comfy, closed-toed shoes. Hiking shoes or work boots would also be handy, but sandals are not recommended because of the sandy landscape. Jeans or long, durable pants are good to bring along because you're likely to be greeted by some quite enthusiastic dogs, cats, and other critters.

Where to Stay

Angel Canyon Guest Cottages are the primary onsite lodging and must be reserved several months in advance. These eight guest cottages overlook the horse pastures and are nestled in the red cliffs of Angel Canyon near the Best Friends Welcome Center. Each has one bedroom, a sitting room, and kitchen. The cottages start at $125 per night double occupancy. For Best Friends members, high season rates (March 1–November 30) are $110 per night, and during low season (December 1– February 29), the member rate is only $85 per night. Basic memberships are $25 annually.

A smaller alternative to the cottages, Angel Canyon Guest Cabins are also conveniently located on sanctuary property. Each has a studio setup with one queen-size bed, a kitchenette, and private bath. Cabins are $82 per night and can accommodate two people. Member rates are discounted to $70 during high season and $55 in low season. Make your reservations for the cottages and cabins through the Best Friends Volunteer Office.

Another option are the three cute-as-a-postcard **Kanab Garden Cottages (435-644-2020,** www.kanabcottages.com), just five miles outside the sanctuary. All are fully furnished with separate bedrooms, full kitchens, and washers and dryers and can sleep up to eight people comfortably. Rates start in the $150 neighborhood depending on the number of people and duration of the stay.

Best Friends also has relationships with nearby hotels and inns that offer discounts to visitors and volunteers. Of those, you'll find solid chain options such as **Best Western** and the **Quality Hotel** as well as a few unique places. **Coral Cliffs Townhomes (1-800-707-9706** or **435-616-0948,** www.cctownhomes.com) feature four units with full kitchens, washers and dryers, and modern, spacious digs starting at $115. The aptly named **Victorian Charm Inn (1-800-738-9643** or **435-644-8660,** www.victoriancharminn.com) is a B&B with 20 themed guest rooms marked by period pieces and luxuries such as Jacuzzi tubs starting at $99. Contact the Best Friends Volunteer Office for a current list of participating hotels.

If cleaning out cat boxes has taken a toll on your muscles, you can stay at one of three nearby spa resorts. **Flanigan's Inn (1-800-765-7787** or

435-772-3244, www.flanigans.com) in **Springdale** offers contemporary rooms and suites starting in the $119 range, and its Deep Canyon
Adventure Spa has a full menu of therapeutic and luxury services. The
world-renowned **Green Valley Spa and Resort (1-800-237-1068** or
435-628-8060, www.greenvalleyspa.com) in **St. George** offers all-
inclusive spa-and-stay packages that start at $495 double occupancy for
three-night stays. **Red Mountain Spa (1-877-246-4453** or **435-673-
4905,** www.redmountainspa.com) is a top-notch destination spa with a
focus on outdoor adventures (read more about it in Chapter 9).

Savvy Sister

Karma points aside, a 2007 study conducted by the Corporation
for National and Community Service found a significant connection
between volunteering and good health. The study found that people
who volunteer have lower mortality rates, greater functional ability,
and lower rates of depression later in life than those who don't volunteer. Who needs Botox?

Global Volunteers

Dubbed the "granddaddy of the volunteer vacation movement" by *USA
Today*, **Global Volunteers (1-800-487-1074,** www.globalvolunteers.
org.) was established in 1984 as a nonprofit, nongovernmental organization that strives to wage peace throughout the world by helping establish mutual understanding between people of diverse cultures. That's
a mouthful for sure, but the underlying goal is simply to build bridges
of understanding between people of diverse cultures by involving them
in one-on-one service projects. The function of "servant-learner" volunteers is to serve local people by sharing talents with them. Projects
include tutoring children, teaching conversational English or business
skills, renovating and painting community buildings, assisting with
health care or natural resource projects, and nurturing at-risk kids.

Each year, Global Volunteers coordinates up to 200 teams of volunteers who contribute to long-term human and economic development
projects. From all backgrounds and of all ages, volunteers work with
and learn from people worldwide. Programs are offered in Australia,

Brazil, China, the Cook Islands, Costa Rica, Ecuador, Ghana, Greece, Hungary, India, Northern Ireland, Italy, Jamaica, Mexico, Peru, Poland, Portugal, Romania, South America, Tanzania, Vietnam, and of course, the United States.

The Volunteer Program

All U.S. program fees are $995 but by applying online, you'll save $100. The program management encourages Internet enrollment because it speeds up the application process. The only hitch is that you must agree to receive and send materials and correspondence via the Internet. North American programs in Costa Rica, Jamaica, and Mexico start at $1,895 (after Internet discount). Additional discounts are available for former volunteers, students, and groups. The fee directly supports the ongoing development work of the host community and covers project materials, the volunteer's meals, lodging, ground transportation, emergency medical evacuation insurance, team leader services, and other project expenses.

You'll need to cover airfare and all project-related expenses. As a reminder, fees including airfare are tax-deductible under current U.S. laws.

The Global Volunteers official service program starts on the first Saturday of your service program with the evening meal. Programs are seven days.

Meals on these trips are plentiful and consist of American fare mixed with the local culture. Depending on the location, most teams prepare their own breakfasts and lunches, and dinners consist of a variety of options from local restaurants or are prepared by local cooks.

Where You'll Go

From the hills of Appalachia to the prairies of Minnesota and the mountaintops of Montana, you and your girlfriends can help these communities improve their living conditions and empower them to build better lives.

The **Minnesota Work Projects** are focused on tutoring new immigrants in the communities of **Austin** and **Worthington.** These rural

Midwestern cities have become home to thousands of immigrants from across the globe— southeast Asia, Mexico, Russia, Sudan, Somalia, Bosnia, and Ethiopia (to name a few). As a Global Volunteer, your job will be to assist in teaching conversational English to these new citizens and address the social challenges faced by both children and adults in school and at work. Even if you've never formally taught in a classroom, you can be a valuable resource for these diverse communities by helping them communicate effectively and realize their potential.

The starting point for this trip is Minneapolis-St. Paul. The drive to Austin and Worthington from the airport averages three to four hours. Worthington volunteers stay in cabins on a lake while lodging is dormitory style in Austin.

The **Montana Work Projects** serve the Blackfeet Nation community, which sits along the main route to **Glacier National Park** near the **Canadian border.** Isolated on a reservation in a sparsely populated area, the Blackfeet people face both cultural and building challenges. Volunteer work varies depending on the immediate needs of the reservation and might include painting or repairing playground equipment or landscaping family recreational areas. Team members can volunteer at the Eagle Shield Senior Center, Early Childhood Center, the Boys & Girls Club, Blackfeet Community College, and Blackfeet Care Center.

You'll fly into Great Falls, Montana, where from there the drive to the reservation takes about three hours. In Browning, Montana, you'll camp out in Early Childhood Center classrooms.

The **West Virginia Work Projects** focus on renovating homes and tutoring children in the coal-mining towns deep in the "hollers" of **Appalachia.** This rural region of southern West Virginia is designated as a federal empowerment zone because of high poverty levels and limited job opportunities. As a Global Volunteer, you will help repair and renovate former coal-company houses so that low-income families can live affordably. You'll work alongside and be a mentor to participants in the local Youth Build program and will help young adults study for their General Equivalency Diplomas (GEDs) and learn construction skills. You may also have the opportunity to assist with an after-school program at the Beards Fork Community Center.

The gateway airport for this trip is Charleston, West Virginia. Beards Fork is an hour drive from the airport, where you'll shack up dorm style with your volunteer group.

STOP *Bad Trip*

With the recent surge in "Voluntourism," a few hastily contrived volunteer trips have popped up that do more harm to the local communities than good—especially abroad. Global Volunteers co-founder Michele Gran suggests choosing volunteer programs firmly rooted in the long-term development of the host community and that commit sufficient time to contribute to development work. Also, she warns to resist the urge to give money or gifts directly to local people. Ethical organizations channel volunteer contributions through community leaders and local institutions.

Earthwatch Institute

So maybe you're not one for science. (I know I'm not.) But what if you paired up traveling to exotic locations with serving as a scientific assistant of sorts? **Earthwatch Institute (1-800-776-0188 or 978-461-0081,** www.earthwatch.org) is an international volunteer organization that supports science by offering the public unique opportunities to work alongside leading field researchers. Their mission is to engage people worldwide in scientific field research and education to promote the understanding and action necessary for a sustainable environment.

In 2008, Earthwatch sponsored some 130 research projects in more than 40 countries and 20 states in the United States. Since its founding in 1971, the organization has supported nearly 1,350 projects in 120 countries and 35 states. More than 90,000 volunteers have contributed an incredible 11 million hours to essential field work.

Earthwatch expeditions are not tours, not ecotourism, and not adventure travel. They are instead short-term volunteer opportunities that directly assist scientists in their field research. In some cases, you'll work in areas inaccessible to tourists—pristine regions that only researchers are allowed to enter.

The Volunteer Program

Earthwatch team members share the costs of research expeditions and cover food and lodging expenses with a prorated contribution. In 2007, expedition costs ranged from $199 to more than $4,000, averaging $2,500 for one- to twenty-day team durations. No prior skills are required (except scuba certification for diving projects). Research teams are usually small groups of between 4 to 15 people.

All projects are led by researchers and their field staff. These principle investigators are not tour leaders or Earthwatch representatives and have a rich, scientific background encompassing years of experience at leading field research teams. Each has his or her own leadership style. They all share an enthusiasm and passion for their subject that you will find infectious, and they value your work and your questions.

Most projects are ten to fourteen days long, but one-week, three-week, and weekend opportunities are available. The researchers you work with come from all over the globe. They apply to Earthwatch Institute for grants that support their work by simultaneously organizing volunteers to assist them in the field and funding the research. Topics span a wide range of scientific study including climate change, endangered species, history of civilizations, sustainable development, and the state of the oceans.

Most projects are suitable for every fitness level. To fully enjoy your expedition and contribute to the research, be sure to assess the physical requirements of your group. All volunteers are required to have a health exam and have an Earthwatch health form signed by a doctor within one year prior to the start date of the expedition. Projects are classified as very easy, easy, moderate, very active, and strenuous. Consult the Earthwatch website (www.earthwatch.org) for a complete description of each ranking.

Powder Room

You don't have to travel far to find a volunteer opportunity, so why not get your local girlfriends together for a practice run before a big trip? VolunteerMatch catalogs thousands of volunteer opportunities by location and type. Visit www.volunteermatch.org to find one near you.

Where You'll Go

Oh, the places you'll go! On the easy side, the **Mammoth Graveyard** site in **Hot Springs, South Dakota,** is a fifteen-day trip that explores an ancient geologic-hydrologic trap where mammoths met their fate. After a few initial days of learning excavation techniques, Earthwatch volunteers will help excavate both relatively sterile areas as well as areas pregnant with bone.

You'll welcome showers at a comfortable motel located close to the site, where you will share same-gender rooms with two double beds, television, and a full bath with laundry facilities a short walk away. Enjoy hearty, family-style meals prepared by a local cook. Team members and staff rotate for "kitchen police" duties. This trip runs $2,746 and is based in Rapid City, South Dakota.

As a volunteer on the moderately ranked **Marine Mammals of Monterey** trip, your days will be spent either onshore observing sea otters near **Elkhorn Slough,** the third-largest wetland along the California coast, or on board an outboard-powered vessel in Monterey Bay's blue waters looking for bottlenose dolphins, humpback whales, and other marine mammals.

Your volunteer team will stay in a comfortable beach house at the **Pajaro Dunes Colony** near **Watsonville** with shared rooms, two bathrooms, and decks. Volunteers and project staff members share cooking and light cleanup. The menu will be healthy and varied, with lots of salads, fruits, and casserole dishes. This ten-day trip is $2,746 and will rendezvous in Monterey, California.

Another moderately paced ten-day trip too scenic to resist is the **Alaskan Fur Seals** expedition. You will spend four-hour blocks each day in the blinds at the fur seal rookery observing seals and recording data on their numbers, genders, and ages. Getting to the rookery requires a half-mile hike over rocky tundra, during which you will carry a backpack containing spotting scopes, data sheets, and snacks. After your shift in the blinds, you'll upload your data and prepare your gear for the next day. Additional activities might include working with Island Sentinel, the local monitoring group, to observe sea lions or to assist with the reindeer census.

Teams will share rooms and one bathroom in a historic house with all modern conveniences in the village of **St. George.** A cook will prepare dinners of standard American fare, such as pizza and chicken, as well as some local favorites, such as halibut fish pie and reindeer stir-fry. Teams will make their own breakfasts, snacks, and lunches and pack thermoses of hot drinks for field work. The adventure starts in St. George Island, Pribilof Islands, Alaska, and is $3,246.

Probably the most challenging trip but an amazing way to observe wildlife is the **Wild Horses of the Outer Banks** excursion based in **New Bern, North Carolina.** With a hand-held GPS unit and a data sheet, you'll trek this nine-mile-long island in small teams searching for groups, or harems, of horses. You'll observe the harems and collect data on location, herd composition, behavior, and individual identity. You'll likely see five to seven harems a day, taking short breaks for lunch, swims, or naps. In the late afternoons, you'll have some time to enjoy the beach, read, or just relax before dinner. During the expedition, you'll head back to **Beaufort,** where you may have the opportunity to visit the **Foundation for Shackleford Horses.** You can also take advantage of your time on the mainland to stock up on any items you need, to eat out, or to visit attractions such as **Blackbeard's house** or the **North Carolina Aquarium.**

Shackleford Island is uninhabited, so be prepared to rough it. You'll have your own tent, but showers are scarce—and you'll have to learn leave-no-trace bathroom procedures. You will help prepare simple meals such as cereals, sandwiches, fruit, pasta, burritos, and snacks. While in Beaufort at the beginning, middle, and end of the expedition, you'll stay at a local inn—allowing you to enjoy the luxuries of showers and air conditioning. This fifteen-day trip is $2,346.

What to Bring

Once you register for an Earthwatch expedition, you will be sent an Expedition Briefing containing a full list of everything that you'll need to bring with you. Certain projects may require camping equipment; others specify clothing for certain types of weather conditions. But most require no more than your favorite pair of tough pants and an old work shirt.

Powder Room ———————————————————————

For further reading, check out *Volunteer Vacations: Short-Term Adventures That Will Benefit You and Others* (ninth edition) by Bill McMillon, Doug Cutchins, and Anne Geissinger (Chicago Review Press, 2006). The book profiles 150 organizations that run volunteer adventures in the United States and around the world.

More Volunteer Vacations

Spend one- to six-weeks on the **Appalachian Trail Conservancy** (**304-535-6331,** www.appalachiantrail.org) Trail Crew to rebuild and maintain the 2,175-mile **Appalachian National Scenic Trail,** a 250,000-acre greenway that extends from Maine to Georgia. Once you reach a base camp, most expenses are covered, and trips include shelter, food, transportation to and from work projects, tools, safety equipment, and group camping gear at no charge.

Help maintain national parks, forests, and wilderness areas across the United States through **Wilderness Volunteers** (**928-556-0038,** www. wildernessvolunteers.org). Trips last about a week and cost around $219. The 2008 itinerary included trips across the United States ranging from Caladesi Island State Park in Florida to Olympic National Park in Washington.

Check out the roughly 90 service trips the Sierra Club (**415-977-5500,** www.sierraclub.org) runs each year. Trips range from helping with research projects at whale calving grounds in Maui to assisting with archaeological site restoration in New Mexico to trail maintenance in the back country of Big Sur in California. Week-long trips run about $475 per trip and include all meals and camping arrangements.

Vision Quests and Mystical Experiences

In This Chapter

* Witch trials and tall tales in Salem, Massachusetts

* Ghost hunting in historic Savannah, Georgia

* Visit with the spirits in the psychic capital of Cassadaga, Florida

* Vortex walks and chakra realignment in Sedona, Arizona

* More mystical getaways

The funny thing about girlfriends is that we stick together, even when things get a little weird. In fact, the wackier the experience, the closer your bonds often become. Years ago, shortly after the passing of my mother, a girlfriend proposed that three of us pile in a car for a ten-hour road trip to The Middle of Nowhere, Texas, to catch a touring celebrity psychic. Next thing you know, we were crammed together in a hot high school auditorium as the medium tried to piece together random chit-chat from the spiritual world. When it was all over, hundreds of sad-faced souls piled out of the auditorium, heartbroken that their dead Uncle Harry didn't have the decency to even say hi. (I know—I was one of them.) It was an enlightening experience, all right. But enlightenment came in the form of a lesson I learned later that night: never get in a steamy hot Jacuzzi after downing a super-size margarita made with cheap tequila. You might pass out. I also learned that laughing your way through a heartbreaking situation with friends is a gift more valuable than a chirp from beyond. But secretly, I would do it again—especially with friends.

In this chapter, we'll explore destinations where the supernatural world and the material world collide. We'll take a walk on the spiritual side of life, look at witchcraft from a new perspective, follow in the footsteps of ghosts, take a dip into spiritualism, and get our chakras polished and pretty and put back into their proper places.

Witch Watch: Salem, Massachusetts

Most of us picture **Salem** as a place where cloaked, crooked-nosed hags scurry down the street hugging their books of magic while dark clouds hang over leafless trees that rustle eerily in the heavy sea breeze. Well, you might actually see that—especially in October when the Halloween festivities last all month long. But the fact is that Salem is a colorful, thriving town with a rich maritime past, quaint shopping and restaurants, lush gardens, a world-renowned art museum, and buildings that span four centuries of architectural grandeur.

> **Powder Room**
>
> Get psyched for your Salem trip with a movie night travel-planning party. Rent *The Crucible*, the 1996 adaptation of Arthur Miller's account of the trials, or the 1995 version of *The Scarlet Letter*, the story written by Salem native Nathaniel Hawthorne where Demi Moore plays an alluring Hester Prynne.

And it also happens to be the site of the infamous witchcraft trials of 1692, which for good or bad, are laced into the fabric of the town's heritage.

Witch Walk

The walkable town of Salem is spattered with historical sites and museums that attempt to shed light on its history and a few that make light of its notoriously shady past. Put on your walking shoes or catch the Salem Trolley, which makes stops at all the major sights—and let's go on a witch walk.

Start with a stop at the **Salem Witch Museum (978-744-1692,** www.salemwitchmuseum.com). Housed in a former Unitarian church built in the mid-1800s, the Salem Witch Museum is the first place to go to understand the witch trials from a historical perspective. You'll be ushered into a darkened auditorium where stages built into the walls come alive as the story unfolds. Don't let the menacing statue that guards the museum fool you. Although his stern countenance might imply otherwise, the statue is of beloved Salem founder Roger Conant, who died in 1679 before the witch trials took place.

Next, pay your respects to the victims of the witch hunt at the **Salem Witch Trials Memorial.** Adjacent to the Old Burying Point, Salem's oldest cemetery, the memorial was dedicated in 1992 to commemorate the 300th anniversary of this black mark in American history. The innocent pleas of the falsely accused are inscribed in stones that line a walkway leading to granite benches with the names of the 14 women and 6 men who died, along with the methods and dates of their executions.

Wrapped in mystery and lore, **The House of the Seven Gables (978-744-0991,** www.7gables.org) formally called the Turner-Ingersoll Mansion is the oldest seventeenth-century wooden mansion in New England and was said to have inspired author Nathaniel Hawthorne to write his legendary novel of the same name. The mansion and grounds are on the National Register of Historic Places and hide a secret staircase, which you'll see as part of the guided tour. Reacquaint yourself with Hawthorne's novel before you go, because you might run into ghosts of his characters along the way. General admission is $12 and includes a visit to the relocated site of Hawthorne's childhood home. Special events held throughout the year, such as the Spirits of the Gables, are $14.

Another rambling seventeenth-century home with a notorious past is **The Witch House** (more accurately, The Corwin House; **978-744-8815,** www.corwinhouse.org). The only surviving building in Salem with a direct tie to the 1692 trials, the home was where witch trial judge Jonathon Corwin lived for more than 40 years. Take the guided tour for insights into the court proceedings and period culture. Guided tours are $10; self-guided tours are $8. The house is the site of live, scary storytelling events in October.

The architecturally exquisite **Peabody Essex Museum (1-866-745-1876** or **978-745-9500,** www.pem.org) is much more than a witch stop and presents collections and exhibitions from New England and across the globe. Considered one of the nation's preeminent collectors of Asian art, the three-story museum and campus features parks, period gardens, and 24 historic properties. Stay on theme with a stop by the Phillips Library to see a rotating display of the original witchcraft trial documents. No ordinary library, Peabody's research and documentation division features a restored interior with grand white columns, gold leaf accents, and crystal chandeliers. Museum admission is $15; half-day use of the library is $10.

Finally, wind up your tour with a stop at any number of mystical witch shops and gift stores. **The Oracle Chamber (978-745-9988,** www. theoraclechamber.com) specializes in "magickal" herbs, gems, and candles and offers psychic readings by appointment. Need a new goddess wand? Stop by **The Broom Closet (978-741-3669,** www.broomcloset. com) for spell supplies, books, and gifts. Snag a voodoo doll, a broomstick, or a protective trinket at **Hex (978-666-0765,** www.salemhex. com), the Old World Witchery.

Where to Stay

Revel in the area's history with a stay at the centrally located **Salem Inn (1-800-446-2995** or **978-741-0680,** www.saleminnma.com), which comprises three outstanding period structures with 40 rooms and suites—each of which have been carefully restored and decorated.

The **Captain West House,** an imposing four-story brick structure, was built by a Salem sea captain in 1834 and has 23 rooms, suites, and family suites with kitchenettes on four floors. The nonsmoking **Curwen House** is a restored 1854 Italianate Revival wood frame structure with 11 richly decorated rooms and suites offering creature comforts such as double Jacuzzis and fireplaces. The Colonial-style **Peabody House** was built in 1874 and has four family suites and two honeymoon suites. Inn rates start at $129 and include a buffet continental breakfast.

Savvy Sister

Recognized as the "Official Witch of Salem" in the 1970s by then Governor Michael Dukakis for her community service, Salem resident Laurie Cabot formed the Witches League for Public Awareness to dispel myths in the media about witches. She has since written a number of books and runs a "Witch Shoppe" called **The Cat, The Crow, and The Crown** in the **Pickering Wharf shopping district.** For more information, visit www.lauriecabot.com.

The elegant **Hawthorne Hotel (1-800-729-7829 or 978-744-4080,** www.hawthornehotel.com) is also located in the heart of historic Salem. Built in 1925 when more than 1,000 Salem residents purchased stock to create a modern hotel, the Hawthorne is now designated as an Historic Hotel of America. The hotel still strives for a contemporary edge with amenities such as complimentary wireless Internet and a fitness studio. Each of the 93 rooms is tastefully furnished with eighteenth century–style reproductions that capture New England's charm and character. Rates start at $104, but check the website for a handful of excellent package deals.

The Hawthorne is also home to a separate bed and breakfast. Built in 1808, the **Suzannah Flint House** (www.suzannahflinthouse.com) offers three charming guest rooms and one suite with a large living and dining area. Each room features hardwood floors, oriental carpets, decorative fireplaces, TVs, private baths, and coffee makers. Rates start at $99 and include breakfast. Make reservations through the Hawthorne Hotel.

Even if you don't stay at the hotel, stop by the **Tavern** at the Hawthorne for an upscale pub atmosphere or by **Nathaniel's,** where the seasonal cuisine is freshly prepared and artfully presented in the elegant dining room. Nathaniel's serves lunch, dinner, and Sunday jazz brunch.

Powder Room

Halloween starts early in Salem, where the haunted festivities kick off with an evening parade the first weekend of October and continue all month long. Crash a costume party, attend a Halloween ball, or hit the psychic fair for a Tarot card reading. If you decide to visit in October, book your accommodations early. Find out more at www.hauntedhappenings.org.

For a free Salem Visitor's Guide, call **1-877-725-3662** or **978-744-3663,** or visit www.salem.org.

Ghost Whisperer: Savannah, Georgia

Shaded by majestic moss-draped oaks and dotted with mansions of historical significance and curb appeal of a grandiose nature, **Savannah** is the perfect city to enjoy the company of your friends. But beneath the city's polished Southern charm lies another side that has earned it a reputation as America's most haunted city. The more than 20 squares that shape the city's historical district have been the site of battles, devastating hurricanes, fires, plagues, and voodoo. Hauntingly beautiful cemeteries and houses with chilling pasts all set the scene for spooky tales and supernatural phenomena. Go to Savannah to enjoy the comforting cuisine, the lively atmosphere, and the abundant parks—but save time for a walk on its darker side.

Ghost Trails

Founded in 1733, Savannah is one of America's oldest cities—and sprinkled among its locals are quite a few residents of a spiritual nature (or so the ghost stories go). Here are a few of the many ways to get your britches scared off in America's most haunted city:

* **Take a ride in a hearse.** You heard me—a real, live, former working hearse from **Hearse Ghost Tours** takes you and your crew past cemeteries and mansions as the guide scoops on all the grisly tales that went on behind the closed doors of Savannah's most beautiful homes. This one has a novelty feel, and be forewarned of tipsy co-passengers—but the 90-minute, $15 tour is fun nonetheless. For more information, call **912-695-1578** or visit www.hearseghosttours.com.

* **Go for a trolley ride.** The haunted trolley tours are great for a cheap thrill. **Old Town Trolley** offers The Ghosts and Gravestones Night Tour, where you'll tour the Sorrel Weed House (featured on the SciFi Channel's *Ghost Hunters*). The tour is just under 90 minutes and costs $25. For more information, call **912-233-0083** or visit www.trolleytours.com. The locally owned **Oglethorpe Trolley Tours** also offers a ghostly 90-minute night ride through the streets of historic Savannah for $22. For more information, call **1-866-374-8687** or **912-233-8380,** or visit www.oglethorpetours.com.

* **Take a walk by candlelight.** Founded by James Caskey, author of *Haunted Savannah* (Bonaventture Books, 2006), **Cobblestone Tours** offers a dimly lit but enlightening look at the tragic and chilling tales that shaped the city's history. Two tours are available nightly for $10 (with online coupon). For more information, call **912-604-3007** or visit www.ghostsavannah.com.

Chick Wit

Just do it. Stop thinking about what might happen back at home without you, and start thinking about what will happen if you don't go. Girlfriend getaways are a must for your sanity—not to mention that the rejuvenation will make you a better wife, mom, sister, or girlfriend. Stop contemplating, and start planning.

—Stephanie, project manager

* **Have dinner and a movie (sort of).** The **Savannah Movie Tours'** *Midnight in the Garden of Good and Evil* package is a real trip for fans of the book and movie of the same name. The four-hour tour stops at pivotal locations from the story—including the **Mercer House,** where you'll see first-hand the site of the infamous shooting and get a peek inside of the fabulous life of its illustrious owner. You'll stop at Bonaventure Cemetery and learn about Minerva the voodoo priestess and visit the graves of people from the story. The engaging tour is $253 and includes a meal at the celebrated **Clary's Café,** a book and DVD of *Midnight in the Garden of Good and Evil*, a souvenir cap, and a CD of photos from your journey. The tours were created by filmmaker and Savannah native Ron Higgins (known as "Hollywood Ron"), who also hosts scary and not-so-scary movie tours that take you to famous movie sites (including the bench seen in *Forest Gump*). For more information, call **912-234-3440** or visit www.savannahmovietours.net.

* **Get up close and personal with the spirits.** Not for the scaredy pants, the two-hour **Sixth Sense Tours** were created by parapsychologist Shannon Scott and are among the most informative and creepy of the tours. The walking route and stories vary by guide, but you'll tour homes and locations with gory pasts and walk away with a new appreciation for why Savannah is considered the nation's most haunted city. Chances are, you'll also see a ghost. The nightly tours are $18; the longer and scarier midnight tours are $36.50. For more information, call **1-866-666-3323** or visit www.sixthsensesavannah.com.

Still haven't had the bejesus scared out of you? Take a few walking tours on your own. Open to the public from dawn to dusk, the **Bonaventure Cemetery (912-651-6843)** is both beautiful and eerie with its spectacular oaks, lush landscaping, and elaborate headstones and statues. The site of the *Ghost Hunters* show, the 1840s **Sorrel Weed House (912-236-8888,** www.sorrelweedhouse.com) offers informative historical tours through its landmark halls. History tours or evening candlelight tours start at $10. Even the **birthplace of Juliette Gordon Low (912-233-4501),** the founder of the Girl Scouts, is said to be haunted. Historical tours are $8, or check with local tour companies for a more haunted perspective.

Finally, stop for a bite (but keep an eye on your back). The **Olde Pink House** (912-232-4286) is hard to miss—it's pink—and serves well-received seafood and low-country favorites. Keep an eye out for the ghost of the wealthy Savannah resident who built the house, James Habersham, who reportedly has run into his share of unsuspecting diners. **The Pirates' House** (912-233-5757, www.thepirateshouse.com) is also a famous spot to refuel with pub fare and spirits served on the same grounds once frequented by pirates. Several of the local touring companies will take you to the restaurant's **Rum Cellar,** where tunnel passages lead to the river and unsuspecting sailors were reportedly shanghaied.

Where to Stay

Besides ghosts, the historic district is buzzing with beautiful antebellum inns and hotels. You might want to bunk up together if you choose to stay at the stately **17Hundred90 Inn and Restaurant.** Constructed in 1790 as the name implies, the inn is rumored to be haunted by the spirit of an early nineteenth-century ghost named Anna Powers. As the story goes, desperately in love with a married seaman, Anna threw herself to her death from the third-floor balcony just as the sails of his ship left her sight and headed out to sea. Rooms are charming and comfortable, and most have fireplaces. Rates start at $129 and include breakfast at the downstairs restaurant. Book Room 204 if you want the best chance of an Anna sighting. *912-236-7122. www.17hundred90.com.*

You can also experience the 17Hundred90 Inn with The Hauntings Dinner & Tour, which for $40 includes an evening walk through the neighborhood and dinner—all sprinkled with haunted details. For more information, call **912-234-3571** or visit www.hauntingstour.com.

Two convenient midrange choices with distinct personalities are the **Azalea Inn & Gardens** (1-800-582-3823 or 912-236-2707, www. azaleainn.com) and the **Dresser Palmer House** (1-800-671-0716 or 912-238-3294, www.dresserpalmerhouse.com). At the Azalea, splurge on the Cotton Exchange room with a massive king-size bed and jetted bathtub. Rates start at $170 and include breakfast. At the Dresser Palmer, stay in the white-bricked Wisteria Room, which boasts a fireplace and whirlpool tub. Rates start at $129 and include a Southern breakfast and evening wine and cheese.

Back on the ghost trail, the exquisitely restored **Kehoe House (1-800-820-1020,** www.kehoehouse.com) is an elegant B&B with an equal share of ghost tales and modern comforts. The 1892 Renaissance Revival mansion is rumored to be haunted by twins born to the Kehoe family who died while playing in the chimney (shiver). All but 2 of the 13 rooms have king beds with elegant furnishings, hardwood floors, and exceptional views. Complimentary amenities include coffee and tea service all day, a full breakfast, afternoon tea, evening wine and hors d'oeuvres, and nightly turndown service.

For more Savannah B&Bs and inns, visit www.bedandbreakfastsofsavannah. com or www.romanticinnsofsavannah.com. For more information about visiting Savannah (including special offers and travel guides), call **1-877-SAVANNAH** or **912-644-6401,** or visit www.savannahvisit.com.

Ⓧ *Savvy Sister*

When is the best time to hunt for ghosts? The hours between 9 P.M. and 6 A.M., according to Tom Ogden, author of *The Complete Idiot's Guide to Ghosts and Hauntings, Second Edition* (Alpha Books, 2004). Pick up the book for more ghostly tips, or visit the unofficial ghost hunters' website Hollow Hill at www.hollowhill. com.

Psychic Visions: Cassadaga, Florida

You won't find five-star restaurants and luxury hotels in the town of **Cassadaga, Florida.** Instead, you'll find a mystical destination where spiritual healing has drawn tourists and soul seekers for more than a century. About 30 minutes west of Daytona Beach and north of Orlando, Cassadaga is one of those quirky small towns you might pass right by if you didn't know to look for it. The community was established in 1894 when George P. Colby, a medium from New York, choose the site for a spiritualist camp. A hamlet of psychic mediums and healers now call it home, and it's a haven where people at a cross-roads or in need of closure with a departed loved one go for internal peace and spiritual guidance. Cassadaga's neighboring town of Lake Helen is a storybook slice of Old Florida style—and together, the area offers a peaceful yet enlightening getaway.

Road to Enlightenment

Although you might be drawn in by the beckoning signs that hang in windows or in yards, make your first stop the **Cassadaga Spiritualist Camp Bookstore & Information Center (386-228-2880,** www. cassadaga.org) in the center of town. Besides books, gifts, and tour information, you'll find a board that is updated daily with names of mediums certified with the Cassadaga Spiritualist Camp who are offering readings that day. The kind folks at the camp will encourage you to be open-minded and choose the name of a medium that you are drawn to for your reading.

The center also offers a calendar full of weekly events and tours. You can take a two-hour historic tour of Cassadaga and learn more about the architecture, homes, spirits, and the Colby Memorial Temple. The Nighttime Orb Photography tours take you to energy spots such as the Spirit Pond, believed to be a portal to the spiritual world. Tours start at $15, or you can make a donation to attend weekly healing workshops and talks.

You'll find about a dozen or so independent psychics just across the street from the camp. You can also visit the **Cassadaga Hotel & Psychic Center (386-228-2323,** www.cassadagahotel.net) for a "Spirit Burger" at the **Lost in Time Café & Sports Bar** or to schedule time with a reader at the Psychic Center.

For a diversion, take a step back in time to **Lake Helen,** where quaint historic homes line the streets and a lake by the same name sets a picturesque backdrop. Or explore the revived historic Main Street of nearby **DeLand** or head to **Blue Spring State Park** in **Orange City,** where you'll see manatees during the cooler months and enjoy lake recreation in the warmer months. Read more about these towns at www. visitflorida.com.

Where to Stay

The charming **Ann Stevens House** in Lake Helen is a short walk from the camp and offers a true immersion in Old Florida style and hospitality. Built in 1895 by Ann C. Stevens, a prominent spiritualist, the inn is on the National Register of Historic Places. Each of the 10 rooms offers a private bath, TV, phone, free wireless Internet service, and a dose of individual personality. The Laredo Room is a popular choice for its log cabin feel and its horse trough bathtub. The Cross Creek room is Old Florida at its best with a sunny color scheme, wicker accents, hardwood floors, and a sleepy veranda. Both have king beds and a day bed for bunking up. Besides a Girlfriend Getaway Package customized to your preferences, the inn offers a few other brow-raising options such as the Séance Package and the Past Life Regression Experience. The gracious innkeepers are quick to offer guidance on choosing a reader or exploring the area. Rates start at $130 and include a full country breakfast. *1-800-220-0310 or 386-228-0310. www. annstevenshouse.com.*

Cabin on the Lake is another charming Lake Helen retreat. The two-story log home offers three cozy rooms with TV, wireless Internet, and refrigerators. Inn pluses include a wooden deck that overlooks a manicured lawn and lake, a full English breakfast served daily, and weekend bistro lunches by request. The inn will arrange for an evening of private psychic readings onsite. *386-951-2684. www.cabinonthelake.com.*

Shake Up Your Chakras: Sedona, Arizona

Sedona is known worldwide as a place of natural beauty marked by craggy landscapes layered in hues of reds and speckled with evergreens and cacti. But like Savannah, Sedona has another side. Whether it's because of the vortexes said to inhabit the rock formations or the inspirational setting itself calling out like a beacon, Sedona has attracted a community of New Age healers, psychics, and intuitives. It's this metaphysical soup of awe-inspiring scenery and positive good vibes that has secured Sedona's place in ShermansTravel's "Top 10 Girl Getaways" in the world for spiritual renewal (read more at www.shermanstravel.com).

Soul Searching

Beyond Sedona's art galleries, Pink Jeep Tours, and hiking trails galore is a path toward a greater connection between mind and spirit. Here are a few ways to get a tune up under your spiritual hood.

* **First stop: The Center for the New Age.** At the crux of the two major roads that pass through Sedona sits a modest book and gift store with gemstone jewelry, crystals, New Age music, and a global collection of ethereal trinkets and statues. Upstairs, the center offers readings by appointment. You can choose a reader from a wall of brochures or chat with the store keeper about who might be available. Like Cassadaga, let your intuition guide you. I've been to the center many times myself and have some-times walked out after a few minutes. Other times, a reader's face popped out at me and I was whisked off to a private session. The center is also the place to get information about vortex tours, aura photography, chakra balancing, and energy healing. Energy clinics, psychic circles, and workshops are offered weekly at the center. Call or check the website before you go for a list of spe-cial events, and if you plan to visit on a weekend, book a reading before you go. *928-282-2085. www.sedonanewagecenter.com.*

* **Visit a vortex.** Sedona is believed to have at least seven major vortex centers where a powerful swirling energy escapes to the surface of the rock. You can purchase a vortex map or book at the Center for the New Age and plan a hike to one yourself (or take a guided tour). For a more spiritual view of the energy centers, popular Sedona psychic Angel Lightfeather offers an off-the-map Sacred Soul Journey Vortex Tour (2 hours for $360 per person). *928-451-1222. www.angelsangelsangels.org.*

* **Have your aura captured on film.** Aura photography might sound a little hokey, but it's the interpretive reading of your photo that might give you insights into your path. Now that I'm out of the closet as a New Age dabbler, I'll admit that I get my aura photo taken every couple years and find it fascinating to watch as the colors shift and drift over time. Aura photography is offered at several places in town. The Mystical Bazaar offers aura photos as well as psychic readings, mystical vortex tours, shamanic journeys,

and aura cleansing ceremonies. *928-204-5615*. *www.mysticalbazaar. com*.

* **Go deep with an intuitive group journey.** The New Age centers and bookstores will introduce you to a number of spiritual journeys. Follow one that speaks to the group, or check out the InnerVision 12 Intuitive Journeys. A half-day Intuitive Journey for three or four people is $275 each. *1-888-641-1212 or 928-203-0793*. *www. innervision12.com*.

(STOP) Bad Trip

If you're truly in search of some spiritual spark or morsels of enlightenment, invite Debbie the Doubter on your *next* girlfriend getaway—but not this one. While completely understandable in some ways (come on, can a camera *really* capture your aura on film?), a constant barrage of scoffing and skepticism can dampen the spirit of an otherwise uplifting experience.

Where to Stay

Central to Sedona's bustling uptown area and on the banks of Oak Creek, the **Four-Diamond Amara Resort & Spa** is an inviting boutique resort wrapped in a contemporary, thoughtful vibe. The 100 guest rooms surround visitors in plush practicality with pillow-top mattresses, luxury linens, spa robes, and WiFi workstations. Outdoors, a heated saltwater pool, hot tub, and fire pit blend with the spiritual scenery. The artful restaurant and the boutique spa offer the final blissful touches. Rates start at $139, but check the website for several enticing packages. Girls Get Grounded is a 2-night package that includes a $20 credit per person each day for the **Gallery on Oak Creek** restaurant, a personal crystal or vortex guide book, complimentary wine and cheese, and your choice of a spa service or psychic reading. *1-866-455-6610 or 928-282-4828*. *www.amararesort.com*.

Located in Sedona's historic arts district, **El Portal** offers a heavenly slice of only the best aspects of this rustic Southwest design style. The Grand Canyon suite, for example, is sheltered by a vaulted log beam and rafter ceiling that joins a full-length river rock fireplace. The flagstone floor, oak furnishings, and stained glass accents punctuate the rustic ambiance. The room has a king-size bed, a twin-size daybed, a private patio, a luxurious bathroom with a soaking tub and double sinks, and plenty of extra seating. The other rooms are just as spectacular, and each has a subtle design theme of its own. All include TVs and free Internet service. An acclaimed restaurant is onsite, and a concierge is available to arrange tours and trips. Rates start at $179 off season (January, February, June, September, and December) and include breakfast and afternoon hors d'oeuvres and drinks. Check the website for seasonal specials, including package deals just for women. *1-800-313-0017 or 928-203-9405. www.elportalsedona.com.*

For a more intimate creekside setting, the **Briar Patch Inn** is a quaint bed and breakfast nestled along the banks of Oak Creek, surrounded by lush gardens and red rock mountain views. The 18 spacious cottages are scattered throughout the nine-acre property and offer a cozy southwestern décor with Native American arts and crafts. All cottages have a private entrance and patios and a full kitchen or kitchenette, and all but two have wood-burning fireplaces or stoves. With one king and two twin beds, the Creekside cottage is ideal for a group of four and has the plus of being so close to the creek that it actually flows beneath the patio. Cottages start at $205. *1-888-809-3030 or 928-282-2342. www. briarpatchinn.com.*

For more information on traveling to Sedona or to request the **Experience Sedona Guide,** call **1-800-288-7336** or **928-282-7722,** or visit www.visitsedona.com.

More Mystical Destinations

The mantra at **The Ashram** (818-222-6900, www.theashram.com), located outside **Los Angeles,** is, "A commitment of a week ... a change of a lifetime." And by all accounts, the people who go swear by the spiritual enlightenment that comes from near starvation and numbing physical workouts that start at the crack of dawn. The always smiling and encouraging staff keeps you going while New Age touches such as chakra balancing help to mentally purge stress. A week at The Ashram will set you back $4,000, but the rate is all-inclusive.

Crazy lady or genius? You be the judge with a visit to the **Winchester Mystery House** (408-247-2101, www.winchestermysteryhouse.com) in

San Jose, California. A construction project that started in 1884 and lasted 38 years, the Victorian mansion was the work of Winchester Rifle heiress Sarah L. Winchester. Mystery swirls around her true intent on building staircases that lead nowhere and using the number 13 as a prevailing design theme, but whatever it was, the sprawling mansion is as creepy as it gets. Tours are held daily, and many nearby hotels—such as the **Hotel DeAnza** and the **Dolce Hayes Mansion**—offer getaway packages that include a trip to the mansion. Special Flashlight Tours are given every Friday the 13th and around Halloween.

An hour north of **Buffalo, New York,** the village of **Lily Dale (716-595-8721,** www.lilydaleassembly.com) is the spiritual sister community of Cassadaga, Florida, and is also a hub for healers and psychics. The town is open to tourists during the summer for a $10 gate fee, or you can schedule a reading almost any day of the week. Stay on the grounds of the nearby **Chautauqua Institution** or in Lily Dale at the **Maplewood Hotel,** which is rumored to be haunted.

Festivals and Special Events

In This Chapter

* Experience the sounds, tastes, and heritage of Louisiana
* Delight in a euphonic feast of classical and world music in Colorado
* Celebrate the onion's famous cousin in California
* Kick up your spurs at a rodeo in New Mexico
* More fairs and festivals

Here's what I know about festivals, fairs, concerts, and special community events: you'll eat really bad food, you'll blow way too much cash, and you'll have a blast. The build-up and the planning that goes into special events is often what brings a community together and gives shape to its traditions. As an "outsider," these events give you a front-row seat to witness the sights, sounds, tastes, and culture of a geographical area.

In this chapter, we'll take off on getaways built around an event that happens just once a year. So ... no excuses! You'll have plenty of time to start planning now.

Culture: New Orleans Jazz & Heritage Festival

The **New Orleans Jazz & Heritage Festival (504-410-4100,** www. nojazzfest.com) is a cultural celebration that unites thousands of musicians, chefs, artists, and craftspeople with locals and visitors from across the globe. Since 1970, when the headliners were Mahalia Jackson, Duke Ellington, and Fats Domino (among many other musical greats), the concept hasn't strayed much from its original concept when it was envisioned as a large daytime fair with multiple stages featuring a wide variety of indigenous music styles, food booths of Louisiana cuisine, and arts and crafts booths along with an evening concert series.

Now known by most simply as Jazz Fest, the seven-day shindig kicks off the last weekend of April at the **Fair Grounds Race Course** just minutes from the historic **French Quarter.** Eleven stages of simultaneous music are complemented by an unparalleled **Food Fair** offering a dizzying array of authentic Louisiana cuisine and a **Heritage Fair** of one-of-a-kind crafts. The New Orleans Jazz & Heritage Festival and Foundation is the nonprofit organization that uses the proceeds to fund year-round community development activities in the areas of education, economic development, and cultural programming.

The music showcases Louisiana's diverse heritage, and not only will you hear the best in contemporary and traditional jazz but also blues, R&B, gospel, Cajun, Zydeco, Afro-Caribbean, folk, Latin, rock, rap, country, bluegrass, and everything in between. The 2008 season welcomed an amazing roster of performers: the Neville Brothers, Stevie Wonder, Billy Joel, Jimmy Buffett, Tim McGraw, Santana, Frankie Beverly, Sheryl Crow, Widespread Panic, Dr. John, Al Green, Diana Krall, Keyshia Cole, Robert Plant, and Alison Krauss.

Tickets for the past season were $50 for the first weekend, $40 for a midweek pass, and $50 for the final weekend. VIP tickets and experiences are available.

Visit the website for a list of nearby hotels that offer special Jazz Fest rates. For more travel information, contact the **New Orleans Metropolitan Convention & Visitors Bureau** at **1-800-672-6124** or **504-566-5003,** or visit www.neworleanscvb.com.

Savvy Sister

Events of this size wouldn't be possible without the help of a crew of volunteers. Consider rallying the girls to volunteer at an event. You'll work your butts off, but you'll get free admission and the chance to interact with folks who are out to have a good time. Inquire early about volunteering to get the cushiest positions.

Classical and World Music: Colorado Music Festival

For music of a more classical nature, the **Colorado Music Festival** (**303-449-1397,** www.coloradomusicfest.org) in **Boulder, Colorado,** has been thrilling audiences since 1976. The festival presents a summer season of classical music concerts at the historic Chautauqua Auditorium in Boulder. Emerging talent from Europe, Asia, South America, and the United States joins CMF musicians in performances that inspire and engage concert-goers of all ages. Under the skilled baton of Music Director Michael Christie, the CMF thrills audiences of nearly 20,000 each season with programming that embraces the most beloved classical music repertoire while integrating world music and the works of exciting twentieth-century composers. The six-week series kicks off late June and wraps up early August.

The 2008 season kicked off with a performance of Barber's *Violin Concerto* with protégé Shannon Lee, a Canadian-born violinist who made her debut with the Dallas Symphony Orchestra at age 12. The season featured an appearance by the internationally acclaimed St.

Petersburg String Quartet; young pianist Adam Golka for a performance of Brahms' *Piano Concerto No. 1*; a world music series of the world's top ukulele players; Irish traditional music; and a Brazilian guitar quartet. The season closed with a performance by Grammy-winning mezzo-soprano Kelley O'Connor.

Sunday evenings feature the CMF Chamber Orchestra, Tuesdays bring chamber music and world music ensembles, and Thursday and Friday evenings showcase the full CMF Festival Orchestra. The Colorado Music Festival Chamber Orchestra also performs in Estes Park on select Monday evenings throughout the summer. A free Patriotism & Pops concert is held outdoors at the Performance Park Pavilion to celebrate the Fourth of July.

Ticket prices range from $12 to $45. All concerts begin at 7:30 P.M., and performances are at **Boulder's Chautauqua Auditorium.** A National Historic Landmark built in 1898, the all-wood structure is known as one of the best acoustical venues in Colorado.

Stay on the historic grounds at **Chautauqua (303-442-3282,** www.chautauqua.com) in one of the lodge rooms or cottages. Ranging from efficiencies to three-bedroom, two-bathroom units, cottages start at $99 and lodge rooms start at $71. Amenities vary greatly depending on which you choose, but the bonus of staying on property is the affordable dining hall for three meals per day and access to the tennis courts, parks, and hiking trails.

For more accommodation options and information about things to do in Boulder, contact the **Boulder Convention & Visitors Bureau** at **1-800-444-0447** or **303-442-2911,** or visit www.bouldercoloradousa.com.

Powder Room

If you're a fan of Shakespeare, plan your visit to coincide with the **Colorado Shakespeare Festival,** which runs mid-June through mid-August at the **Mary Rippon Outdoor Theatre.** For more information, call **303-492-0554** or visit www.coloradoshakes.org.

Produce: Garlic Festival

In the small farming and ranching community of **Gilroy, California,** garlic is king. And for the last 30 years, during the last full weekend of July, the town of Gilroy has sent up a pungent smoke signal signifying its place as the Garlic Capital of the World with its annual **Garlic Festival (408-842-1625,** www.gilroygarlicfestival.com).

The heart of the Gilroy Garlic Festival is Gourmet Alley, a gigantic outdoor kitchen where the flamboyant "Pyro Chefs" fire up garlic-laced calamari and scampi in huge iron skillets over blazing fire pits. An army of dedicated volunteers prepares other Alley favorites, such as penne con pesto, stuffed mushrooms, pepper steak sandwiches, garlic sausage sandwiches, Pacific Rim garlic chicken stir-fry, and—of course—garlic bread.

Besides the food, the festival boasts three stages where jazz, rock 'n' roll, country, blues, reggae, and swing keep things rocking while strolling musicians keep garlic revelers engaged in the action. The festival also features some 100 artists and craftspeople from across the country who peddle handcrafted treasures such as hats, pottery, stained glass, original jewelry, paintings, and sculptures.

Think you've got the best garlic recipe? The Great Garlic Cook-Off is part of the festivities—so if you plan to go, submit your recipe early so you can be in the running with the hundreds of other amateur chefs who take part. Starting in December, the Gilroy Garlic Festival staff puts out a call across the United States and Canada for the most creative and delicious garlic recipes. Eight finalists are chosen by a professional food consultant and are invited to prepare their creations at the festival. Celebrity judges pick their favorites, and the winner is appropriately honored with a crown of garlic and goes home $1,000 richer. Cash prizes are awarded to all finalists. Hey—even if you don't win, you'll pick up tips from other garlic aficionados and a few new recipe ideas to perfect for future cook-offs. Past winners have included Chai-Steeped Chicken Breasts with Oriental Aioli, Basil and Garlic-Stuffed Sea Scallops Wrapped in Prosciutto, and Garlic Seafood Soup. Garlicky desserts are welcome, too.

General admission to the garlic affair is $12 daily.

Stay at the quaint **Gilroy Fitzgerald House Bed & Breakfast.** Originally constructed in 1885, the Queen Anne–style home offers two rooms and a suite all wrapped in Victorian San Francisco charm. Single rooms start at $135, and the suite—which sleeps up to 3—starts at $175 and includes a freshly prepared breakfast. *1-888-847-6421* or *408-847-6421*. *www.gilroyfitzgeraldhouse.com.*

For more nearby lodging (and garlic recipes, of course!), contact the **Gilroy Visitors Bureau** at **408-842-6436** or visit www.gilroyvisitor.org.

Powder Room

Garlic heads who can't book it to the West Coast can get their taste of the fun at the **Hudson Valley Garlic Festival** in **Saugerties, New York,** about fifteen minutes outside the scenic **Catskill Mountains.** A tradition in the area for more than 20 years, the East Coast festival is held the last full weekend of September. Stay at a local bed and breakfast in Saugerties to bask in your garlic getaway. Get the details by calling **845-246-3090** or by visiting www. hvgf.org.

Ride 'Em, Cowboy: Rodeo! de Santa Fe

This one's for my dear girlfriend Kari, who has a secret penchant for rodeos. The cat's out of the bag, Kari, because you're not the only one who gets a thrill from watching a professional bull rider strut his or her stuff. A **Santa Fe, New Mexico,** tradition since 1949, the **Rodeo! de Santa Fe (505-471-4300,** www.rodeodesantafe.org) is an annual event now ranked among the top 100 rodeos in the nation. The four-day shindig is held in late June, usually the last full weekend of the month. Dust off that 10-gallon hat and cowboy boots for a weekend of cowgirl fun set against the beauty of the Santa Fe backdrop.

The festivities kick off a few weeks before the rodeo rolls into town with a crowning of the Rodeo Royalty court, including the queens and princesses. This is no beauty contest. The girls are chosen based mainly on their riding skills, and besides a crown and a sash, the queen also gets a cash scholarship award. A parade the weekend before gets the show on the road, and then the rodeo starts midweek and runs through Saturday.

Competitive events include individual and team roping, bull riding, steer wrestling, barrel racing, and saddle and bareback bronco riding. Rodeo clowns are ever present, and the event features a carnival midway, food, and souvenirs.

Rodeo! de Santa Fe takes place at the city rodeo grounds, just a short drive from downtown Santa Fe. General admission is $10, and parking is $5.

Stay at the enchanting **Inn of the Five Graces (505-992-0957,** www. fivegraces.com), which offers 24 lavishly decorated and supremely comfortable suites with feather beds, wood-burning fireplaces, lavish baths, living areas, kitchenettes, and a delightful décor that harmoniously blends Old West with Asian styles. Rooms start at $300 and include a full breakfast, historical walking tours, and an arrival amenity. Information on seasonal packages is available on the website.

For dining, activities, and more lodging options or to request a free visitor's guide, contact the **Santa Fe Convention and Visitors Bureau** at **1-800-777-2489** or **505-955-6200,** or visit www.santafe.org.

Powder Room

Not a bull riding fan? Santa Fe kicks up the dust with events throughout the year. Another one of acclaim and distinction is the ArtFeast (505-603-4643, www.artfeast.com) in late February. An annual event for more than a decade, the weekend is dedicated to showcasing the best artists, chefs, wine, fashion, and homes that the city has to offer. Funds raised support art programs for Santa Fe's youngsters. Tickets for the various events start at $50.

Other Festival and Event Destinations

With more fairs and festivals than you can count, Wisconsin loves a party. In May, **Jazz on the Vine** mixes live contemporary jazz with wine tasting at **The Osthoff Resort** in **Elkhart Lake.** The village of **Little Chute** hails in summer with the **Great Wisconsin Cheese Festival** in early June. The three-day event features cheese-carving demos, curd-eating contests, music, food, and activities galore. **Oshkosh** kicks it up mid-summer with the famed **Country USA music festival—** five days of country music's hottest singers plus food, shopping, and activities. **Oktoberfest** kicks off in **Chippewa Falls** the third week-end in September with Bavarian dancing, sauerkraut eating contests, beer and brat slinging, and German heritage activities. For more on these events, nearby lodging, and free travel maps and guides, call the **Wisconsin Department of Tourism** at **1-800-432-8747** or **608-266-2161,** or visit www.travelwisconsin.com.

Savvy Sister

Festivals, fairs, and events bring together communities on a large scale. But when's the last time you took a day off for a celebration on a smaller scale with your girls? Use an excuse like the Super Bowl, the Kentucky Derby, or a two-for-one sale on strawberries at the market to throw a celebration of your own. Any day is a good day for a party, right?

Baltimore, Maryland, boasts America's largest municipally produced arts festival that remains free and open to the public. Held in mid-July, **Artscape (1-877-BALTIMORE,** www.artscape.org) is a three-day celebration of the arts featuring continuous musical performances by local, regional, and national talent on four outdoor stages, indoor and outdoor visual arts exhibitions, film, theater, the Artists' Market with crafts and works of art for sale, opera, dance, fashion, literary arts activities, and more.

UFO Fest (www.ufofest.com/ufofest07/) in **McMinnville, Oregon,** started nearly 10 years ago as a way to honor the famous 1950 Trent sighting in which two local citizens witnessed and photographed a UFO (said to be among the most credible images of UFOs to date). The festivities include a costume parade, entertainment, food (alien ears, anyone?), and expert panels and guest speakers who address alien abductions and other close encounters. The festival is held in mid-May and takes place along the city's old main street in and around the funky and historical **McMenamins Hotel Oregon (1-888-472-8427** or **503-472-8427,** www.mcmenamins.com).

For people watching, you can't beat the annual **How Berkeley Can You Be? Parade and Festival (510-644-2204 ext. 12,** www.howberkeleycanyoube.com) in **Berkeley, California.** The one-day event kicks off with a parade where locals strut their "Berkeley-ness," followed by a festival with music, dancing, and food. Retreat from the zaniness with a stay at the **Claremont Resort & Spa (1-800-551-7266** or **510-843-3000,** www.claremontresort.com), an elegant and historical hotel nestled in **Berkeley Hills.** The Claremont is located on 22 acres of landscaped gardens and features an award-winning spa, aquatic facilities, tennis club, and exceptional California cuisine at the four-diamond **Jordan's** restaurant. The resort offers several heavenly packages. The Spa Renewal Getaway Package includes accommodations, two spa treatments, and unlimited use of the fitness center and spa facilities for $450 per night (double occupancy). How relaxed can you be?

Rock Band Camp and Other Fantasies

In This Chapter

* ✱ Rockin' out at Ladies Rock Camp
* ✱ Hang gliding over the dunes of the Carolina coastline
* ✱ Cruising to the Caribbean
* ✱ More fantastic getaways

I was destined to be a rock star. If only I could carry a tune. And if I could play a musical instrument. Oh, and if I could get up in front of a crowd of people without hyperventilating. But it's never too late, right? If you've always fantasized about playing in a rock 'n' roll band, strapping on wings and soaring above the clouds, or cruising the high seas without a care in the world, this is the chapter for you. These getaways raise the bar on fun and come fully padded with plenty of time to relax and reconnect.

Rock Star: Ladies Rock Camp

What started as an annual fundraiser to support the Rock 'n' Roll Camp for Girls, **Ladies Rock Camp (503-445-4991,** www. girlsrockcamp.org) in Portland, Oregon, has become so popular that it's now a regular event held two or three times per year. Based in **Portland, Oregon,** Rock 'n' Roll Camp for Girls is a nonprofit organization with a mission of mentoring girls and building their self-esteem through music creation and performance. Ladies Rock Camp allows you to support their mission by letting go of inhibitions and rocking out. It's good fun for a good cause. Everybody wins!

⚥ Savvy Sister

If you've always wanted your own guitar, Daisy Rock not only makes the girliest-looking guitars on the market (think Cosmic Pink and Vintage Ivory Pearl), but it designs the instruments in a way that works for chicks of all ages. The slim neck profile fits smaller hands, and the body of the guitar is contoured in a way that fits our curves. Rock on. More at www.daisyrock.com.

The weekend day camp is open to women 19 and older at all levels of musical experience. Female instructors with experience song writing, playing, recording, and touring lead the group. Besides forming your weekend band and practicing your instruments, you'll prepare for a live show on your last evening of Rock Camp. You'll also get a taste of the workshops that the girls experience during their camp, such as self-defense, song writing, and screen printing.

The weekend kicks off on Friday with a welcome lunch and then moves right on to instrument instruction, band practice, and workshops until you stop for dinner and end the day with a movie screening. Saturday is spent practicing for the next day's big show with breaks for lunch with a local rock band and time to create and print your band merchandise. Saturday wraps with a party—give karaoke a shot, practice your songs, or just hang out. Sunday is the big day as you prepare for your evening performance at a local club. (No stage fright allowed.) Although the club seats up to 300 people, the audience is mostly family and friends, and the rest understand that the show is a charity event—not a Rolling Stones concert. The show wraps up with an after-party celebration.

Tuition for the Ladies Rock Camp weekend is $350 and includes beginner to advanced lessons on your instrument of choice—drums, bass, keyboards, vocals, or guitar—as well as weekend use of Rock Camp instruments. The fee also includes meals and all activities.

Volunteers are a necessary part of the success of the camp, so even if you have no musical inclination at all, be sure to inquire about volunteering so you don't miss out on the fun.

Once you book your spot, you'll get information about group rates at local hotels. Lodging rates vary, but ask about the **Silver Cloud Inn** (**1-800-205-6939,** www.silvercloud.com/08home.htm), which is the cushiest spot to stay closest to the venue. Also ask about "Teri's famous list" or download it from the website for an insider's guide to clubs, shops, restaurants, and things to do. Rides to and from the airport are usually available on request. Meals are catered and are generally well-rounded and healthy. Notify the staff of dietary restrictions or needs when you sign up.

Powder Room

New York City has its own version of Ladies Rock Camp. **Willie Mae Rock Camp for Girls** is a nonprofit summer day camp also supported through annual adult camps. Find out more by calling **212-777-1323** or by visiting www.williemaerockcamp.org. For a truly surreal experience, **Rock 'n' Roll Fantasy Camp** allows participants to learn from celebrity musicians with one- or five-day packages at locations throughout the United States. Get details at **1-888-762-2263** or by visiting www.rockcamp.com.

Fly Girl: Hang Gliding

Named one of the "Best Outfitters on Earth" by National Geographic Adventure in 2007, **Kitty Hawk Kites (1-800-334-4777,** www. kittyhawk.com) was founded by a pioneer in hang gliding in 1974. Since then, it has become the premiere place to learn hang gliding. Not only are the Kitty Hawk Kites instructors among the best in the biz, but the place where you'll learn is also just a couple miles from the very spot where the Wright Brothers caught the wind in their historic flight a century ago. Dune hang gliding lessons are conducted at the training school in **Jockey's Ridge State Park,** home to the largest natural living sand dune on the East Coast. Located in **Nags Head, North Carolina,** the soft sands and gentle ocean breezes of Jockey's Ridge provide the perfect site for learning to hang glide.

The beginner dune hang gliding lesson is about three hours and includes a training film, ground school, log booklet, and all the equipment for your hang gliding lesson. Classes are no more than five students per instructor. Your first hour will be spent in basic ground school, after which you'll gear up and head to the dunes to prepare for takeoff. Once you make the scenic walk to the top of the dunes, you'll make your first solo flight. An instructor will run alongside you until the wind takes hold of the glider—and off you'll go for anywhere from 30 to 100 yards at 5 to 15 feet above the sand. You'll make a comfortable landing either on your feet or on the wheels of the glider on the soft sands of Jockey's Ridge. The instructor will carry the glider, where you'll take four more flights. Beginner dune lessons are $89.

Once you've taken the beginner course, you can move on to an advanced lesson where you spend the three hours flying and refining your skills. Advanced lessons are $79. Other options include a 2,000-foot tandem lesson, which is a 10- to 15-minute high-flying ride across the coastline ($129), or an airport mile-high tow, a tandem ride that climbs to more than 5,000 feet for 30 minutes ($249).

Kitty Hawk also offers parasailing, kiteboarding (kind of like wind surfing but with a kite above you to keep you afloat), air tours, and water sport lessons.

Go buy a kite! Once you've experienced the thrill of floating through the air, try your hand at kite flying. Kitty Hawk Kites just happens to be the largest retailer of kites in the eastern United States and can fit you with a snazzy single or dual-line kite that reminds you of your hang gliding experience long after the wind dies down.

Stay in one of the **Wilbur & Orville Wright Court cottages (252-441-7331,** www.obxlodging.com) in **Kill Devil Hills,** between Kitty Hawk and Nags Head and less than a mile away from the Wright Brothers Memorial. The beach-side, white-washed cottages have two to six bedrooms with kitchens, TVs, and homey amenities. Some are oceanfront, and all have access to the Days Inn pool next door. Book early; these gems go fast in the summer. Weekly rates start at $595 during off season, which starts late September and runs through late May. Rates double during the peak summer months.

For more Outer Banks lodging and activities information or to request a free travel guide, call **1-877-629-4386** or **252-473-2138,** or visit www.outerbanks.org.

Bad Trip

According to the folks at Jockey's Ridge State Park, the sand on the dunes can get uncomfortably hot during the summer months and can top out at 30 degrees warmer than the air temperature. So if it's 95 degrees, the sand will be 125 degrees. Ouch! Find more dune tips, cautions, and park information at www.jockeysridgestatepark.com.

Caribbean Queen: Cruise

Why go on a cruise? For starters, what better way to wave bon voyage to stress, roles, and responsibilities for a week and just hang with the girls? Cruise ships come in every shape and form and offer trips to fit most budgets. Here are some options.

Snagging the number one slot for the third consecutive year in the large-ship category as voted by *Condé Nast Traveler* readers in 2008,

Celebrity Cruises (1-800-437-3111 or **305-539-6000,** www.celebrity. com) has been a top pick among persnickety cruisers for its consistent delivery of a comfortably sophisticated, upscale cruise experience with impeccable service and exceptional dining. The only downside might be choosing among the extensive recreational and entertainment options offered aboard their fleet. Of the Caribbean-bound ships, *Century* recently unveiled upgraded Concierge Class staterooms that feature fresh-cut flowers, a menu of luxurious pillows (choose from Conformance, body, goose down, or Isotonic pillows), plush duvets, pillow-top mattresses, upgraded bathroom amenities such as double-thick bathrobes, personalized stationery, and VIP dining preferences and special event invitations. The ship houses a pool, four restaurants, five lounges, shops, and a spa for pampering at sea. Celebrity also sails to the Panama Canal, Alaska, Canada/New England, the Galapagos Islands, Hawaii, and other international ports.

Norwegian Cruise Line (1-800-327-7030 or **305-436-4000,** www. ncl.com) boasts the youngest fleet in the industry and provides guests with flexible dining and activities with its signature **Freestyle Cruising** experience. In June 2008, the cruise line also became the first to offer cosmetic medical spa treatments, including injections and facial fillers at sea. Of the ships that cruise to the Caribbean, *Norwegian Pearl* features 10 restaurants, 13 bars and lounges, 2 swimming pools, a casino, a bowling alley, and a rock-climbing wall. *Norwegian Pearl* offers five- and nine-day sailings to the Western and Southern Caribbean and seven-day Alaska and nineteen-day Panama Canal itineraries. Norwegian also sails to the Panama Canal, Alaska, the Mexican Riviera, Bermuda, Hawaii, Canada/New England, and other international ports.

> *Powder Room*
>
> Get the news before you cruise! Find cruise ship news, deals, and reviews on Cruise Critic at www.cruisecritic.com. Get more bargains at www. cruise.com, www.cruisecheap. com, or www.cruisedeals.com.

Among the ultra-luxury liners, **Cunard Line (1-800-728-6273,** www. cunard.com) has long been synonymous with flawless service and ships of stately grandeur. Of them, *Queen Mary 2* has racked up accolades for extraordinary touches such as the largest ballroom at sea, a library of more than 8,000 books, the only planetarium at sea, superb gourmet dining prepared by world-class chefs, and **Canyon Ranch SpaClub**—a 20,000-square-foot full-service spa and health club. The spa is complete with a gym, weight room, co-ed Aqua Therapy pool, whirlpool, herbal sauna, Finnish sauna, reflexology basins, aromatic steam room, and relaxation lounge. Cunard ships sail to the Caribbean, Mediterranean, Canada/New England, the Canary and Atlantic Islands, and Northern Europe along with trans-Atlantic crossings, world cruises, and holiday getaways.

More Fantastic Adventures

Tired of losing to the boys on poker night? Plan a getaway to a **World Poker Tournament (WPT) Boot Camp (1-866-978-2668,** www. wptbootcamp.com). The WPT Boot Camps are held about once a month at top casinos in New Jersey, Las Vegas, and other locations and are taught by the nation's top poker professionals—including competitive female poker players. The two- and three-day camps are geared for the novice to the advanced player and start at $1,695. The boys won't know what hit 'em!

Starting in the 1950s, **Outward Bound (1-866-467-7651,** www. outwardboundwilderness.org) has built a reputation for instilling self-reliance and personal growth through hands-on experience and physical challenges—especially in the younger population. But you're never too young for a challenge, and Outward Bound answers that call with wilderness experience for adults. The adult programs are broken down by age groups (adults 18+, adults 23+, and adults 30+) and emphasize self-reliance, responsibility, teamwork, confidence, and compassion as well as environmental and community stewardship. From canoeing in Maine to backpacking in California, each trip is geared toward challenge, reflection, and camaraderie. Women-only trips are also available. Four-day trips start at $775; seven-day trips start at $1,195.

Space camp isn't just for kids. The **U.S. Space & Rocket Center** in **Huntsville, Alabama,** offers **Space Academy for Adults (1-800-637-7223** or **256-721-7150,** www.spacecamp.com) for a realistic astronaut experience. You'll train for a simulated space shuttle mission, feel what it's like to blast off on a mission, and experience a simulated walk on the moon. Three-day programs start at $449; six days start at $899.

Fly above **Salt Lake Valley** in **Utah** at the **Super Fly Paragliding Academy** (**801-255-9595,** www.paraglidingacademy.com). Earn your wings with a tandem flight, where after a short briefing, you'll take off with a professional tandem pilot for 15 to 50 minutes depending on flying conditions. Pilot certification courses are also offered. Tandem flights are $125; pilot courses are $1,200.

Vegas, Baby!

In This Chapter

* Watch true LOVE bloom at The Mirage
* See and be seen at The Palms
* Get wet at MGM's hippest pool on the Strip
* Experience off-the-Strip luxury at Red Rock
* Reach a new culinary high at Mandalay Bay
* More Vegas getaways

What can I say about Vegas that hasn't already been said? It's an unabashed, bold wonderland where over-the-top luxury is an everyday occurrence. It's a landscape dotted with hotels of unusual size that is at once beautifully alluring and ridiculously kitschy. Vegas is a place that invites you to leave your inhibitions at home and reinvent yourselves if only for a long weekend. Love it or hate it, Vegas is a place where girlfriends flock to laugh, let go, and revel in fantasy. In this chapter, we'll take a fly over just some of the many getaway opportunities that await … only in Vegas.

Best in Show: The Mirage

3400 South Las Vegas Boulevard, Las Vegas, NV 89109. **1-800-374-9000** *or* **702-791-7111.** *www.mirage.com.*

Sprawling more than 100 acres, The Mirage sits mid-Strip fronted by its famous volcanic light show and tropical foliage. A landmark destination since its opening in 1989, the resort had a major facelift in 2008—from top-to-bottom room renovations to an upgrade of the iconic volcano, which features an all-new audio and visual spectacle that will have you shaking your head and whispering, "Only in Vegas." The grand interior is reminiscent of a Polynesian paradise where palm trees tower 60 feet above waterfalls and pools that meander through a forest of rich tropical flora, including banana trees, elephant ears, and tropical orchids. From shopping and poolside dozing to throwing the dice and playing the slots, The Mirage serves up an oasis of options—but if you want to be dazzled, go for the really big show.

Show Stopper

Presented exclusively at The Mirage, Beatlemania was reinvented with the 2006 premiere of The Beatles **LOVE** by Cirque du Soleil. LOVE unites the magic of Cirque du Soleil with the spirit of The Beatles to create a moving and visually stunning experience. LOVE was born from a personal friendship between the late George Harrison and Cirque du Soleil founder Guy Laliberté and is a magical mystery tour into the heart and soul of The Beatles's music through an exploration of the aesthetic, political, and spiritual trends of the 1960s.

Inspired by the poetry of the lyrics, the creative team designed scenes alive with colorful characters in extravagant costumes. Through stunning visuals, the show captures the essence of love that John, Paul, George, and Ringo inspired during their adventures together. The international cast of 60 performers channels a raw energy with high-energy fusions of urban, freestyle dance, aerial performance, and fast-paced athleticism that make LOVE a visual and musical feast.

LOVE is performed Thursdays through Mondays with two shows nightly at 7 and 10 P.M. Tickets start at $93.50 and can be reserved online, by phone, or at The Mirage box office. For tickets and more information, call **1-800-963-9634** or **702-792-7777,** or visit www. cirquedusoleil.com.

○ Savvy Sister

What is it that makes Vegas shows so dazzling? In the case of LOVE, the custom-built 360-degree theater at The Mirage features panoramic sound from three speakers in each seat equaling about 6,500 total speakers, high-definition video projections with 100-foot-tall moving images, and a complicated lighting system completely hidden from audience view. The farthest seat from center stage is less than 100 feet, while the closest seat is just a couple feet from the stage edge. Translation: there are no bad seats.

After the show, keep the good vibrations flowing with an evening at **The Beatles Revolution Lounge (702-692-8383,** www. thebeatlesrevolutionlounge.com). Inspired by the spirit of The Beatles and created by Cirque du Soleil, the lounge features cutting-edge, interactive experiences that create a psychedelic sensory environment and a contemporary interpretation of The Beatles's era. Each night is an evolutionary journey where both the music and interior transform, resulting in an eclectic nightlife adventure. The **Abbey Road Bar,** located in front of the lounge, is a full-service bar that reflects the Revolution experience.

More Juicy Options

It's a city that never sleeps, so why should you? Here's more to do at The Mirage:

* Visit **Siegfried & Roy's Secret Garden and Dolphin Habitat (702-791-7188,** www.miragehabitat.com). More than just a tourist diversion, the garden is a research and educational facility where you can become a dolphin trainer for a day or take a group tour for a look behind the scenes. General admission is $15.

* Leave your modesty in the room and head to the **Bare Pool Lounge** (702-791-7442, www.barepool.com), an adults-only pool where tops are optional for European-style sun bathing (go on, be brave!) with two dipping pools, private daybeds and cabanas, and VIP service. Or, keep your assets covered and head to **The Mirage pool,** where interconnected lagoons and grottos are surrounded by tropical foliage. Bare is $10 on weekdays and $20 on weekends.

* Indulge in one of the 15 restaurants and cafés, from creative American bistro cuisine at **Stack** and eclectic Asian dishes at **Japonais** to the ultimate great American burger at **BLT Burger.** Reservations are suggested for fine-dining restaurants. Call **1-866-339-4566.**

* Catch a headliner show where a parading cast of characters such as Jay Leno, Ray Romano, Kevin James, and Lewis Black perform standup most weekends. Tickets start at $65. For tickets and more information, call **1-800-963-9634** or **702-792-7777.**

* Banish preshow beauty woes with a stop at **Kim Võ Salon** (702-791-7474) and get a "Hairtini" cocktail conditioner, makeup, brow plucking, or luxurious nail service.

Rooms and Rates

Thanks to the remodel, gone are the late 1980s digs and in their place, a refined and tranquil décor. From luxury amenities to modern furnishings, the resort's 2,765 Deluxe and Tower Deluxe rooms feature pillow-top mattresses, down comforters, feather pillows, cotton robes, 42-inch LCD TVs, iPod/MP3-compatible clock radios, Internet access, and personal amenities. Nonsmoking floors are available on request.

The resort's indulgent suites—Petite, Hospitality, Tower, and Penthouse—also reflect a modern residential feel with clean lines, vivid color palettes, and upgraded amenities ranging from his and her baths and wet bars to separate living and dining areas.

Standard room rates start at $119. Watch the website for hotel promotions and air travel packages.

See and Be Seen: Palms Casino Resort

4321 West Flamingo Road, Las Vegas, NV 89103. **1-866-942-**7777 *or* **702-942-**7777. *www.palms.com.*

Celebrity sightings are an everyday occurrence in Vegas. Seems they flock to the city of sin just to blend into the crowds. And the smart and ever-so-stylish **Palms Casino Resort** is one of many places where spotting a celebrity is likely—in fact, it was the site of Britney Spears's first nuptials (remember that?). But if you don't come eye to eye with a celebrity, you'll certainly feel like one yourself with the surreal nightlife scene. Grab your party shoes, push-up bra, and false eyelashes, and let's go live large at the swanky clubs of The Palms.

Party Scene

Throw your dice at the upscale **Playboy Club,** where dealers wear vintage-style Roberto Cavalli–designed Playboy bunny getups complete with ears, bow tie, and bunny tail. Located in the Fantasy Tower, the club is an ingenious marriage of an ultra-lounge and gaming venue complete with roulette, blackjack, and slots. One wall of the club is plastered with 60 plasma screens displaying the riches from the *Playboy* archives while another all-glass wall offers dramatic views of the Strip. Decadence bounces off the spectacular **Diamond Bar,** made from 10,000 diamond-shaped crystals, and the Philippe Starck–designed black Baccarat crystal chandeliers that illuminate the gaming tables. Specialty cocktails evoke a throwback to the original Playboy Club era, but contemporary creations along with a global wine list and champagne are also available to top off the extravagance. Open daily at 8 P.M. to about 4 A.M. with a cover charge of $40.

Located just above the Playboy Club is the **Moon Nightclub (702-942-6832),** a boutique venue at the top floor of the Fantasy Tower that boasts spectacular sky views from a celestial retractable roof. The high-end nightclub offers a visually stunning main room with an elaborate bar, lounge, and illuminated dance floor. A palette of yellow, gold, nickel, and silver gives the room a mystical lunar aura, and unique glass floor tiles display a dazzling spectrum of color. The incredible night sky, 35 feet above the dance floor, becomes part of the décor after the roof retracts. The full-service bar offers specialty "moon drinks" along with classics, top champagnes, and an extensive wine list. Get dressed to the hilt and head to Moon after it opens at 10:30 P.M.

Another celebrated nighttime hot spot is **ghostbar (702-942-6832)**, which sits high above the glittering expanse of Las Vegas on The Palms's 55th floor. Indoors, the scene is set with seductive shadows and a sleek, chic ultra-lounge attitude and an ethereal color scheme of silver, white, greens, and grays. Floor-to-ceiling windows offer a dramatic view of the night sky and city below while above, a 30-foot ghost-shaped ceiling soffit changes colors as a deejay spins an eclectic music mix. Lounge on the super hip furniture or escape the fray in an intimate nook or VIP lounge. Outdoors, the dramatic sky deck provides a panoramic view of the Vegas night lights with a glass inset in the floor offering a jaw-dropping view straight down. Posh seating areas are enhanced with a fiber-optically lit drink rail running most of the circumference of the deck. Order up a "Ghostini" or enjoy a wide variety of cocktails, wines, and champagnes. Ghostbar is open nightly from 8 P.M. until late, and super-fab nightlife attire is required.

Chick Wit

Vegas is a fast and easy girlfriends' getaway. The only downside is sore, aching feet from tooling around all day and night in designer shoes. My advice is to suck it up and wear your ugly comfy shoes for shopping; otherwise, you'll end up at the Bellagio shops buying a pair of Chanel flats for $400 just to get back to the hotel. Been there, done that—and I don't even wear flats!

—Kari, marketing director

More Juicy Options

What, you want more? Here's a sampling of other Palms diversions:

* You'll need plenty of beauty sleep before your up-all-night bar-hopping adventure. Catch up on your zzz's in a cabana by the opulent pool, spanning some two acres of true-blue heaven.

* Book a beauty stop at **Amp Salon** (**702-942-6909**) for a sweat-proof, dance-proof, go-all-night Airbrush Makeup Application, or arrange for a makeup artist to come to your room. Prices vary.

* No cocktails on empty stomachs, ladies! Start the evening at one of the eight alluring restaurants. The celebrated **Nove Italiano** (**702-942-6800**) turns out classic Italian fare with a contemporary twist while **N9NE Steakhouse** (**702-933-9900**) is heralded for its bold take on American cuisine.

Rooms and Rates

Deluxe Guestrooms and Junior Suites at The Palms offer spacious comfort and are available with two double beds or one king-size bed. You'll find the usual amenities along with super-comfy beds, Internet access, complimentary newspapers, and Aveda bath products.

The Palms is also home to the pimped-out and plush Fantasy Suites tucked among the Superior Guestrooms in the 53-story Fantasy Tower. Of them, the Hot Pink Suite is a sprawling sweet suite awash in reds and pinks with silver accents and touches of fur. Extras include an over-sized Jacuzzi tub, steam shower, Hollywood-style dressing vanity and mirrored terrazzo bubble floor, a two-way fireplace, plasma TVs, bathrobes, and a decked-out entertainment center. You can find packages such as the Hot Pink Suite Party Package that for $1,200 per person includes a fully stocked bar, bar snacks, VIP entry into Rain nightclub, and spa access.

Rooms start as low as $89. Keep an eye on the website for special packages and value dates.

Coolest Dip: MGM Grand Hotel & Casino

3799 Las Vegas Boulevard South, Las Vegas, NV 89109. **1-877-880-0880** *or* **702-891-7777**. *www.mgmgrand.com.*

Guarded by the 100,000-pound bronze lion statue—the largest bronze statue in the United States—the **MGM Grand** sits majestically on the

Strip adorned by water fountains, Atlas-themed statues, and lush land-scaping. Designed to capture the drama of Hollywood, the MGM is a bustling behemoth where the din of the casinos is mellowed by plush rooms, lavish lounges, and a Grand Pool complex of five separate pools, whirlpools, and a lazy river. Shopping and gambling are a given, but for an experience like no other, a new ultra hip dip has been unveiled that redefines poolside lounging.

The Cool Pool

It sounds almost naughty, but then again, it *is* Vegas. The new **Wet Republic Ultra Pool (702-891-3563,** www.mgmgrand.com/wetrepublic) is centered around an alluring 53,000-square-foot ultra-pool concept that combines a nightlife vibe with poolside relaxation. And although the name may have you thinking otherwise, Wet Republic is not a topless pool area like Bare at The Mirage and is instead an adults-only mecca for people who like to party while the sun's still up. Wet Republic is a playground for grownups with intimate spaces complemented by elite VIP service, high-end amenities, and renowned entertainers—oh, and a killer pool.

Blanketed with a South Beach vibe, Wet Republic features two spec-tacular saltwater pools, eight individual pools and spas, exclusive VIP bungalows, party cabanas, spacious daybeds, and extra-large chaise lounges. The ultra-mod bungalows are decked out with plush king-size day beds, teakwood furniture, giant flat-screen TVs, a DVD library, a fully stocked mini fridge, ceiling fan, telephone, and sheer draperies for privacy. Cabanas have oversized couches and ottomans with many of the bungalow amenities. The 80 deluxe chaise lounges placed through-out the poolscape are adjustable on both ends, allowing you to soak up the rays throughout the day without having to move your chair.

Adjacent to the main pool area, an open-air ultra lounge delivers on the "daylife" party promise. At its focal point is a 60-foot marble-topped bar with a custom glass base inset with chartreuse silk and bamboo. A huge sundeck is located between the lounge and the saltwater pools that transforms into a stage for celebrity guests and entertainers at weekly and monthly events and offers a perfect view from every angle. Set against the backdrop of a glistening water wall, a booth elevated above the pool area plays host to celebrated DJs as they keep the tunes rockin' until the sun goes down. Underwater speakers in the main pools keep the grooves bumping in every square inch of the destination.

Signature cocktails and premium bottle and pitcher service are yours for the asking. You can order up elegant poolside bites such as Lobster Gazpacho Gelée and Toro Tuna Tartare, Green Papaya and Shrimp Summer Rolls, or Kobe Sliders. Frozen-Stem Strawberries with Grand Marnier Fudge and delicious assortments of marshmallow s'mores provide the sweet ending.

Wet Republic is open daily from 10 A.M. to 6 P.M. Cover charges and bungalow and cabana rental costs vary.

More Juicy Options

And if that's not enough, here are just a few of the many MGM options:

* Stay up all night at one of the seven MGM bars and clubs. Among them, **Studio 54** is a modern interpretation of the original and kicks it up with deejay-spun, high-energy dance tunes. **Tabú Ultra Lounge** serves up a more sophisticated vibe with classic lounge music that evolves into progressive vocal blends throughout the evening—but not at a pace that you have to shout above to mingle. For table and booth reservations, call **702-891-7279.**

* Choose from nearly 20 restaurants and cafés to feed your cravings. Go for the bold Mexican flavors of **Diego (702-891-3200)**, or savor dishes crafted from family farm–raised ingredients at **Tom Colicchio's Craftsteak (702-891-7318)**. MGM also houses casual favorites such as **Emeril's (702-891-7374)**, **Wolfgang Puck Bar & Grill (702-891-3000)**, and 'wichcraft for gourmet sandwiches on the go. Reservations are recommended at most dining establishments by calling the individual restaurants or reserving your table online at www.mgmgrand.com.

* Take in the thrills of **KÀ (1-866-774-7117** or **702-531-2000,** www.cirquedusoleil.com), a creation of Cirque du Soleil that combines acrobatic performances, martial arts, puppetry, multimedia, and pyrotechnics to tell the saga of separated twins with linked destinies. Show times are Tuesdays through Saturdays with two shows nightly at 7 and 9:30 P.M. Tickets start at $69.

* Take a break from the casino din at the **Grand Spa & Health Club (702-891-3077).** The spa's signature 75-minute Nirvana Massage is a multicultural experience with Ayurvedic oils with Abhyanga massage, Shirodhara hot oil placement, hot stones, a cool eye mask, a foot balancing massage, and customized music (starting at $245).

Rooms and Rates

MGM Grand is home to some 5,000 diverse guest rooms, suites, and luxury lofts—each laced with the Hollywood glam, Art Deco style of the hotel. The Grand Tower rooms are the most affordable and offer a classic motif with custom black-and-white marble bathrooms, thick cotton towels, roomy closets, wireless Internet, and personal items. The boutique-style West Wing features 700 rooms with king-size beds decked out with pillow-top mattresses and body pillows, flat-screen TVs, and bathrooms with oversized showers and TVs embedded in the mirror. MGM Grand's boutique hotel, **The Signature,** is a nongaming, nonsmoking hotel set within three distinct towers—each featuring 576 suites with a gated entrance, elegant lobby, and 24-hour concierge service.

> STOP *Bad Trip*
>
> Coffee hounds take heed: in-room coffee makers in hotels on the Strip are rare. Rumor has it (my only confirmation is a fuzzy conversation with a Vegas taxi driver) that coffee makers were banned in hotels of certain mega proportions for safety reasons. If your day doesn't start until caffeine is flowing through your veins, locate the closest coffee joint in the hotel the night before, and you won't panic come morning.

Standard room rates start in the $99 neighborhood. Watch the website for seasonal special offers.

Stripped Off: Red Rock Casino, Resort & Spa

11011 West Charleston Boulevard, Las Vegas, NV 89135. **1-866-767-7773** *or* **702-797-7777.** *www.redrocklasvegas.com.*

Despite the cheeky taglines that Las Vegas has managed to tack onto its name, destinations with laid-back sophistication do exist. And topping that list is the **Red Rock Casino, Resort & Spa.** Embraced by locals and the "been-there, done-that" resort traveler, Red Rock exudes a cool, boutique vibe punctuated by a chic décor that echoes the rich hues of the nearby Red Rock Canyons.

A 10-mile hop from the Strip, the Resort goes out of its way to offer a true resort experience. The separate hotel and casino entrances keep guests from having to plod through the dizzying dings of the slots and smoky haze to access their rooms. Also, unlike the massive Strip cribs, the pool isn't a mile trek across the hotel property and is instead at the heart of the horseshoe-shaped resort. The central three-acre backyard pool deck is flanked by private cabanas, swim-up gaming tables, and more than enough lounge chairs to eliminate the up-before-dawn fight to reserve a seat. Once you've seen the dancing fountains and the blue-faced trio pounding on giant drums, head to Red Rock Resort where relaxation and cool sophistication underline a refreshing Vegas experience.

The Off-the-Strip Experience

With nine distinctive dining destinations, the swinging **Cherry Nightclub, Lucky Bar, Rocks Lounge,** and arguably the most technologically advanced casino in Vegas, revelers aren't without a wildly relaxing place to prop up their tired feet at the end of the day:

∗ Dine at one of the 10 restaurants and eateries. Among the latest to open, **Hachi** offers modern Japanese cuisine infused with a variety of cultural influences from around the world. For more casual fare, **Salt Lick BBQ** brings Texas's world-famous BBQ restaurant. For fine-dining reservations, call **702-797-7576.**

＊ Shake your tushies at the **Rocks Lounge,** where house band Zowie Bowie ignites the tiger-striped dance floor on Friday and Saturday nights. The ever-tan and glam duo of Chris Philips and Marley Taylor and their backup band pump out the Rat Pack favorites in their first set, followed by a high-voltage hip hop set.

＊ Catch a flick at the 16-screen onsite **Regal Cinemas** theater featuring high-back reclining chairs. General seating and private VIP viewing boxes are available. Tickets are $10 and up. Get a current movie listing at **702-221-2283.**

＊ Luxury bowling? Isn't that an oxymoron? Not at Red Rock, where they boast the largest luxury bowling center in Vegas. Check out **Cosmic Bowling** on Friday and Saturday nights with hot tunes, glow-in-the-dark lanes, and special lighting effects until 2 A.M. Cosmic Bowling is $4.50 per person and regular play is $3.75 per person. For VIP suites reservations, call **702-797-7356.**

＊ For the ultimate in relaxation, the 25,000-square-foot spa boasts a sleek, ultra-mod atmosphere with 20 treatment rooms, a fitness center, salon, and an outdoor adventure spa program. Try a signature service like the Ashiatsu Massage (80 minutes for $190), where therapists manipulate muscles using their feet while supporting themselves with bars suspended from the ceiling. Or, try a more tranquil Cucumber Green Tea Facial (50 minutes for $145). For appointments and more information, call **702-797-7878.**

Rooms and Rates

The lavish guest rooms reflect the resort's rich colors and materials. Exotic woods, marble, crystal, and elegant fabrics adorn each room. Filled with luxury amenities, including 42-inch high-definition plasma televisions, Bose sound systems with iPod connectivity, guest robes and slippers, in-room martini bars, and 15-inch LCD televisions in the bathrooms, all rooms offer spectacular views of the Las Vegas Strip or the Red Rock mountains. In addition to its standard guest rooms, the hotel offers six styles of suites, including one-of-a-kind custom villas and penthouse suites.

Rooms start from $160 with hotel specials available on the website.

Culinary Climax: Mandalay Bay Resort and Casino

3950 Las Vegas Boulevard South, Las Vegas, NV 89119. **1-877-632-7800** *or* **702-632-7777.** *www.mandalaybay.com.*

Dare I say that I saved the best for last? As far as posh service, endless exclusive entertainment, and exclusive dining options, **Mandalay Bay** certainly has carved out its place among the top hotels on the Strip. The AAA Four Diamond Award–winning resort is a lush, tropical destination awash in intricately carved stone statues, spectacular fire pots, cascading waterfalls, mythical architecture, and tropical landscaping. The feeling of a vibrant paradise starts in the hotel's registration lobby, home to a 14-foot-high saltwater aquarium reminiscent of South Pacific coral reefs and filled with dozens of aquatic species, including eight types of angelfish. Throughout the 60-acre property, thousands of palm trees create the sense of a sheltering oasis.

Eating Las Vegas

Dining at Mandalay Bay is a far cry from the complimentary all-you-can-eat Vegas buffets of yore. You'll find tons of tempting options scattered throughout the resort, the attached Mandalay Place, and the boutique hotel inside the resort, **THEhotel.** Of the many options, here's a quick trip down the pathway toward culinary heaven:

* **StripSteak** (702-632-7414) is the first steakhouse by acclaimed chef Michael Mina. The classic menu is punched up with modern twists and exquisite tastes that come from corn-fed, all-natural meat, line-caught seafood, and fresh, seasonal produce.

* **Fleur de Lys** (702-632-9400) is the work of preeminent chef Hubert Keller, who shares his talent and finesse for contemporary French cuisine with multicourse, prix-fixe dinners. The elegant main dining room features 30-foot walls of cultured stone and a live floral sculpture of more than 3,000 fresh-cut roses.

* **Aureole** (702-632-7401) is chef Charlie Palmer's legendary restaurant that boasts its place among the finest in the United States.

The centerpiece of the establishment is a spectacular four-story wine tower. World-famous "wine angels" use a high-tech suspension system to gracefully retrieve each order.

∗ Located atop THEhotel, **Mix (702-632-9500)** brings together culinary art, cutting-edge interior design, and astounding vistas of The Strip. The Las Vegas debut of famed chef Alain Ducasse, Mix offers contemporary and classic French and American dishes with global accents as well as signature dishes from sister restaurants in Paris, France, and Monte Carlo, Monaco.

∗ **Rumjungle (702-632-7408)** is a lively spot for Latin American dishes and striking visuals, such as a dancing fire wall that transforms magically into a soothing wall of water. Walls of rum and spirits rise to the ceiling in an illuminated bar while a tropical-inspired Brazilian Rodizio-style feast features meats cooked over a giant open fire pit.

For fine-dining reservations, call **702-632-7200** or reserve your table online at www.mandalaybay.com.

More Juicy Options

Work off your dining adventures with a stroll through Mandalay Place or any of these other options:

∗ Indulge in aquatic relaxation at **Mandalay Bay Beach,** where the 11-acre playground offers a wave pool, lazy river, three swimming pools, jogging track, and 2,700 tons of real sand. The area is home to the **Beachside Casino** and the private, adults-only **Moorea Beach Club** for European-style sunbathing. Moorea has a cover charge of $10 for women (men have to plunk down $40 to $50 to get in).

∗ Take a fascinating walk through the **Shark Reef Aquarium,** featuring more than 2,000 dangerous and unusual aquatic animals swimming safely behind gigantic walls of glass. Fourteen exhibits allow you to view more than 100 aquatic species, including 15 types of sharks. Adult admission is $15.95.

* Get in touch with your playful side at **Eyecandy Sound Lounge & Bar** (702-632-7777), where interactive touch tables, revolutionary sound stations, and a touch-activated, multicolored dance floor creates a unique sensory experience.

* Recover from your Vegas adventure at one of two spas. **Spa Mandalay** (1-877-632-7300) is a huge and wonderful pampering palace with miles of relaxation spaces and diverse treatment selections. The chic **Bathhouse** (1-877-632-9636) inside THEhotel is an architectural wonder that hides a mindful water lounging area with separate hot and cold plunge pools, swirling whirlpools, eucalyptus steam rooms, and redwood saunas.

Powder Room

Newbie gamblers can ward off first-timer fears with a complimentary gaming class, offered by most major resorts on the Strip. Among them, Circus Circus, Excalibur, and Luxor offer free table game lessons; times and locations vary so call the hotel directly for details. For more tips about visiting Las Vegas, check out www. vegas.com.

Rooms and Rates

Each of Mandalay Bay's deluxe rooms offers 550 square feet of comfort and style marked by warm textiles in soft earth tones and artfully designed furnishings. Lofty pillow-top beds with triple sheeting, plasma TVs, an iHome clock radio for your iPod, cordless phones, lighted closets, floor-to-ceiling windows, and Internet access grace the bedrooms—while in the bathrooms, you'll find LCD TVs, multijet spa tubs with separate showers, twin vanities, and bath amenities. Rates start at $120, but check the website for promotions and land and air packages.

For more help planning your Vegas getaway, including special offers and a free **Visitor's Guide,** call **1-877-847-4858** or visit www. visitlasvegas.com.

More Vegas Destinations

Planet Hollywood is back, baby! Stripped down and fully renovated in 2007 on the former site of the Aladdin, the **Planet Hollywood Resort & Casino** (1-866-919-7472 or 702-785-5555, www. planethollywoodresort.com) offers up 2,600 movie-themed rooms and suites as well as the chance to take a dip in Hollywood culture. The resort boasts the latest in technology with 5,000 Panasonic high-definition plasma TVs in public areas and guest rooms. Dine at one of eight already-famous restaurants, including **Koi** from Los Angeles and **Strip House** from New York. Catch "Stomp Out Loud" in the 1,500-seat Showroom, splurge at the **Miracle Mile Shops** with 170 stores, or bliss out at the **Planet Hollywood Spa** by Mandara. Rates start at $99.

The **Venetian Resort-Hotel-Casino** (1-877-883-6423 or 702-414-1000, www.venetian.com) stakes its claim as the largest property in the country to receive AAA's Five Diamond and Mobil Four-Star Awards and is arguably among one of the world's most luxurious resorts. Recreating Venice's legendary landmarks, the resort is located in the heart of the Las Vegas Strip and features **The Grand Canal Shoppes,** an indoor streetscape complete with gondolas and singing gondoliers, the **Canyon Ranch SpaClub,** world-class gaming, exquisite restaurants, the **Guggenheim-Hermitage Museum,** and extensive entertainment options such as the **Phantom-The Las Vegas Spectacular and Blue Man Group.** Rates start at $169. Check the website for suite specials and entertainment packages.

Platinum Hotel (1-877-211-9211 or 702-365-5000, www. theplatinumhotel.com) offers an alternative to the bigger-is-better Vegas pleasure principle with style, sophistication, and attentive but unobtrusive service. Ideally located a little more than a block off the Strip, the 17-story Platinum is a nongaming, nonsmoking hotel with 255 fashionably appointed one- and two-bedroom suites, indoor and outdoor swimming pools, a fitness studio, and restaurant. The **Well Spa** is the place to go for a secluded, intimate spa treatment. The hotel offers fabulous views of the Vegas skyline and is within walking distance of **Caesar's Palace,** the **Bellagio,** and the **Venetian.** Rates start at $159.

Resources

Travel Companies that Cater to Women

Adventure Divas
206-328-9519
www.adventuredivas.com
Diva Tours follow in the steps of the award-winning PBS
Adventure Divas television series for all-inclusive travel odysseys
that span the globe.

Adventure Women
1-800-804-8686 or 406-587-3883
www.adventurewomen.com
Adventure Women designs and organizes domestic and international vacations for women who want to experience an active,
out-of-the-ordinary adventure vacation.

Adventures in Good Company
1-877-439-4042
www.adventuresingoodcompany.com
Adventures in Good Company specializes in women-only outdoor trips in North America, Europe, and beyond that range from hiking, canoeing, sea kayaking, dog sledding, cross-country skiing, rock climbing, backpacking, and horseback riding.

Call of the Wild
1-888-378-1978 or 530-642-1978
www.callwild.com
Call of the Wild has offered adventure travel for women since 1978 and arranges group trips to Alaska, Hawaii, California, Arizona, Mexico, Peru, and New Zealand.

Eurynome Journeys
207-236-0110
www.wanderwoman.com
Eurynome Journeys offers leisurely paced travel itineraries for women traveling alone or in small groups to Greece, Ireland, and in the United States.

Girlfriend Getaways
1-800-829-9161
www.girlgetaways.com
From the publishers of *Budget Travel*, this website focuses on travel destinations for women (including special deals and packages).

Gutsy Women Travel
1-866-464-8879
www.gutsywomentravel.com
With travel programs designed especially for busy women, Gutsy Women Travel offers all-inclusive trips for small groups in North America, Latin America, Europe, and beyond.

Mariah Wilderness Expeditions
1-800-462-7424 or 530-626-6049
www.mariahwomen.com
Mariah offers women's whitewater rafting trips in California and international adventure tours to Costa Rica, Baja, Peru, and Tierra del Fuego.

Red Lotus Tours
509-264-8444
www.redlotustours.com
Red Lotus offers women-only tours and volunteer opportunities that explore exotic destinations such as Peru and Nepal.

Serendipity Traveler
1-800-975-2357 or 978-879-7464
www.serendipitytraveler.com
Serendipity Traveler creates thoughtful and enriching travel experiences for women with destinations throughout Canada, the United States, Italy, and beyond.

Wild Women Expeditions
1-888-WWE-1222 or 705-866-1260
www.wildwomenexp.com
Wild Women Expeditions is an all-women outdoor adventure company operating across Canada that offers paddling, hiking, fly-fishing, and cycling expeditions.

Wild Women Travel
1-800-800-7583
www.wildwomentravel.com
Wild Women Travel offers women a variety of worldwide travel packages and custom trips designed to offer itineraries packed with unique, unusual, interesting, and exciting features with a feminine flavor.

Women Traveling Together
1-800-795-7135 or 410-956-5250
www.women-traveling.com
Women Traveling Together offers women-only tours through the United States, Canada, Europe, and beyond that provide authentic experiences including outdoor adventures, special events and holidays, cultural immersion, and cruises.

Online Travel Guides

Go Girlfriend
www.gogirlfriend.com
A blog-style website aimed at arming female travelers with tools and information to travel with confidence.

Journeywoman
www.journeywoman.com
A collection of tours, tips, and articles for women who travel.

Tango Diva
www.tangodiva.com
An online magazine focused on travel adventures for women flying solo.

Travels with Tish
www.travelswithtish.com
"Tish," the travel expert, scoops on vacation options, deals, and ideas for girlfriend getaways.

Vagablond
www.vagablond.com
An online magazine cataloging firsthand, worldwide travel experiences with a focus on food, wine, and shopping.

Women on the Road
www.women-on-the-road.com
Advice and resources for women who travel on their own.

Women Travel Tips
www.womentraveltips.com
A collection of articles and tips for female travelers.

Magazines

Travelgirl
770-451-9399
www.travelgirlinc.com
Aimed at active women who enjoy traveling, this magazine examines lifestyle issues such as when it's safe to travel while pregnant, tips for planning an out-of-town bachelorette party, and reviews on travel-friendly products.

Women's Adventure
1-800-746-3910
www.womensadventuremagazine.com
Aimed at female outdoor enthusiasts, this magazine explores destinations, gear, products, and close-to-home ways to enjoy nature.